Transitions to Better Lives
Offender readiness and rehabilitation

Andrew Day, Sharon Casey,
Tony Ward, Kevin Howells and
James Vess

WILLAN
PUBLISHING

Published by

Willan Publishing
Culmcott House
Mill Street, Uffculme
Cullompton, Devon
EX15 3AT, UK
Tel: +44(0)1884 840337
Fax: +44(0)1884 840251
e-mail: info@willanpublishing.co.uk
website: www.willanpublishing.co.uk

Published simultaneously in the USA and Canada by

Willan Publishing
c/o ISBS, 920 NE 58th Ave, Suite 300,
Portland, Oregon 97213-3786, USA
Tel: +001(0)503 287 3093
Fax: +001(0)503 280 8832
e-mail: info@isbs.com
website: www.isbs.com

First published 2010

ISBN   978-1-84392-718-1 paperback
          978-1-84392-719-8 hardback

British Library Cataloguing-in-Publication Data

A catalogue record for this book is available from the British Library

FSC
Mixed Sources
Product group from well-managed
forests and other controlled sources
Cert no. SGS-COC-2482
www.fsc.org
© 1996 Forest Stewardship Council

Project managed by Deer Park Productions, Tavistock, Devon
Typeset by GCS, Leighton Buzzard, Bedfordshire
Printed and bound by T.J. International, Padstow, Cornwall

ONE WEEK LOAN

Contents

Figures and tables

Figures

Tables

Abbreviations

AMI	Adaptations of motivational interviewing
ARCQ	Anger Readiness to Change Questionnaire
ASPD	Anti-social personality disorder
ATSA	Association for the Treatment of Sexual Abusers
CBT	Cognitive behavioural treatment
CLAHRC	Collaborations for Leadership in Applied Health Research and Care
CVTRQ	Corrections Victoria Treatment Readiness Questionnaire
DSM-IV-TR	*Diagnostic and Statistical Manual of Mental Disorders*, 4th edn, text revised
DSPD	Dangerous and Severe Personality Disorder
EssenCES	Essen Climate Evaluation Scheme
FoSOD	Facets of Sexual Offender Denial
GLM	Good Lives Model
GLP	Good Lives Plan
GPS	Goal positioning system
MI	Motivational inverviewing
MMPI	Minnesota Multiphasic Personality Inventory
MORM	Multifactor Offender Readiness Model
NIHR	National Institute of Health Research
ORS	Outcome Rating Scale
PCI	Personal Concerns Inventory
PCI-OA	Personal Concerns Inventory – Offender Adaptation
PCL-R	Psychopathy Checklist – Revised (Hare)
PDO	Personality disordered offender

RCQ   Readiness to Change Questionnaire
RCQ-TV   Readiness to Change Questionnaire [Treatment
                 Version]
RCT   Randomised controlled trials
RNR   Risk–need–responsivity
SE   Supportive-expressive (therapy)
SOCRATES   Stages of Change Readiness and Treatment Eagerness
                 Scale
SRS   Session Rating Scale
STRS   Serin Treatment Readiness Scale
TA   Therapeutic alliance
TRCRS   Treatment Readiness Clinical Rating Scale
TTM   Transtheoretical model
URICA   University of Rhode Island Change Assessment
VRS   Violence Risk Scale
VRS-SO   Violence Risk Scale – Sex Offender
VTRQ   Violence Treatment Readiness Questionnaire
WAI   Working Alliance Inventory

Acknowledgements

This book is the product of a long-term collaboration between a group of clinical and forensic psychologists who are interested in the field of offender rehabilitation. Over the last ten years the group has investigated different aspects of treatment readiness, publishing a number of journal articles on the topic (for a full list of these articles, see page 252). Parts of this book draw on these articles, but they have been rewritten and collated for the purposes of this volume. In addition, we have invited others with particular expertise in this field to prepare chapters. We are very grateful to them for their contributions. We would also like to extend our thanks to Brian Willan, Julia Willan and their colleagues at Willan Publishing as well as Bill and Michelle Antrobus and the rest of the team at Deer Park Productions for their support with this project.

Authors and contributors

Sharon Casey completed her PhD in forensic psychology in 2004. Her areas of expertise include offender assessment, juvenile offending, programme evaluation, and psychology and the law. Dr Casey has been a collaborator with other members of the group on several publications and projects, and has been involved in the completion of a number of competitively tendered research consultancy and consultancy projects. Dr Casey has also worked with a number of government agencies in both South Australia and Victoria and supervised a large number of Psychology Honours and Masters theses.

Andrew Day is a clinical and forensic psychologist who is interested in research and practice in the area of offender rehabilitation. He is currently an Associate Professor with the Centre for Offender Reintegration at Deakin, in the School of Psychology, Deakin University, Australia. His most recent books include *Writing Court Reports* (2007, Australian Academic Press), *Anger and Indigenous Men* (2008, Federation Press) and *Integrated Responses to Domestic Violence: Research and Practice Experiences in Working with Men* (2009, Federation Press).

Laura J. Hanby, MA, is a PhD candidate in forensic psychology at Carleton University, Ottawa, Ontario, Canada. Her research examines the relationship between offender competencies, correctional programme performance and offender change. She has recently been involved in a range of research projects, including the role of psychological assessments in parole decision-making, the relationship between the therapeutic alliance and sex offender programme performance, and the variability in treatment engagement by type of violent offender.

Kevin Howells is Professor of Forensic/Clinical Psychology in the Institute of Mental Health at Nottingham University. He is also Head of the Peaks Academic and Research Unit at Rampton Hospital, with a responsibility for service evaluation and research relating to the Dangerous and Severe Personality Disorder initiative at the hospital. He is a chartered forensic and clinical psychologist and has long-term clinical and research interests in cognitive behavioural treatments, anger, violence, treatment readiness and, latterly, therapeutic climates in forensic units. He is a Fellow of the British Psychological Society and has worked in the UK, Australia and the USA.

Sharon M. Kennedy received her PhD in clinical psychology from the University of Ottawa in 1990 and currently works with the Correctional Service of Canada as an Area Psychologist for Greater Ontario and Nunavut District at the Ottawa Parole Office. In addition to her responsibilities at the Ottawa Parole Office, Dr Kennedy is a part-time lecturer at the University of Ottawa in forensic psychology. She has worked as a consultant and trainer for the National Institute of Corrections, International Community Corrections Association, the American Probation and Parole Association, the Canadian Training Institute, the Department of Youth Services in Ohio, and the Federal Bureau of Prisons. Her current research interests include risk/need assessment, violent offenders, and treatment responsivity and readiness to change.

Christina Kozar has worked as a forensic psychologist within correctional environments since 1997, largely in the delivery of offending behaviour programmes. She is currently a PhD candidate at Deakin University and is examining the relationship between the therapeutic alliance and outcomes in offending behaviour programmes for clients who are personality disordered.

Mary McMurran is Professor in the University of Nottingham's Institute of Mental Health. She joined HM Prison Service in 1980 and worked up the ranks to become Head of Psychology Services at a young offenders' centre. After qualifying as a clinical psychologist, she became Head of Psychology Services at Rampton Hospital and then at the East Midlands Centre for Forensic Mental Health. In 1999, she was awarded a five-year Senior Baxter Research Fellowship by the NHS's National Programme on Forensic Mental Health Research and Development. She has written over 100 academic articles and book chapters. Her edited text, *Motivating Offenders to Change* (Wiley, 2002) was commended in the British Medical Association's 2003 Book Competition. She is a Fellow of the British Psychological Society and former Chair of the Society's Division of Forensic Psychology. In 2005, she was recipient of the Division of Forensic Psychology's Lifetime Achievement Award. She was founding co-editor of the British Psychological Society journal *Legal & Criminological Psychology*.

Donna L. Mailloux, MA, is a PhD candidate in forensic psychology at Carleton University, Ottawa, Ontario, Canada. Her research has included the areas of sex offender programming and assessment, learning disabilities, treatment readiness and responsivity, offender change, hostage-takings and psychopathy. She has published research relating to juvenile and adult populations for both males and females.

Ralph C. Serin was employed with Correctional Service Canada from 1975 to 2003 in various capacities. He is presently an Associate Professor at Carleton University in the Department of Psychology where he teaches forensic and correctional psychology courses. He has published in the areas of parole, treatment readiness and responsivity, risk assessment, psychopathy, sexual offenders, and the assessment and treatment of violent offenders. Current research topics include correctional programming (evaluation, measurement of readiness and gain, factors influencing programme drop-out); violent offenders (pathways to desistance, typologies, specialised intervention and management); and decision-making (strategies, competencies, and factors influencing accuracy).

James Vess has over 25 years of clinical and research experience with forensic populations. He received his PhD in clinical psychology from Ohio State University in the United States, and then served in a variety of treatment, assessment, and supervisory roles at Atascadero State Hospital, the maximum security forensic psychiatric facility in California. He was subsequently a Senior Lecturer at Victoria University of Wellington, where his research focus was primarily on risk assessment with violent and sexual offenders, as well as public policy dealing with high-risk offenders. He is now a Senior Lecturer at Deakin University and a member of the Clinical Forensic Research group of the recently formed Centre for Offender Reintegration at Deakin. He has also remained active in forensic practice, and has provided expert witness evidence in a variety of High Court and Court of Appeals cases for Preventive Detention and Extended Supervision in both New Zealand and Australia.

Tony Ward, MA (Hons), PhD, DipClinPsyc, is a clinical psychologist by training and has worked in the forensic field since 1989. He has taught clinical and forensic psychology at the Universities of Canterbury and Melbourne, and is currently Professor of Clinical Psychology at Victoria University of Wellington, New Zealand. He has over 260 publications and his recent books include *Rehabilitation: Beyond the Risk Paradigm* (with Shadd Maruna, Routledge, 2007) and *People Like Us: Desistance from Crime and Paths to the Good Life* (with Richard Laws, Guilford, in press). His research interests centre on rehabilitation, forensic ethics and cognition.

A Melodious Poem

It is our motivation, good or bad, that determines
the quality of our actions.
When our motivation is pure,
Even the rough earth looks friendly and the roads we walk safe.
When our motivation is poor,
Even a good home feels cold and the road we walk lonely.

Since all is dependent on our intention,
Being consumed by the mean spirit of envy,
Driven always by hatred and desire,
Do you not think this is the cause of our suffering?

Oh you intelligent people, think about it seriously.

Lama Tsong Khapa the Great
(thirteenth century, trans. S. Rigzin, in Fallon 2005: 243)

Part One

What is Treatment Readiness?

Chapter 1

The Multifactor Offender Readiness Model

These are particularly challenging times for researchers and practitioners who seek to work with offenders in ways that will assist them to live better lives. A range of different perspectives currently inform this work, from those that emphasise the rights of victims and communities to those that emphasise the rights of individual offenders. In many parts of the world, more and more people are being imprisoned and for longer periods of time. Communities are becoming more risk aversive and punitive in their attitudes towards offenders and there would appear to be a growing determination to make individuals pay severely for transgressions against the state. At the same time significant effort is put into rehabilitating offenders and helping them to plan for a successful reintegration back into society. Indeed, the last twenty or so years have seen significant investment in the development and delivery of offender rehabilitation programmes across the western world, in both prison and community correctional (probation and parole) settings, and support for rehabilitative ideals is perhaps now more clearly enshrined in public policy than perhaps at any time in the past. That is not to say, however, that the value of offender rehabilitation is universally recognised, and it is in this context that interest in issues such as human rights, offender dignity, and the values of offender rehabilitation has grown (see Ward and Birgden 2007; Ward and Maruna 2007).

The socio-political context in which any work with offenders takes place ensures that attempts to reintegrate or rehabilitate offenders will almost certainly come under a high level of scrutiny, both public and professional. It is now more important than ever that rehabilitation providers can demonstrate that their efforts are effective in reducing rates of reoffending or, at the very least, consistent with those practices that have been shown to be effective in other settings. Most correctional agencies have now developed accreditation and quality assurance systems designed specifically to ensure that the programmes offered meet basic standards of good practice. There are thousands of controlled outcome studies from which to determine the types of intervention that are likely to be effective (Hollin 2000), the results of which, when aggregated, offer consistent and persuasive evidence that offender rehabilitation programmes can, and do, have a positive effect on reducing recidivism. Furthermore, it is clear that these reductions are likely to be of a magnitude that is socially significant. It has also become apparent that programmes that adhere to certain principles are likely to be even more successful in reducing recidivism (Andrews and Dowden 2007). It is this knowledge that has led to the development of a model of offender management commonly known as the 'what works' or 'risk–needs–responsivity' (or RNR) approach, based largely on the seminal work of Don Andrews and James Bonta.

The RNR approach centres around the application of a number of core principles to offender rehabilitation (primarily the risk, needs, and responsivity principles), each of which seeks to identify the type of person who might be considered suitable for rehabilitation initiatives. Perhaps most progress here has been made in the area of risk assessment, with recent years seeing the development and validation of a wide range of specialist tools designed to help identify those who are most likely to reoffend. The logic is compelling – if the goal of intervention is to reduce recidivism, then effort should be invested in working with those who are the most likely to reoffend, rather than those who probably will not. It is possible to meaningfully categorise offenders into different risk brackets using a relatively small set of variables (such as the age at first offence or the number of previous offences). A focus of current work in this area is on the identification and assessment of those risk factors that have the potential to change over time. These 'dynamic' risk factors, or what have become known as 'criminogenic needs' (see Webster et al. 1997), are particularly important in determining treatment targets (that is those areas of functioning that might be addressed within offender rehabilitation programmes). In comparison, the third major tenet of the RNR approach – responsivity – has been somewhat neglected. This term is commonly used to refer to those characteristics of individual offenders (such as motivation to change) that are likely to influence how much they are able to benefit from a particular programme.

In many respects, the RNR approach has revolutionised correctional practice. It has promoted the idea of community safety as the primary driver behind correctional case management, and given offender rehabilitation programmes a central role in the sentence planning process. The approach has had a major impact on practice in relation to offender assessment and the selection of appropriate candidates for intervention around the western world. It has, however, had less influence on the actual practice of offender rehabilitation (see Andrews 2006; Bonta *et al.* 2008), and significant gaps in knowledge remain (Andrews and Dowden 2007). Critics of the RNR model have, in a range of different ways, drawn attention to how the model struggles to inform the process of programme delivery, and how psychological and behaviour change takes place. This may be, in part, because the RNR model was developed as an approach to offender management rather than psychological therapy. It may also perhaps relate to difficulties in the way in which some of the key terms (notably risk and needs) have been conceptualised, and in particular how the overarching focus on risk can be experienced as demotivating for individual participants in rehabilitation programmes, ultimately contributing towards high rates of programme attrition and a lack of rehabilitative success (Thomas-Peter 2006; Ward and Stewart 2003). While the notion that offender rehabilitation is something that can be done to someone, possibly even without their consent, has appeal, it is also therapeutically naive. The gains made in the area of offender assessment and selection have not, in our view, been matched by progress in the area of offender treatment, where concerns are commonly expressed about issues of offender motivation and engagement in behaviour change, therapist skill and training, programme integrity, and the social climate of institutions in which interventions are delivered.

Perhaps nowhere are these issues more apparent than in the areas of treatment readiness and responsivity. It is our contention that work in this area has been hampered by a lack of conceptual clarity about the construct of responsivity, how it might be operationalised, and how it might be reliably assessed. In this book, we explore the idea that even greater reductions in recidivism than those demonstrated in programmes that adhere to the evidence-based principles of risk and needs can be made when programmes are able to be responsive to individual needs. We discuss the meaning and nature of the term 'treatment readiness' and how this might inform the rehabilitative process. Readiness is proposed as an overarching term that encompasses both the internal components of responsivity (offender motivation, problem awareness, emotional capacity to engage with psychological treatment, goals, and personal identity), as well as those external components that may be specific to the environment in which treatment is commonly offered.

Our interest in the notion of treatment readiness arose out of work in which we examined the effects of anger management programmes offered to offenders (Howells *et al.* 2005; Heseltine *et al.* 2009). These evaluations suggested that anger management training, at least of the type commonly offered in Australian prisons at the time, was unlikely to be particularly effective in bringing about behavioural change – in this context this referred to physical aggression and violent behaviour of a criminal nature. At the time, prison administrations across Australia dedicated considerable energy and resources to the development and delivery of anger management programmes to violent offenders, and so these apparently weak treatment effects required some explanation. A number of hypotheses were proposed, including those relating to the selection of appropriate candidates, the matching of the intensity of the intervention to the level of risk and need, and the extent to which those who are imprisoned for violent offending might be considered to be ready for treatment. In a subsequent paper, Howells and Day (2003) developed the notion of treatment readiness by identifying seven impediments that potentially inhibited the effective treatment of offenders presenting with anger problems (see Table 1.1).

This work was subsequently elaborated into a more general model of readiness which was then applied to all forms of offender rehabilitation programming (Ward *et al.* 2004b). The Multifactor Offender Readiness Model (MORM) proposed that impediments or barriers to offender treatment can reside within the person, the context, or within the therapy or therapeutic environment. The following definition of treatment readiness was put forward: *the presence of characteristics (states or dispositions) within either the client or the therapeutic situation, which are likely to promote engagement in therapy and which, thereby, are likely to enhance therapeutic change.* According to this definition, readiness to change persistent offending behaviour requires the existence of certain internal and external conditions within a particular context (see Figure 1.1). Offenders who are ready to enter a specific treatment programme are thus viewed as possessing a number of core psychological features that enable them to function well in a particular rehabilitation programme at a particular time.

Table 1.1   Impediments to readiness for anger management

Number	Description
1	The complexity of the cases presenting with anger problems. This includes the coexistence of mental disorders with aggressive behaviour.
2	The setting in which anger management is conducted.
3	Existing client inferences about their anger problem. For example, inferences indicating that the anger was viewed as appropriate and justified.
4	The impact of coerced or mandatory treatment.
5	The inadequate analysis of context of personal goals within which the anger problem occurs. It is possible that the expression of anger could increase the likelihood that important personal goals are achieved.
6	Ethnic and cultural differences.
7	Gender differences in the experience and expression of anger.

Source: Adapted from Howells and Day (2003).

Individual or person readiness factors are cognitive (beliefs, cognitive strategies), affective (emotions), volitional (goals, wants, or desires), and behavioural (skills and competencies). The contextual readiness factors relate to circumstances in which programmes are offered (mandated vs voluntary, offender type), their location (prison, community), and the opportunity to participate (availability of programmes), as well as the level of interpersonal support that exists (availability of individuals who wish the offender well and would like to see him or her succeed), and the availability of adequate resources (quality of programme, availability of trained and qualified therapist, appropriate culture). It is suggested that these personal and contextual factors combine to determine the likelihood that a person will be ready to benefit from a treatment programme. Those who are treatment ready will engage better in treatment, and this will be observably evident from their rates of attendance, participation, and programme completion. Assuming that programmes are appropriately designed and delivered, and they target criminogenic need, higher levels of engagement are considered likely to lead to reductions in levels of criminogenic need and a consequent reduction in risk level. The model thus incorporates whether or not a person is ready to change his or her behaviour (in the general sense); to eliminate a specific problem; to eliminate a specific problem by virtue of a specific method (such as cognitive behavioural therapy); and, finally,

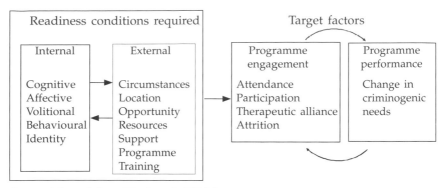

Source: Adapted from Ward et al. (2004b).

Figure 1.1 Original model of offender treatment readiness

to eliminate a specific problem by virtue of a specific method at a specific time.

To be treatment ready, offenders must not only recognise that their offending is problematic, but also make a decision to seek help from others. This implies a belief that they are unable to desist from offending unaided. Once the offender makes a genuine commitment not to reoffend, he or she may then be taught the relevant skills and strategies in treatment to help achieve this goal. The decision to seek help may also be affected by factors such as which services are available, attitudes or beliefs about those services, beliefs about the importance of privacy and autonomy, or that problems are likely to diminish over time anyway. The extent to which a behaviour or a feeling is defined as a problem will, in part, be determined by cultural rules and norms relating to what is acceptable or appropriate (for example women generally have more positive attitudes towards help-seeking than men: Boldero and Fallon 1995), and in environments where certain types of offending are considered normative, it is unlikely that the individual will see his/her offending as problematic. Other contextual factors, such as poverty, may also influence the decision to recognise a particular behaviour as a problem. Of course, an offender may be ready to work on a particular problem, but not necessarily one that the therapist views as relevant and central to his or her offending; to be treatment ready, both the treatment provider and the offender have to agree on both the goals and the tasks of the treatment.

The MORM was developed in a way that distinguishes between three distinct although related constructs: treatment motivation, responsivity, and readiness. The constructs of motivation and responsivity are conceptualised as somewhat narrower in scope than that of readiness (see Table 1.2). Furthermore, readiness directs us to ask what is required for successful entry into a programme, while the concept of responsivity focuses attention on what it is that can prevent treatment engagement. Ward *et al.* (2004b) suggest that the responsivity concept has not really developed conceptual coherence and, as such, is often poorly operationalised as a list of relatively independent factors (see Serin 1998). We suggest that treatment readiness may be a better model because of its greater scope, coherence, testability, and utility (fertility).

Our aim in writing this book is to describe, collate, and summarise a body of recent research, both theoretical and empirical, that explores the issue of treatment readiness in offender programming. The book is divided into different sections. In the first, we unpack our model of treatment readiness and how it has been operationalised. Ralph Serin and colleagues also describe their understanding of the notion of treatment readiness (Chapter 2). We then discuss in Part Two how the construct has been applied to the treatment of different offender groups. In Part Three, we discuss some of the practice approaches that have been identified as holding promise in addressing low levels of offender readiness. We have included contributions from a number of authors whose work has stimulated discussion and helped to inform practice in offender rehabilitation. Collectively we hope that these chapters offer a useful resource for researchers and academics alike, describing current thinking and knowledge in this area. We chose to call the book *Transitions to Better Lives* to remind us of the ultimate purpose behind any attempt to rehabilitate offenders – that is, to help individuals learn how to meet their needs in ways that are both personally fulfilling and socially responsible. It is this possibility that motivates practitioner and offender alike and, in our view, lies at the very heart of successful rehabilitation.

Table 1.2 Distinguishing between motivation, responsivity and treatment readiness

Construct	Description
Motivation	Motivation is widely recognised as important in that offenders are usually selected for treatment partly on the basis of being motivated to participate. Professionals typically judge that offenders are motivated when they express regret for their offences, express a desire to change, and sound enthusiastic about the treatments on offer. Motivation in this context relates to whether someone wants to enter treatment; that is, ascertaining his or her level of volition with respect to changing particular target behaviours. There is, however, no consensus regarding what is meant by offenders' motivation and no systematic examination of the factors that influence it (McMurran and Ward 2004), despite it being widely accepted that a major task in treatment is to nurture and enhance motivation to change.
Responsivity	The term responsivity is used to refer to the use of a style and mode of intervention that engages the client group (Andrews and Bonta 2003). Responsivity can be further divided into internal and external responsivity whereby attention to internal responsivity factors requires therapists to match the content and pace of sessions to specific client attributes, such as personality and cognitive maturity, while external responsivity refers to a range of general and specific issues, such as the use of active and participatory methods. External responsivity has been divided further into staff and setting characteristics (Kennedy 2001; Serin and Kennedy 1997). Although responsivity as usually understood in the rehabilitation literature, is primarily focused on therapist and therapy features and thus is essentially concerned with adjusting treatment delivery in a way that maximises learning.

Table 1.2 continues opposite

Table 1.2 continued

Construct	Description
Readiness	The concept of readiness was originally articulated in an offender context by Ralph Serin (Serin and Kennedy, 1997; Serin 1998), although it had previously been used in offender substance use treatment programmes (e.g. DeLeon and Jainchill 1986). It has been broadly defined as the presence of characteristics (states or dispositions) within either the client or the therapeutic situation, which are likely to promote engagement in therapy and which, thereby, are likely to enhance therapeutic change (Howells and Day 2003). To be ready for treatment means that the person is motivated (i.e. wants to, has the will to), is able to respond appropriately (i.e. perceives he or she can), finds it relevant and meaningful (i.e. can engage), and has the capacities (i.e. is able) to successfully enter the treatment programme.

Source: Adapted from Ward *et al*. (2004b).

Chapter 2

The origins of treatment readiness

Ralph C. Serin, Sharon M. Kennedy, Donna L. Mailloux and Laura J. Hanby

The field of forensic and correctional psychology has witnessed an explosion of interest in risk assessment over the past three decades. Encouragingly, many of these risk assessment approaches have evolved from simple aggregation of criminal history factors to the identification of dynamic needs and treatment targets. In turn, this has led to improved clarity regarding programming models for offenders, both in prison and in the community. Concurrently, following the pessimism of Martinson's (1974) 'nothing works' conclusion, a seminal paper by Andrews *et al.* (1990) led the way for an explosion of a new era of correctional rehabilitation. This applied research began to be known as the What Works literature and has been the pre-eminent perspective for offender programming internationally for the past two decades. Strengthened by empirical evidence regarding their utility, correctional programmes have multiplied exponentially, now dotting the correctional landscape in most western countries. Indeed, since the late 1980s the zeal to develop and deliver correctional programmes has continued unabated.

Notwithstanding the enthusiasm of clinicians, it became apparent in the early days of correctional programming that not all offenders embraced change. Although unsurprising, this treatment resistance raised concerns regarding the potential for wasting treatment spots through programme attrition as well as the potential attenuation of effectiveness in evaluation studies. Of note, since these early days of offender programming, evaluations typically now include programme drop-outs within the comparison group to ensure that effect sizes are not unduly inflated (Rice and Harris 1997b, 2005). Hence, the issue of programme attrition has become both a methodological and a practical concern. For those of us (RS and SK) working as part of a large corrections agency committed to offender programming, it became apparent that what was required was some approach to understanding and measuring offender readiness, such that programming efforts were maximised. We therefore saw treatment readiness as but one construct, albeit crucial, to be included in the conceptualisation of treatment response and offender change.

The focus of this chapter is to describe a programme of research relating to the conceptualisation and assessment of treatment responsivity, beginning in 1994. At that time, we viewed treatment responsivity as an overarching term to reflect treatment readiness and interpersonal style factors that would influence treatment performance. Treatment readiness was therefore a requisite component within a model of offender change and any assessment protocol of offender programming. Accordingly, this chapter reviews the related constructs discussed in the literature at that time in order to distinguish the uniqueness of treatment readiness. We provide some observations on recent research regarding offender change and implications regarding our earlier efforts, and comment on the continued theoretical and practical utility of treatment readiness.

At the onset of this research, correctional programmes were evolving from an eclectic mix of programmes (substance use, anger, and sex offender programming) mainly delivered by psychologists to the more current structured programmes now commonly delivered by para-professionals. It was in this context that an appreciation for an understanding of factors that might enhance or mitigate programme participation was conceived. We wanted to develop a model and set of measures that were easy to use by non-psychologists and would inform programme retention and performance. Our logic was that if we could distinguish among programme referrals in terms of treatment readiness, then priming could be provided to those offenders who presented as less ready to participate. Underlying this work was the recognition that programming, regardless of its scope, was intended to be a vehicle for offender change (although this does not mean to imply that change cannot occur in the absence of participation in formal correctional programmes). Nonetheless, change would be more likely to occur if the offender fully participated in the programme. Unfortunately, in these early days there were not the eloquent descriptions of programmes that now exist (McGuire 2001), nor the detailed criteria defining correctional programmes common on most correctional agencies' websites (Correctional Service of Canada 2009).

More recent conceptualisations of offender programming include comments about responsivity, in particular offender motivation, but such language was scarce in 1994 (Michenbaum and Turk 1987).

It should be apparent that advances in programming models and risk assessment were just beginning to take hold in clinical practice as we embarked on our work on our conceptualisation and assessment of treatment readiness. Quinsey (1988) was prescient in noting that improvements in our understanding of treatability were likely to be of greater importance than improved risk prediction.

Prior to 1990 such terms as treatability, motivation, and readiness for change had been used interchangeably. As well, the terms were prominent in the area of mental health in that some legal statutes required a consideration of treatability in a range of criminal justice decisions ranging from the granting of bail to sentencing and discretionary release. Earlier work by Quinsey and Maguire (1983) spoke to the ambiguity of the construct and poor inter-clinician reliability in its assessment. Further, Rogers and Webster (1989) noted that treatability referred to the clinical determination of which patients, under what treatment modalities and circumstances, will respond most favourably. That few clinicians could agree on how to assess treatability led Heilbrun and his colleagues (1992) to seek to develop a scale that reflected the multifaceted nature of the concept. Their effort was substantial but in the end yielded modest reliability and was incredibly labour-intensive. Further, while such efforts might be viable in a mental health setting, it was highly unlikely that such resources would be allocated for assessing treatability in correctional settings. Nonetheless, few clinicians disagreed with the importance of such a construct and there was widespread appreciation that offenders differed with respect to their interest in programming, regardless of demonstrated risk level or nature of identified needs.

At the same time as the issue of treatability was being addressed, work principally in the area of addictions was also germane. Miller and Rollnick's (1991) influential work on motivational interviewing (MI) and the work of Prochaska, DiClemente and Norcross (1992) on readiness for change, as measured by the Readiness for Change Questionnaire (University of Rhode Island Change Assessment), underscored the importance of both motivation and readiness in predicting programme engagement and outcome. The former challenged the apparent interest by some in confrontational approaches to treatment, while the latter underscored the need for viewing change as a stage-based process. Both approaches offered strategies for attending to responsivity issues in offender treatment such that outcomes would be enhanced and both remain important in correctional programming today (Andrews and Bonta 1998). At the time that we began this work it seemed that there were converging lines of research that underscored the need to consider contextual factors that might influence offender programming.

Our goal was to merge these complementary viewpoints of treatability, readiness for change, and motivation, and overlay a corrections interpretation. We also wanted to consider a range of domains that might influence treatment engagement so that there were multiple avenues (targets) to address in order to enhance programme engagement, when needed. We termed this construct 'treatment readiness'. Our expectation was that improved engagement would lead to improved programme performance, which in turn would yield improved programme outcomes. The balance of the chapter describes our conceptual model, the development of an assessment of treatment readiness and related constructs, and comments regarding its application in corrections. Admittedly, much of this viewed the problem through the lens of what an individual offender needed to do to enhance outcomes, but supported by skilled clinicians. This is in contrast to the more multifaceted MORM model described elsewhere in this book.

Conceptual model

Our initial efforts (RS and SK) were to consider the extant literature and to brainstorm regarding how we perceived the different components that influence offender change and how they might be situated. This initial model, then, organised our work plan regarding a programme of research, especially with respect to the development of an instrument to assess treatment readiness. Next, we brainstormed to create an inclusive list of domains that could be obstacles to change, based on our observations during our respective careers as clinical psychologists in corrections. These domains were reviewed and refined to yield a relatively independent (we hoped) series of domains. Given our interest in a behavioural rating strategy rather than self-report questionnaire, we developed a series of anchors to guide assessors. Figure 2.1 presents our conceptual model in 1997. We hypothesised that treatment readiness was more expansive and multidimensional than simply an index of motivation. Indeed, there had just been a clinical rating of offender motivation developed as part of an offender intake assessment but it was not well incorporated into decisions about programming. We hypothesised that a variety of factors would contribute to an overall index of treatment readiness. Further, personality factors, which we termed 'interpersonal style', were hypothesised to interact with treatment readiness, thereby influencing overall treatment response. Finally, we wanted to have an overall conceptual model that provided staff with indices of offender change. At the time we referred to this as 'treatment performance', but now we would likely use the term 'offender competency' (Hanby *et al.* 2009). What should be apparent is that the operationalisation of these three domains (treatment readiness, interpersonal style, and treatment performance) was slightly disconnected from the original conceptual model. That is, interpersonal style is prominent in the assessment protocol but less so in the model. In hindsight, improved clarity regarding the relationship between interpersonal style and treatment readiness would have been desirable.

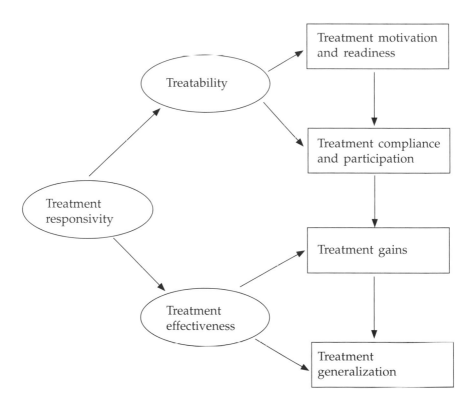

Figure 2.1 Conceptual model of treatment responsivity.

As can be seen in Figure 2.1, treatment response was hypothesised to be comprised of two contributing domains: treatability and treatment effectiveness. Treatability is reflected in indices of treatment readiness and treatment compliance. Specifically, it was hypothesised that treatment readiness would lead to improved compliance and participation, hence meeting the requirement for determining that an individual was treatable, as implied in the earlier research on treatability. Having met the criterion for treatability, it is then of interest to determine if the offender changes as a function of programme involvement and if such change generalises post-programme (upon release). In this manner, recidivism is seen as a failure to generalise gains (assuming gains were real and sufficient to change criminal behaviour). In conclusion, treatment readiness was conceived to be part of a broader conceptual model to understand offender change and treatment outcome. The balance of the chapter, however, focuses on the definition and assessment of treatment readiness, as well as its implications in offender programming.

When this work was initiated our intention was to identify offenders for whom there was concern regarding low readiness so that pre-treatment primers could be provided. In this manner, the treatment readiness assessment would complement motivational interviewing efforts (Anstiss *et al.*, in press), but such efforts would not be routinely applied, rather they would be presumably reserved for a sub-group of programme referrals. The expectation was that such preventative efforts would attenuate programme attrition and in-group misbehaviour. Nowadays most high-intensity programmes for higher-risk offenders utilise some form of engagement or motivational enhancement to address potential treatment readiness (that is obstacles to change) concerns (Polaschek 2009; Serin and Preston 2001).

The initial brainstorming exercise and subsequent review by colleagues yielded an initial 11 factors to consider within the broader domain of treatment readiness. These are listed below. In order to be inclusive and reflect the overall assessment model, the factors for interpersonal style and treatment performance are also provided.

Behavioural rating assessment protocol

Treatment readiness ratings

1 Problem recognition	2 Goal setting
3 Motivation	4 Self-appraisal
5 Expectations	6 Behavioural consistency
7 Views about treatment	8 Self-efficacy

9 Dissonance   10 External supports
11 Affective Component

Interpersonal style ratings
1 Procriminal views   2 Procriminal associations
3 Grandiosity   4 Callousness
5 Neutralisation   6 Impulsivity
7 Procrastination   8 Motivation for anger
9 Power and control   10 Problem-solving
11 Victim stance

Treatment performance ratings
1 Knowledge of programme content   2 Skills acquisition
3 Disclosure   4 Offender confidence
5 Knowledge application   6 Skills application
7 Understanding of criminality   8 Motivation
9 Insight   10 Attendance
11 Disruptiveness   12 Appropriateness
13 Depth of emotional understanding   14 Participation

The treatment readiness and interpersonal style domains of the initial assessment protocol were developed to reflect 11 factors. Each factor (for instance problem recognition) had two representative indices (problem acknowledgement and problem understanding) with behaviourally anchored ratings using a four-point Likert scale and exemplars for each rating. This yielded 22 ratings for each subject for each of the domains of treatment readiness and interpersonal style.

Neither primary author (RS and SK) were directly involved in the delivery, management or evaluation of standardised correctional programmes at the time this work was initiated. Staff directly involved in delivering such programmes were approached regarding participation in research to develop an assessment protocol relating to offender change, but this work was not part of the Correctional Service of Canada's annual research plan. For these reasons, data collection was somewhat sporadic and samples were of convenience. Nonetheless, response from practitioners was favourable and sufficient data were collected to permit refinements of the treatment readiness assessment instrument and an evaluation of its psychometric properties (Serin *et al.* 2007). Initial correlations among items were reviewed and factor analysis was employed to reduce the initial 22-item version to a more useful eight-item version, using data collected on a sample of 262 federally incarcerated offenders who participated in various correctional programs. This abbreviated version has acceptable reliability (alpha = .83) and accounted for 45 per cent of the variance in the treatment readiness factor. Initial normative data regarding male offenders (n = 268), women offenders (n = 29) and sexual offenders (n = 39) are available. It is these eight factors that are listed below and are described in greater detail later in this chapter.

1 Problem recognition
2 Benefits of treatment
3 Treatment interest
4 Treatment distress
5 Treatment goals
6 Treatment behaviours
7 Motivational consistency
8 Treatment support

Essentially, we posit that these final eight items reflect our effort at operationalising the construct of treatment readiness in offenders.

The following excerpt from the user manual presents our view of treatment readiness:

Treatment readiness is a domain that captures an individual's willingness to engage in the treatment process. For some, they see themselves as having very few problems that require therapeutic intervention and do not have any desire to make changes. These individuals tend to be forced into treatment and are reluctant to put forth any effort into changing. Others may be aware of the problems in their lives but are hesitant to make a commitment to change. On the other extreme are those who are committed to changing and are enthusiastic about modifying their behaviours.

The treatment readiness domain is intended to operationalize this continuum in an effort to assist clinicians in determining treatment placement. This domain has excellent internal consistency producing an alpha of .83 in a sample of 265 male offenders entering a cognitive skills program. The items produced factor loadings in the very good to excellent range (.60 to .77) with a mean of .67.

Description of treatment readiness items

Problem recognition

Treatment readiness begins with an appreciation by the offender of the need to change something (friends, substance use, attitudes, problem-solving) in order to avoid future criminality. Problem recognition assesses an offender's awareness that specific criminogenic problems do exist and have contributed to their involvement in offending behaviour. In this manner, intent need not be deliberate and criminal behaviour could be perceived to be accidental or circumstantial; nonetheless, the offender accepts that there is a problem. Problem recognition also addresses the offender's understanding of the impact of these problems (short- and long-term consequences, relation to crime and other lifestyle variables such as financial, employment, family, and interpersonal relationships). Hence, this is more than the offender simply stating they have a problem. Where the offender believes that circumstances or other people are the sole cause of their problems, this reflects an absence of problem recognition. Our inclusion of this item wanted to address both recognition and accountability (Hanby *et al.* 2009). The expectation was that offenders who score higher on problem recognition would be more ready for treatment.

The operational definition from the user manual is: 'Problem recognition assesses an offender's awareness that specific criminogenic problems exist. The first item considers only recognition of specific difficulties. This item assesses the offender's appraisal of their current situation. This is assessed in terms of their understanding and ownership of their problems.'

Benefits of treatment

Another important aspect of treatment readiness is the offender's recognition that there are potential benefits to treatment involvement. The expectation was that offenders who score higher on seeing benefits for treatment would be more ready for treatment. Now, almost 15 years later, we would describe this item in terms of outcome expectancies (Serin and Lloyd 2009): that is, offenders who expect that involvement in treatment will reduce future criminal behaviour and that crime desistance is a valued outcome. Phrased differently, offenders with stronger beliefs in their ability to overcome obstacles involved in giving up crime through programming will more readily attempt to give up crime, continue to strive against setbacks and ultimately succeed.

The operational definition from the user manual is: 'This item is intended to tap into an offender's views regarding the overall benefits of participating in treatment. An offender who describes the long-term benefits (lifestyle stability such as employment, relationships, no crime) *and* short-term benefits (earlier release, fewer release conditions) of treatment would be assessed as recognizing the benefits of treatment.'

Treatment interest

The next treatment readiness item is very similar to the benefits of treatment item. The intent was to capture whether the interest in treatment reflects both internal and external reasons. Those offenders who can identify that treatment participation will be of value to themselves as well as to others would be considered most ready for treatment, thus heading towards a path of crime desistance. Individuals tend to adopt a particular style of explaining life events, whether internal (caused by features within the person) or external (caused by others, the environment or chance). When desisting from crime, it may be most adaptive for offenders to reject blame for their criminal history and current problems (external) while still holding themselves responsible for finding methods for staying crime-free (internal) (Maruna and Mann 2006). Others have noted the need to seek resources and a requirement for active effort in the change process (Moulden and Marshall 2005).

Treatment distress

Although negative affect can be a precursor to criminal involvement (Pithers *et al.* 1989; Zamble and Quinsey 1997), our experience and some research regarding individuals suffering from anti-social personality disorder (Alterman and Cacciola 1991) suggested that some distress was also important in influencing offender commitment to change. More recently, this viewpoint has been supported by physiological assessment where cortisol levels were related to treatment response (Fishbein *et al.* 2009). Essentially, offenders who present as indifferent and lacking in some emotional distress were hypothesised to be less ready than offenders whose distress regarding their current circumstance prompted them to consider change.

Treatment goals

Another aspect of our conceptualisation of treatment readiness is setting realistic treatment goals. Goal-setting assesses an offender's ability to identify and realistically create treatment goals. This item considers the knowledge and skills necessary for treatment gain. Again, nowadays we might incorporate the issue of outcome expectancies (how effortful is treatment, how viable is the treatment goal, is the treatment goal something developed in conjunction with the offender or proscribed?). More recent work describing approach and avoidance goals in sex offenders (Mann *et al.* 2004) highlights the importance of integrating the identification of goals into a treatment plan in order to enhance programme effectiveness. Moreover, it seemed to us that alerting offenders to the effort required in treatment and the high probability of lapses should ameliorate programme attrition and post-programme failures due to unrealistic expectations.

Treatment behaviours

It is rare that an adult offender who presents for treatment has never had prior experience regarding change efforts. Noting that prior history is often a good predictor of future behaviour, we wanted to include an item regarding treatment behaviours. This can reflect prior treatment experience of the initial two or three sessions of the current programming efforts. This item assesses the offender's motivation for treatment. Behavioural indication of good motivation should reflect, where applicable, timely attendance at interviews and/ or groups, homework completion, compliance with prior treatment, and/or positive comments about treatment as a process not an outcome. Anecdotally, offenders sometimes present for treatment noting a prior positive rehabilitative effort (previously completed a group, or previously seen a psychologist). Yet when enquiries are made to retrieve greater details regarding these experiences, there is a disconnect. That is, the offender cannot remember key learning points. Sometimes they cannot even recall the name of the staff member, despite having just explained how great the programme was and how much they benefited from the experience! At best this is a problem of transfer, at worst an indication that the offender recalls little of the experience and was simply telling you what they thought you wanted to hear.

Motivational consistency

Related to this issue of motivation is one of consistency. This item highlights the importance of an offender's verbal statements *and* their actions regarding treatment. If an offender has not previously participated in treatment then this item refers to behavioural consistency outside of treatment (such as meeting a caseworker). Offenders who state that they are motivated towards treatment, but show incongruence (in poor attendance, being late or infrequent attendance without a legitimate reason, failure to complete homework, and/or stating low motivation to other staff or offenders) would be seen as lacking motivational consistency. Our preliminary research has flagged an issue with this item. It is possible for an individual to be consistently lacking in motivation. In this case we have suggested a score of '0' as the intent is that higher scores reflect greater treatment readiness.

Treatment support

At the time that we created this item as part of the domain of treatment readiness, our clinical work informed the need to include something relating to aftercare and support. Some work regarding the importance of pro-social models was available (Andrews and Kiessling 1980), but it is only more recently that its importance in understanding offender success has been demonstrated (LeBel *et al.* 2008; Maruna 2001; Massoglia and Uggen 2007). Given that we perceive offender change as a process, this item assesses the degree of support for change by others significant to the offender. It is important to allow the offender to determine who is important to them (preferably family, friends, employer, or clergy) and then probe for degree of support from them. Change without support is unlikely to generalize. Of note is that enhancing community support underscores the current re-entry initiative in the United States (Burke and Tonry 2006).

Using the scale

Following the initial interview, the items are scored using a three-point scale and aggregated. Self-reference questions, behavioural anchors, and questions to pose to the offender are all provided in the user manual. For purposes of comparison, normative pre- and post-treatment readiness scores are provided. For offenders who score below average (one standard deviation below the mean), we suggest individual primer sessions to overcome obstacles to treatment engagement following the principles of motivational interviewing (Anstiss *et al.*, in press).

Summary

Throughout the pilot research the feedback we received from programme staff was very positive. Perhaps the absence of an earlier model of treatment readiness augmented its informal use. As well, programme staff found the assessment protocol helpful in structuring their post-treatment reports in that they could systematically comment on changes with respect to treatment readiness, interpersonal style and programme performance. As noted earlier, this modest effort has yielded a user-friendly and short behavioural rating scale that appears to capture meaningful aspects of treatment readiness. More recent research has supported the importance of many of the items and underscores the utility of an assessment of treatment readiness prior to programme involvement.

Empirical support

The results from this pilot research were encouraging in that the revised eight-item treatment readiness rating scale appears reliable; it appears sensitive to change and preliminary norms are now available. However, the absence of inter-rater reliability and concurrent and predictive validity data are disconcerting. For now, sites choosing to use the treatment readiness scale clinically should provide sufficient training with the manual to ensure inter-rater reliability. Nonetheless, interest from other colleagues in other countries has led to some encouraging findings. Unpublished research suggests that the domains of treatment readiness and interpersonal style differentiate among offenders in terms of programme attrition in the United Kingdom (Watson and Beech 2002) and Canada (Stewart 2005). There is also unpublished evidence that treatment readiness is correlated to recidivism in a sample of offenders in Hong Kong (Lee 2005). The eight-item version of the treatment readiness scale has also been used to distinguish among types of sexual offenders (Malcolm 2002), but was not predictive of programme drop-out by sex offenders due to exceedingly low base rates (Latendresse 2006). However, this latter research confirmed the strong relationship between total scores on the original and revised versions.

Implications and new directions

Conceptually, we view treatment readiness as requisite for offender change and the strategies proposed for managing high-risk offenders seem appropriate for engaging offenders who lack readiness for treatment (Anstiss *et al.*, in press; Polaschek 2009; Serin and Preston 2001). Nonetheless, some offenders arrive at treatment ready to change, so there will be heterogeneity among offenders regarding readiness. A review of current literature suggests the concept of treatment readiness remains popular and is particularly salient in understanding violent offenders (Day *et al.* 2009a). Indeed, through numerous papers (Chambers *et al.* 2008; Casey *et al.* 2007; Day *et al.* 2007) these authors have single-handedly refined and underscored the construct as it applies to violent offenders. Moreover, they have applied the construct of treatment readiness to broader models of offender change (Day *et al.* 2006; Ward *et al.* 2004b), suggesting its utility over other models such as the transtheoretical model of change (Casey *et al.* 2005).

With the exception of this recent research regarding treatment readiness in violent offenders, some 15 years later, various terms continue to be used interchangeably – treatment motivation, treatment engagement, and readiness for change. Indeed, in many respects the field has made relatively little progress in understanding offender change and demonstrating its ability to measure such change, although its importance is certainly underscored (McMurran and Ward 2004). It is clear that clinicians continue to struggle with the assessment of these constructs around readiness and treatment engagement, and yet such constructs are critical to our understanding and predicting offender change. As a brief behavioural assessment, we posit that our treatment readiness scale may have potential merit in assisting clinicians to assess treatment engagement and the need for pre-treatment priming. We also believe that a full testing of our model and alternative explanations of offender change is required. As assessment efforts continue, it may be that such a scale and model could inform the development of an assessment protocol.

Since our early research (Kennedy and Serin 1997; Serin and Kennedy 1997), this work has evolved such that we now conceptualise offender change, of which treatment readiness is an important component, to be part of a broader transition by the offender (Lloyd and Serin 2009; Serin and Lloyd 2009). The focus on this transition is markers of interpersonal change in support of successful desistance from crime. We also view treatment readiness as an important competency, one that is requisite for offender change and crime desistance (Hanby *et al.* 2009). Research regarding these refinements to the role of treatment readiness is ongoing, as is research regarding improvements to the assessment of offender change.

Chapter 3

What are readiness factors?

In this chapter we describe in some detail those factors that have been identified in the Multifactoral Offender Readiness Model (MORM), introduced in Chapter 1 of this book. We have adopted the distinction made in the model between internal and external readiness factors, and will begin with a review of internal factors, as these are most commonly associated with current understandings of treatment readiness and, indeed, attempts to modify low levels of treatment readiness (see Chapter 10).

Internal readiness factors

It is those core psychological features that enable offenders to function in a therapeutic context that have attracted most of the attention of researchers and clinicians. These are referred to in the MORM as internal readiness conditions and may be either cognitive (beliefs, cognitive strategies), affective (emotions), volitional (goals, wants or desires), or behavioural (skills and competencies). In this chapter we consider each of these factors in turn. In many ways, it is these characteristics of individual offenders that have attracted the most interest and discussion in relation to both treatment readiness and responsivity. Ways of measuring these readiness factors are discussed later in this book (see Chapter 5), although they are also discussed in relation to violent offenders, sexual offenders, offenders with personality disorders, and those with substance abuse disorders. It is also these internal readiness factors that are most relevant to the clinical and therapeutic approaches to working with low levels of readiness discussed in Part Three.

Cognitive factors

Self-efficacy is one aspect of cognition that has attracted a great deal of attention in relation to treatment engagement. It can be understood as the self-appraisal about how well one can perform actions to deal with a situation (Bandura 1997), and is thought to be related to both enhanced motivation and performance (Bandura and Locke 2003). Chambers and colleagues describe it in the following way: 'Low self-efficacy leaves the individual believing that he/she is unable to learn new social skills, or alternate ways of life, and is thus unlikely to attempt new behaviors' (2008: 281–2). General beliefs about personal change may also influence the likelihood of an individual offender identifying a need for treatment and engaging with a rehabilitation programme. For an individual to take steps to change, he or she must not only believe that the benefits of the action outweigh the barriers, but also experience some trigger to take action, and (in relation to health promotion behaviours), believe that he or she is susceptible to the condition and view the condition as serious (Chew et al. 2002). In terms of offender rehabilitation, this suggests that the offender would need to see his or her offending as likely to recur (that is that s/he is susceptible), that offending is a serious problem, and that the costs of change do not outweigh the benefits (for example not associating with friends who are likely to offend) if he or she is likely to seek out referral to a rehabilitation programme.

More specifically, offenders often hold particular attitudes about treatment in the criminal justice system that can influence the way in which they present to programme providers (Baxter et al. 1995). Expectations about what will happen in programmes will also influence readiness. These can arise from previous experiences of treatment, the experience of the assessment process, or the reputation that programmes and even individual programme staff members have in a particular institution. This area has received surprisingly little attention in the literature, although studies that have been conducted suggest that, generally, offenders are likely to hold quite negative views towards criminal justice agencies (Lyon et al. 2000), and are unlikely to approach correctional staff for help, particularly for emotional support (Dear et al. 2002; Hobbs and Dear 2000).

Offenders also exhibit a number of attitudes, beliefs and thinking styles that potentially either reduce or increase their willingness to engage in a rehabilitation programme. For example, the existence of hostile attitudes and beliefs can result in a tendency to view the world and the actions of others in a negative or cynical fashion, making it difficult to accept that therapists will behave in a trustworthy manner and deliver the kind of interventions that were initially promised. Such beliefs can be understood not only as dynamic risk factors, or criminogenic needs (given the association between particular thinking styles and behaving in anti-social or aggressive ways), but also as factors that will impinge upon an individual's ability to engage with a rehabilitation programme.

Chambers *et al.* (2008) have discussed how holding particular beliefs about an offence may make it less likely that the individual will regard treatment as necessary, as well as how more general, or trait, aspects of cognition potentially influence treatment readiness. For example, what Gibbs, Potter and Goldstein (1995) have referred to as primary self-serving cognitive distortions (self-centred attitudes, thoughts and beliefs that are manifested as a belief in one's own views, needs and expectations to the extent that the views of others are inconsequential or totally disregarded), and secondary self-serving cognitive distortions (such as blaming others, minimising/mislabelling and assuming the worst of others) may both reduce levels of treatment readiness. Chambers and colleagues suggest that strong primary cognitive distortions can seriously impede readiness because the offender believes that he or she already 'knows it all' and, as such, does not see the need for personal change. Secondary distortions support the primary distortions by rationalising and justifying the offending behaviour and serving to protect the offender's self-image following their anti-social behaviour (see Table 3.1).

Affective factors

Howells and Day (2006) have suggested that it is necessary for an offender to have a basic level of emotional control to successfully enter a treatment programme. Serran and colleagues (2003) concept of emotional responsivity identifies three inter-related components of emotion that are thought to impact upon levels of readiness: the access the offender has to emotional states; his or her ability to express such states; and his or her willingness to do this in the therapeutic session (see Table 3.2).

Subjective distress is not only likely to be an indicator of problem severity, but from both a clinical and a theoretical perspective is likely to have motivational properties (Frank 1974). When psychological

Table 3.1 The potential impact of cognitive distortions on treatment readiness.

Cognitive distortion	Potential impact on readiness
Self-centred attitudes and beliefs	May result in little value being assigned to the views of others and even their own long-term interest. This distortion would impact readiness for rehabilitation because these views are likely to foster reactance to suggestions of change.
Blaming others	May lead the offender to believe that the offending was not their fault, and that they are not responsible for their actions. This distortion impacts on readiness for rehabilitation because an offender would believe that their actions are not contingent on controlling their own behaviour. By assigning an external locus of control, these offenders believe that they do not control their offending behaviour; therefore they are unable to change it.
Minimising and mislabelling offending behaviour	Can lead to the belief that behaving anti-socially is admirable and even a service to the community. Change to what is seen as a positive behaviour, which might depict their identity, would be difficult to achieve.
Assuming the worst	May enable anti-social behaviour through ascribing hostile intent to others. Since this is the way a hostile individual views people in general, it is highly likely that they will view the therapist with hostility, thus hindering engagement in the programme.

Source: Adapted from Chambers *et al.* (2008).

distress is experienced, an individual may contemplate behaviour change or become resistant to change. In their review of treatments for depression, Beutler, Clarkin and Bongar (2000) concluded that treatments achieve their greatest effects among those patients who present with moderate to high initial levels of subjective distress. The level of distress with which an offender presents during the reception and screening assessment process may, therefore, be relevant in making decisions about programme referral, although we are not

Table 3.2 Affective readiness factors.

Factor	Description
Access to, and experience of, emotional states	An offender who is unable to access emotional states may be unable to engage in treatment by virtue of being unable to acknowledge and describe past emotional experiences. Given the demonstrated role of strong emotions in the offence chains for both violent and sexual offending, it is essential that such offenders are, or become, able to access and experience such emotions if they are to understand and modify their pathways to offending. While there may be a number of reasons why some offenders do not have access to past emotional states, some level of negative affective arousal may be necessary to motivate some offenders to engage in treatment, given that the goal, at least for some offenders, in attending treatment is likely to be distress or anxiety reduction. Of course, attending a programme may also be a strategy to achieve non-affective goals (such as consideration for parole). A pathological lack of affect would also constitute a barrier to engagement. Support for this suggestion comes from observations that psychopaths perform poorly in treatment (for example Smith, 1999). Psychopathy, as measured by the PCL-R and as understood by clinicians, is primarily a problem of affective deficit, given that shallowness of affect and lack of guilt and remorse are defining features of this condition.
Direct expression of affect	The direct expression of affect refers, for example, to whether the offender who currently feels strong fear, anger or non-specific distress displays these emotions in the therapeutic situation (obvious apprehensiveness, verbal aggression, tearfulness, self-disclosure). For Novaco *et al.* (2001), effective treatment for violent offenders entails the evocation of distressed emotion – it follows that an ability to express emotion is necessary if treatment is to be effective. Why this should, in itself, enhance engagement is not obvious,

Table 3.2 continues overleaf

Table 3.2 continued

Factor	Description
	except insofar as expression may sometimes assist the individual to acknowledge the extent and intensity of their emotions, or, as Serran *et al.* (2003) have suggested to directly activate latent offence-related schemas. It is also possible that the direct expression of emotion is functional not for the client, but for the therapist, whose knowledge about the client's subjective states is improved by the opportunity to observe the client.
The willingness of the client to admit to, and reflect on, their experience and expression of emotions in the therapeutic session	To be unwilling, or unable, to acknowledge emotional reactions in front of others in a therapeutic situation (for example a rehabilitation group) is to preclude the possibility of working therapeutically to understand and modify these emotions. Emotions form one domain of potentially painful experiences which may be disclosed or not (another being details of the offence). In prison environments, self-disclosure is a particularly sensitive topic. Disclosure of personal information or about offences may place the individual at risk from other prisoners and offenders may also be reluctant to disclose personal issues to prison staff.

Source: Adapted from Howells and Day (2006).

aware of any empirical research that has directly addressed this question.

Another potentially important (and related) component of readiness will be the individual's emotional reaction to both their offence and their status as 'offender'. The relationship between distress that is attributed directly to the offence (guilt, shame, remorse; see below), and distress that is attributed primarily to the consequences of imprisonment (coping, adjustment) is another area that warrants much further investigation. It may be, for example, that pre-treatment levels of distress will only be a significant engagement factor when certain attributions are made about the causes of that distress.

Given that most offender rehabilitation programmes target medium to high-risk offenders, and given the high weighting of previous offences in most methods of assessing risk, the great majority of offenders being assessed for programmes will have established histories of offending. The conferral of the status 'offender' for these participants will be long-standing. There will, however, be others who are referred following one-off offences: those who have no significant history of offending, such as some perpetrators of domestic homicides. Intuitively, it might be predicted that individuals in this group would have stronger negative, emotional reactions to their offence and to their offender status. Among such offenders, emotions of guilt, shame and remorse may be particularly common. Once again we know of no empirical studies investigating potential differences in these emotions in one-off as opposed to repetitive offenders, though the high incidence of subsequent suicide in domestic homicides would suggest that there are stronger guilt, shame and remorse experiences in this group (West 1965).

In order to assess the potential influence of offence-related emotions such as guilt, shame and remorse on readiness for treatment there are two requirements. First, these emotions need to be defined and differentiated. Second, possible mediating mechanisms need to be identified. Proeve (2002) has suggested that the cognitions that characterise guilt and shame have different foci. In guilt, the individual's focus is on the act, while in shame it is on the self (Tangney 1999).[1] It has been suggested (for example Lewis 1995; Proeve 2002; Proeve and Howells 2002) that shame can be distinguished from guilt in terms of the self-evaluative components of emotion. Although guilt may involve focusing on aspects of the self that lead to the transgression, typically the self is not negatively evaluated in a global way as is the case with shame where the self is seen as inferior, incompetent, or otherwise bad.[2] Thus it would appear that shame and guilt can be distinguished to some degree in terms of their phenomenology and accompanying cognitive and behavioural processes. There are also indications that shame is more strongly associated with other psychological variables that might impair readiness than is guilt. Shame proneness is associated with

[1]Guilt is also thought to involve a focus on the negative consequences of the act for others and an accompanying belief that the individual has violated a personal, moral standard. A number of action tendencies have been described for guilt, including apologising, undoing damage and attempting to repair the damage done.

[2]Shame also involves an awareness of judgement of the self by others, of the defectiveness of the self in the gaze of the observing other (Taylor 1985).

low empathy, anger, irritability, externalisation, blaming of others for negative events, resentment, suicidal behaviour and psychopathology, whereas guilt tends to show an inverted or no relationship to many of these variables (Bumby *et al.* 1999; Tangney 1991). The action tendency associated with shame appears to be hiding oneself from others, whereas confession and reparation are more salient for guilt. In this context, higher levels of guilt may be associated with increased levels of emotional self-disclosure.

In the above discussion, it is assumed that offenders identify their offending as the problem to be addressed. It is also assumed that offenders are genuinely distressed about their offending: that is, that their offending is ego dystonic rather than syntonic. These are little more than assumptions, and there is a clear need for empirical investigations on this topic. There are also likely to be a number of client characteristics that moderate the effects of each of the three emotional responsivity factors outlined above. Individuals differ in terms of the extent to which they experience emotions, express emotions and generally describe their experiences in emotional terms. Gender, gender role stereotypes, cultural values, and personality factors (such as a pervasive lack of trust in others) are all relatively stable characteristics that will influence the level of treatment engagement (see Table 3.3).

In summary, affective factors appear closely related to motivational structures and consequently the desire to enter a behaviour change programme. However, these factors remain poorly understood, difficult to assess reliably, and not well investigated empirically. There would appear to be a strong case for further research exploring the association between different affective states and styles and treatment readiness.

Personal goals, volition, and identity

Volition refers to the formation of an intention to pursue a certain goal and the development of a plan to achieve the goal in question. In the criminal justice context, the exercise of volition requires the ability to consent to treatment programmes, and to make informed decisions about participation (Birgden and Vincent 1999). There is also therapeutic value in choice; individuals are more likely to be motivated if they are offered alternative courses of action from which to choose.

Typically, in the offender rehabilitation literature, volitional factors have been understood in terms of motivation to change. Levels of

Table 3.3 Potential moderators of the effects of affective readiness factors.

Factor	Description
Gender and gender role stereotypes	Men and women may differ in display rules and in the influence of social contexts on emotional expression, such as the gender of other people in the immediate environment. This may have implications for emotional responsivity in male offenders in therapeutic groups. Male violent offenders may be low in emotional responsivity by virtue, in part, of their male gender and ensuing gender-role expectations. This low emotional responsivity would be further exaggerated if male gender-role expectations were particularly extreme and stereotypical in this client group. It is possible, of course, that gender differences in emotion are in part substantial and in part secondary or constructed.
Cultural values	There are likely to be cultural differences in the experience and expression of emotions. These may relate to either categories available within language to label emotions, or to the secondary appraisal process. Averill (1983), for example, has argued that culture not only effects when it is appropriate to be angry, but also the extent to which violence is an understandable response to anger. In addition, there are likely to be significant cultural (and subcultural) influences on the extent to which emotional disclosure is regarded as acceptable. Status effects, for example, are also likely to impact upon levels of disclosure in treatment. Disclosure can make the speaker vulnerable and demonstrate both trust and submission to the other. Research in other settings has shown that disclosure is often associated with social inferiority. Many prisoners, particularly those convicted of violent offences, will be occupied with issues of status and power, and may see disclosure as inconsistent with their self-identity.

Source: Adapted from Howells and Day (2006).

motivation have been shown to be consistent predictors of retention in substance use programmes, and client motivation has also been related to better treatment engagement in such programmes. Joe, Simpson and Broome (1998) concluded that indicators of intrinsic motivation were more important predictors of engagement and retention in treatment than other socio-demographic variables. Client motivation is thus only one of a broader range of responsivity variables considered in offender rehabilitation and in psychological treatments. Nevertheless, motivation is a vital construct to consider.

Human motivation has a long history as a topic of theoretical debate within psychology. Ford (1992) has attempted to integrate a range of findings and concepts from the field of motivation into a Motivational Systems Theory framework. Motivation from this perspective is defined as the 'organised patterning of an individual's personal goals, emotions and personal agency beliefs' (Ford 1992: 78). Thus motivation involves directedness (towards the goal), emotional/affective energising, and expectancies about being able to achieve the goal. The absence of motivation could be due to any of these three components being deficient. Thus a client might be unmotivated for therapy because the therapeutic goal is not important to them, because there are emotional or affective inhibitions to goal pursuit, or because there is a perceived low capability of achieving the relevant goal. Karoly (1993, 1999) has applied goal system constructs to clinical phenomena and to treatment. He defined goals as 'imagined or envisaged states towards which people intentionally aspire and actively work to bring about (or to avoid, in the case of negative goals) (1999: 274).[3] Personal goals can be conceptualised at three different levels: the latent, the phemonenological and the external observer (Austin and Vancouver 1996). Latent goals may be outside of phenomenal awareness while phenomenological goals are experienced directly and are (presumably) capable of self-reporting. External observers may infer goals from features of the individual's behaviour.

---

[3]Previous researchers have used different terms to describe goals of this sort. Emmons (1999), for example, investigated 'personal strivings' while Little (1983) described 'personal projects'. Ford (1992) distinguishes three types of goals, based on their level of prioritisation by the cognitive regulatory system: wishes, current concerns and intentions. Personal goals are thus cognitive representations and potential self-regulatory mechanisms by means of which behaviour is activated and coordinated.

Personal goals need to be understood in terms of content. What does the individual want? The emphasis in goal system theory tends to be on tangible, task-specific incentives rather than on broad, higher-order incentives, such as control or competence (Karoly 1999). Other dimensions of goals in Karoly's framework include goal topography, structure, process representation, dynamics, modality of representation, procedural predispositions, mindset effects, social context effects and interface with emotion. Goals are widely believed by researchers and theorists to be hierarchically organised, cascading from higher order goals to goals at the level of local and briefly experienced psychophysiological states.

Ford (1992) has attempted to define the necessary conditions for achievement and competence from a goal systems perspective. For the purposes of the present discussion, we can substitute 'achieving rehabilitation goals' for achievement/competence, the latter terms having been used because of the educational/developmental context of much goal system research. Ford's analysis, when extended to the field of readiness for treatment, would suggest the following as necessary conditions for achieving therapeutic goals:

1 Personal goals are constituted by, supportive of, or consistent with the therapeutic goal.
2 Emotional states are congruent with therapeutic goal pursuit and achievement.
3 Capability beliefs are present (regarding the achievability of therapeutic goals).
4 Positive context beliefs are present (perceived supportiveness of the environment in achieving therapeutic goals).
5 Actual capability/skill exists.
6 Actual environmental/contextual support exists.

Issues of treatment motivation have been directly addressed by goal theorists, albeit briefly. Karoly, for example, stresses the need to examine treatment targets in the context of broader client goals and the motivational salience of change. He also suggests that 'therapeutic failures of various kinds (premature termination, resistance, relapse etc) can result from the therapist-assessor's failure to appreciate the structural relation between time-limited treatment goals and life goals in general' (1993: 279). Karoly (1999) makes the point:

Assuming that a 'therapy goal' represents a to-be-achieved destination, it must be borne in mind that the instantiation of any new trajectory or pathway is always accomplished in the context of existing and projected pathways and hierarchically distant aspirations. Therapy goals that help achieve, or are consistent with, meaningful higher order goals stand a better chance of long-term success than do therapy goals that are at odds with higher order goals or values. (1999: 264–5)

In summary, goal systems theory would suggest that the offender who has goals that are incompatible with implicit or explicit rehabilitation goals will be low in readiness. Additionally, the absence of effective self-regulative strategies and processes in relation to goal attainment would also be a determinant of the occurrence of the presenting clinical problem (for example anger difficulties) and would, in turn, form an impediment to effective change in therapy. The goal system perspective indicates that determining the client's goal structure and associated self-regulative skills are key components of pre-treatment readiness assessment.

There have been two bodies of work in the field of offender rehabilitation that consider the role that the personal goals of offenders might play in behaviour change programmes. The first focuses on the personal concerns of offenders and is discussed by Mary McMurran in Chapter 11. The second is a broader rehabilitation theory, the Good Lives Model, which suggests that a focus on the primary goods sought by an individual offender is likely to improve both treatment engagement and programme outcomes. This approach is discussed in Chapter 4.

A number of other constructs overlap with the notion of personal goals. The subject factor of personal identity, for example, is one that is likely to be of particular importance. In seeking to achieve goals, we construct personal identities (Emmons 1999), a term that refers to the kind of life sought, and relatedly, the kind of person that an individual would like to be. Ward et al. (2004b) suggest that, for example, if an offender decides to pursue a life characterised by service to the community, a core aspect of his or her identity will revolve around the primary goods of relatedness and social life. The offender's sense of mastery, self-esteem, perception of autonomy and control will all reflect this overarching good and its associated sub-clusters of goods (such as intimacy, caring, honesty). They argue that the important issue for readiness is that an individual's personal identity must allow for the possibility of an offence-free lifestyle (and includes the possibility of change) and is not based too strongly on being an 'offender' (also see the reference to practical identities and values in Chapter 4). Of course, personal, cultural and social needs all impact on personal identity and, as such, should also inform programme development and delivery. That said, rehabilitation programmes are often developed in ways that do not cater well for the needs of particular groups such as culturally and linguistically diverse clients, and those with lower incomes and less education.

Behavioural factors

Behavioural factors include possession of the basic communication and social skills necessary to participate successfully in treatment. These are assumed to be necessary conditions for *entering* a rehabilitation programme and are not to be confused with the skills that are expected to be acquired *during* treatment. In other words, if an individual is unable to initiate and maintain basic conversations with others, then he or she is not 'ready' for treatment. The nature of the required skills or competencies will depend on the methods of delivery and the content of the particular treatment programme. A programme with a large educational component will require different competencies (such as literacy) than will a programme based primarily on role-playing and rehearsal of core behavioural skills (confidence in group setting) or a programme with a significant component of intellectual analysis of the antecedents for the person's offences (verbal ability, capacity to discuss thoughts, feelings and behaviour in front of other group members).

Given the prevalence of mental disorders (Hodgins and Muller-Isberner 2000) and intellectual disability (Day 2000) in offender populations, it is also important to note that the existence of mental illness or intellectual disability may functionally disable these important core skills and prevent the individual concerned from successfully functioning in groups or having the necessary attention and concentration abilities to acquire new skills. Although these may be regarded as both affective and cognitive readiness factors, the negative symptoms associated with conditions such as schizophrenia and mood disorders (even when the disorder is in remission) may mean that the individual is unable to arrive at programme sessions on time, sit for an extended period with concentration on group activities, engage and empathise with the problems expressed by other group participants, or organise and carry out homework tasks.

External readiness factors

The focus of the above discussion has been on internal readiness factors – those characteristics of offenders, such as motivation, beliefs about treatment, emotional regulation styles, that are likely to influence performance in a rehabilitation programme. We now turn our attention to those readiness factors that lie outside of the individual offender. By external factors we are referring to those characteristics of the environment, or the context, in which rehabilitation is offered that impact on an individual's ability to engage with a particular programme. Although some of these factors may appear obvious, they are often overlooked in terms of their potential impact on programme outcomes. For example, rehabilitation programmes need to be available within the agency or institution in which the offender is located. Sentence planning requirements sometimes mean that prisoners are moved to locations in which programmes are not offered, perhaps as a result of limited bed space.

Whether a programme is offered in an institutional or a community setting will have implications for whether certain skills can be meaningfully taught. Location will influence the degree to which family members can visit regularly and support the rehabilitation process. The encouragement of other prisoners, prison officers, community corrections officers, and clinicians for the offender to enter a specific programme may also be critical. If offenders are placed in prison units characterised by guardedness and suspicion, they may be less likely to volunteer to participate in programmes that they know will require self-disclosure and openness. In addition, the existence of rewards for successfully completing a rehabilitation programme is also potentially significant. In some jurisdictions prisoners are only considered eligible to apply for parole if they can demonstrate that they have addressed the causes of their offending by participating in and completing a programme. Programmes also need to be adequately resourced. Despite the considerable need for treatment, there is evidence to suggest that existing offender rehabilitation programmes tend to be over-burdened, and that many offenders receive either very limited treatment or none at all. The ability to provide meaningful treatment programmes requires the presence of skilled and trained staff and the physical resources necessary to run the programme in a given setting. In our view, these all represent important readiness factors.

Factors such as when programmes are offered, for example in relation to stage of sentence, may also play an important role in whether offenders see an opportunity for treatment participation. Initial contact with the criminal justice system (conviction and sentencing) will for some (but by no means all) be a critical event that leads the offender to reflect on the need for change. Those who are approaching release from prison may not have sufficient time to complete a programme and consequently not be offered one; conversely, they may be more ready to participate as the possibility of early release on parole draws closer. Alternatively, offenders might prefer to wait so they can access community treatment programmes on a voluntary basis. Those beginning long sentences may feel that they will have multiple opportunities over the course of their sentence and as such feel no immediate pressure to attend.

In summary, then, it is suggested that the extent to which a person is ready for treatment will extend beyond his or her psychological characteristics and those of the treatment itself. The focus should be just as much on whether the environment is right for successful rehabilitation to take place as on individual factors such as motivation to change. Too often, in our experience, rehabilitation programmes are offered without adequate planning, resourcing, or adequate consideration of the context in which they take place. We would suggest, however, that by far the most significant external component of treatment readiness lies in relation to the level of coercion placed upon the individual to attend a particular programme. This is included here as an external readiness condition as many offenders are pressured, if not legally obliged, to participate in rehabilitation programmes independently of their desires to do so.

Level of coercion

The use of the criminal justice system to force offenders to receive psychological treatment is one of the most controversial aspects of service provision. As Day, Tucker and Howells (2004) have observed:

> Whilst many practitioners are uncomfortable with the perceived infringement of civil liberties associated with enforced treatment, coercion is not inherently unethical. Paying taxes and obeying laws related to dangerous driving are also coerced, but these forms of coercion are accepted by most as promoting the general good. Indeed, the legal system and the act of imprisonment itself are based on coercion. (2004: 259)

Marlowe and colleagues (2007), in their discussion of compulsory substance use treatment, further suggest that the intrusion of a judge into the treatment process can be disruptive or harmful to the development of a therapeutic relationship. They suggest that 'clients may be hesitant to confide important information to their counsellors for fear the information would be disclosed to the court and used against their legal interests', and that 'being "treated like a criminal" by being brought into court on a regular basis might elicit counterproductive feelings of resistance or reactance' (2007: S5). Their conclusion is that judicial monitoring can elicit iatrogenic effects. Nevertheless, coercing offenders to attend rehabilitation programmes is increasingly accepted as an appropriate course of action, particularly for those who are regarded as posing a continuing threat to public safety. It is sometimes seen as the only effective means to ensure that offenders attend programmes (Burdon and Gallagher 2002).

Coerced treatment needs to be distinguished from pressured treatment, although both have objective and subjective dimensions. One of the difficulties with any consideration of the effects of coercion is the lack of consistency with which the term is defined. For example, it is commonly assumed that because a programme is mandated, there is a high level of coercion, and yet when asked participants may report that they do not feel coerced. Coerced or compulsory treatment can be defined from three different perspectives: legal social controls (civil commitment, court-ordered treatment, diversion-to-treatment programme; see Wells-Parker 1995; Wild 1999, 2006); formal social controls (mandatory referral to employee assistance programmes providing addiction treatment, usually following employer drug testing; see Lawental *et al.* 1996); and informal social controls (threats, ultimatums initiated by friends and family members; see Room *et al.* 1991; Hasin 1994). Day *et al.* (2004) suggest that:

> Coercion and pressure are not simple objective facts. The person may feel coerced and pressured into treatment even when there is no objective requirement to engage in treatment. Equally, the person may be objectively coerced (for example by a court) but have little subjective sense of being coerced (for example, when treatment is congruent with their own goals and aspirations). The term coercion often implies being forced to do something against one's will, and includes an implicit evaluative component that compliance will in some way be unpleasant or aversive. Being pressured into a course of action is a similar concept, although

with pressure the person will be able to exercise a higher degree of choice about compliance. (2004: 260)

Typically offender rehabilitation programmes are coercive in the sense that there are negative consequences for non-participation in treatment, although the nature of these consequences may vary significantly across jurisdictions. Offenders who refuse treatment may, for example, find it to be impossible to reduce their security classification, which in turn may have an impact on the living conditions and freedoms they will experience during their imprisonment. Grubin and Thornton (1994) reported that nearly half (41 per cent) of sexual offenders in the UK said that they would participate in treatment only in order to gain parole. Hutchins (2003) has described the process as follows: 'if the offender does not complete the program satisfactorily, parole is virtually routinely refused when the offender is first eligible. If refused, a date is fixed by the Board when parole will be considered again and it is suggested to the inmate that he/she do a ... program whilst in custody and before the next hearing' (2003: 1).

An important consideration here is whether coercing offenders into attending programmes (or placing legal pressure on them to attend) is likely by itself to lead to lower levels of treatment readiness. In their review, Day *et al.* (2004) suggest that it is the individual's perception of coercion that is more likely to determine treatment readiness, and even when clients do perceive that they are being coerced, then pre-treatment anti-therapeutic attitudes can change over the course of a programme. Day *et al.* (2004) have argued that given that perceptions of coercion will not always reflect the objective situation, it becomes important to identify when and how legal pressure is perceived as coercive. They suggest five factors that might influence the extent to which legal pressure is perceived as coercive (see Table 3.4), which might also be reframed as aspects of treatment readiness.

It is proposed then that the legal context in which offender rehabilitation is offered, and in particular the extent to which legal pressure is placed on the offender to participate in a programme, will be an important determinant of treatment readiness. Of course, the impact of such external readiness factors can be understood in terms of their influence on internal factors, such as beliefs and attitudes about the appropriateness or value of programmes. Wild, Newton-Taylor and Alletto (1998) have suggested that the most appropriate way to understand coercion is in relation to the concept of motivation. When offenders perceive that they are being coerced into treatment, they are more likely to see their participation as controlled by

Table 3.4 Influences on perceptions of coercion

Factor	Description
Agreement on the need for treatment	In order for an offender to accept coercion into treatment, he or she will also need to see his or her offending as likely to recur (that s/he is susceptible), believe that offending is a serious problem, and that the costs of change do not outweigh the benefits (such as not associating with friends who are likely to offend). He or she will also need to have some confidence that the treatment can be effective. It may be that an individual's perceived level of coercion is linked with their personal treatment goals.
The aversiveness of the treatment	The more unpleasant or distressing that treatment is thought to be, the more likely it is that pressure to attend will be perceived as coercive. For some offenders the thought of being asked to disclose personal information in a group setting is acutely distressing.
Information about the treatment	Levels of perceived coercion may be lower when offenders are clear about what they are being coerced to do. Providing offenders with information about the treatment and convincing them that rules would be enforced are among the most effective forms of coercion. Including offenders in the decision-making process may also reduce perceptions of coercion.
Relationship with the source of the pressure	Views about the legitimacy of the courts to make decisions, and confidence in the legal process may also affect the extent to which legal pressure is perceived as coercive. Informal pressure from family and friends will also be perceived differently according to the importance of these relationships to the offender.

Table 3.4 continues opposite

Table 3.4 continued

Factor	Description
Personality factors	Individual differences in perceptions of coercion exist over and above that of referral source. Psychological reactance, for example, can be understood as a motivational state or as a personality trait, and has been defined as the degree to which an individual feels compelled to regain lost or threatened freedoms. As coercion implies a loss or threat to an individual's freedom of choice to attend treatment, it may be that those offenders who score highly on trait reactance would be more likely to perceive coercion. Reactance as a characterological factor is also thought to mediate the effectiveness of various therapeutic interventions, with highly reactant individuals generally having poorer treatment outcomes.

Source: Adapted from Day *et al.* (2004).

external contingencies (such as the requirement to fulfil obligations, to gain parole, or to look good). Deci and Ryan's (2000) model of motivation as occurring on a continuum from extrinsic to intrinsic motivation is useful here, as it suggests that extrinsic motivation can change to intrinsic motivation *via* a process whereby external motivators (socially sanctioned mores or requests) are internalised. For offenders, then, who feel coerced into programmes and who initially show little internal motivation to change their behaviour, it is possible that internal motivation will develop over the course of the programme as they come to personally endorse the values and self-regulations (Deci *et al.* 1999) identified in the treatment.

Conclusion

In summary, there are a number of readiness factors that might best considered as external to the individual offender. Generally, these are features of the environment or context in which programmes are offered that will determine how the individual understands and evaluates the proposed intervention. These are practical issues such as the availability of programmes and the presence of qualified staff to deliver them, through to the pressure to participate, either legally, from those within the correctional environment, or from significant others. The way in which an individual reacts to such pressure is likely to be an important determinant of treatment readiness. However, it is characteristics of individual offenders that are most likely to influence the capacity or ability to engage with a particular rehabilitation programme. This may relate to particular beliefs or attitudes about programmes in general, or the specific programme under consideration, to affective or emotional factors that will influence motivation to participate, and to broader issues related to the individual's goals and extent to which participation is regarded as in his or her best interests. Many of the internal readiness factors described here are also discussed in other parts of the book. These are the aspects of readiness that can be readily assessed, and modified through interventions designed to improve levels of readiness such that offenders are able to participate meaningfully in a programme.

Chapter 4

The Good Lives Model of offender rehabilitation and treatment readiness

The Good Lives Model (GLM) of offender rehabilitation is a strength-based approach by virtue of its responsiveness to offenders' core aspirations and interests, and its aim of providing them with the internal and external resources to live rewarding and offence-free lives. It is closely aligned with positive psychology (Linley and Joseph 2004) because of its stress on promoting offender well-being and its overall positive orientation to treatment, although it was developed independently of this perspective. We propose that rehabilitation theories are composed of three levels of ideas: (1) a set of general assumptions concerning the ethical values guiding rehabilitation, the nature of human beings, conception of risk, and the aims and purpose of rehabilitation practice; (2) a set of general aetiological (causal) assumptions that account for the onset and maintenance of offending; and (3) the practice implications of both of the above. In our view, it is helpful to think of the three levels as ordered in terms of their degree of abstractness, with the general aims and values providing a conceptual foundation for the subsequent levels (aetiology and practice). Each level of the GLM is discussed in greater detail below.

As a rehabilitation theory the GLM comprises a number of ethical, metaphysical, epistemological, methodological, aetiological, and treatment assumptions that are intended to guide practitioners in their work with offenders (Ward and Maruna 2007). In this chapter we will outline the fundamental assumptions of the GLM. Our intention is to provide a reasonably detailed summary of this recent rehabilitation theory and consider its relationship to the MORM model of offender readiness outlined in detail earlier in the book. Because a primary emphasis of the GLM is on offenders' values and their associated good lives plans (GLP) it is much easier to motivate them to engage in treatment (see also Chapter 11).

The Good Lives Model was formulated as an alternative approach to correctional treatment that has the conceptual resources to integrate aspects of treatment not well addressed by the risk–need–responsivity (RNR) model (Andrews and Bonta 2006), such as the formation of a therapeutic alliance, agency concerns, and motivating individuals to commit themselves to treatment and ongoing desistance from offending (Ward *et al.* 2007; Ward and Maruna 2007; Ward and Stewart 2003). The GLM has been most extensively applied to rehabilitation work with sex offenders and therefore the assessment process and interventions consistent with the GLM have been developed in the most detail with this particular population. It important to note, however, that the GLM is a general rehabilitation theory that is applicable to a wide range of problems, including other types of criminal behaviour, and is not restricted to use with sex offenders. It has recently been used effectively in working with individuals convicted of violent, non-sex-related crimes (Langlands *et al.* 2009; Whitehead *et al.* 2007) and also applied to individuals with medical disabilities (Siegert *et al.* 2007).

Principles, aims and values of the GLM

Embodiment, plasticity and cognitive extension

The first major set of theoretical assumptions of the GLM revolve around recent research and theory in cognitive science relating to the nature of human agency. More specifically, this research suggests that: (a) human agents' physical embodiment has a profound impact on their cognitive functioning and interface with the world; (b) human agents are characterised by plasticity of cognitive functioning; and (c) human agents have cognitive systems that incorporate both internal and external components (Ward, in press). The above claims converge on a picture of organisms who are (naturally) designed to act in pursuit of biological, psychological and social goals (Clark 2008). We briefly discuss each of these assumptions in turn.

The claim that human beings are embodied is based on a unified conception of the mind and body and a rejection of dualism. That is, mental properties are thought to be causally dependent upon the body and their form determined in part by the experience of physical embodiment (Johnson 2007; Ward and Nee 2009). Furthermore, the body also plays an important part in altering the environment in ways that facilitate problem clarification and effective action. It is the interface between inner and outer resources that makes it possible for individuals to bring about goal-directed changes in the environment and ultimately within themselves.

The dependence of goal-directed action and psychological functioning upon the body creates a source of vulnerability for human agents and underlines the need to ensure that threats to physical integrity are effectively managed. The provision of adequate food and water, safe and hygienic environments, freedom from physical danger, and accommodation are necessary ingredients of a good life. Typically, this means that individuals need educational and vocational skills to be able to work in order to pay for these essential materials. The fact of being physically vulnerable agents points to our ultimate interdependence and reliance on each other for access to vital goods or at least to the means of providing them for ourselves. Offenders as embodied human agents require the materials needed to protect their physical integrity and subsequent ability to act in pursuit of their goals.

The second assumption concerning the nature of human beings and their capacity for agency trades on the view that they are cognitively versatile animals who are able to quickly adapt to novel situations and acquire new cognitive repertoires and tools with relative ease (Clark 2008). Human beings' sense of self is derived from the ability to effectively change the world and themselves in accordance with their personal commitments (Clark 2008; Korsgaard 2009). From a rehabilitation standpoint, the 'soft' nature of human agency reminds correctional practitioners that enhancing offenders' abilities to achieve better life plans is likely to alter their sense of themselves in ways that are socially beneficial as well as personally fulfilling (Ward, in press).

The third agency-related assumption builds on the fact of human beings' cognitive plasticity and claims that external cognitive resources such as language, computers, other minds, and social and cultural institutions under some circumstances can be viewed as part of people's (extended) minds. In other words, we are not cognitively limited by the biological boundaries of skin and skull and are able to intentionally incorporate internal and external elements when engaged in cognitive tasks. We do not have the space to fully explain this complex and novel idea but point out that it is logically connected to the previous two assumptions (see Ward, in press). It is because human beings are physically embodied that they are able to use tools of various kinds to change themselves and their world. Furthermore, it is their cognitive plasticity and soft agency that enables people to actively incorporate internal and external cognitive resources when engaged in problem-solving activates. The implications of this assumption for offender rehabilitation is that it makes sense to focus our efforts on what matters to people and to realize that external social and cognitive resources may well be actively recruited in offenders' problem-solving routines and strategies. If offenders are quarantined in environments that contain others like them and few pro-social models, the chances are that their beliefs, values and actions will continue to be anti-social in nature.

Primary human goods

The above set of three presuppositions of the GLM centred on human embodiment and agency are the most fundamental ones and the following assumptions are really derived from them. The biological nature of human beings and the supervening of psychological properties on physical processes and structures means that in order for individuals to function effectively their basic needs have to be met (Deci and Ryan 2000). Furthermore, the biological and psychological evidence suggests that all people, including offenders, are naturally inclined to seek certain goals, or what we have called *primary human goods* (such as relatedness, creativity, physical health, and mastery; see Ward and Maruna 2007; Ward and Stewart 2003).

In essence, primary goods are states of affairs, states of mind, personal characteristics, activities or experiences that are sought for their own sake and are likely to increase psychological well-being if achieved (Kekes 1989; Ward and Stewart 2003). In addition to these primary goods, *instrumental* or secondary goods provide particular ways (that is the means) of achieving primary goods: for example, certain types of work or relationships. For instance, it is possible to secure the primary good of relatedness by the way of romantic, parental or personal relationships. The notion of instrumental goods or means is particularly important when it comes to applying the GLM to offending behaviour as it is assumed that a primary reason why individuals commit offences is that they are seeking primary goods in socially and often personally destructive ways.

The psychological, social, biological and anthropological research evidence provides support for the existence of at least ten groups of primary human goods (see Aspinwall and Staudinger 2003; Deci and Ryan 2000; Emmons 1999, 2003; Linley and Joseph 2004; Nussbaum 2006; Ward and Maruna 2007). These include the following:

1 *Life*: The primary good of life incorporates physical needs and factors that are important for healthy living and physical functioning, such as food, water, a physically healthy body, and so on.

2 *Knowledge*: This primary good is based on the notion that human beings are inherently curious and possess the desire to understand aspects of themselves, their natural environments, and other people.

3 *Excellence in play and work*: This primary good refers to the desire to engage in leisure or fun activities for their own sake and to strive for mastery at work-related and leisure or recreational activities.

4 *Autonomy*: The primary good of autonomy refers to the desire to formulate one's own goals and to seek ways to realise these through actions and activities of one's choice without facing undue interference from others (moderated by cultural and social norms).

5 *Inner peace*: The primary good of inner peace refers to emotional self-regulation and the ability to achieve a state of dynamic emotional equilibrium and competence.

6 *Relatedness*: The good of relatedness refers to the natural desire of human beings to establish warm, affectionate bonds with other people. It is noted that these relationships range from intimate, romantic relationships to close family relationships to platonic relationships and friendships.

7 *Community*: The primary good of community refers to the desire human beings have to belong to social groups and to feel connected to groups that reflect their interests, concerns and values.

8 *Spirituality*: The primary good of spirituality refers to the desire to discover and attain a sense of meaning and purpose in life.

9 *Happiness*: The primary good of happiness refers to a hedonic (pleasure) state or the overall experience of being content and

satisfied with one's life, and includes the sub-good of sexual pleasure.

10 *Creativity*: The primary good of creativity refers to the desire for novelty and innovation in one's life, the experience of doing things differently, or engaging in a specific activity that results in an artistic output or other novel or creative product.

An especially significant characteristic of the GLM is that the goods are plural rather than singular and, therefore, a fulfilling life will most probably require access to all the primary goods even though individuals can legitimately vary in the way they value or rank them. This means that there are multiple sources of motivation and that each has their origin in the evolved nature of human beings.

Values and practical identities

The plural nature of the goods sought is likely to result in their differential weightings or endorsement by individuals. While all the primary goods need to be present to some degree (that is, meet a threshold requirement), if persons are to achieve good lives there could be significant differences in the experiences, objects and activities they consider most important. According to Korsgaard (1996), conceptions of practical identity provide 'a description under which you value yourself and find your life worth living and your actions to be worth undertaking' (1996: 101). Thus individuals' sense of identity emerges from their basic value commitments: the goods they pursue in search of better lives. Interestingly, Korsgaard argues that when there are conflicts between different practical identities people have to work hard to establish some degree of unity in their lives, and she suggests that a way of assisting this process is by focusing on our common humanity and our (shared) inherent dignity. The existence of a number of practical identities also means that each of us will draw from a variety of distinct value sources when faced with decisions about how best to act (Korsgaard 2009). For example, a person may value being a father, psychologist, scientist, citizen and member of a political party, and each of these practical identities will exert some normative pressure on his actions and life. At times the aims and subsequent actions arising from the value commitments of each of these practical identities could even conflict. The relevance of variation in value endorsements is that if offenders' sense of themselves and what really matters depends upon the things they most value, then correctional practitioners ought to identify what primary goods are most heavily endorsed and in particular how they are expressed in their lives (Archer 2000; Clark 2007; Emmons 2003).

Because human beings are thinking animals there is a reflective gap between the experience of a desire to act in pursuit of a natural good or incentive, and actually doing so (Korsgaard 2009). This reflective gap allows individuals space to critically evaluate desires and to decide whether or not they are worthy of fulfilment; whether they are really of value. Arguably, problematic actions such as sexual offending partly arise from individuals making faulty judgements and reveal a lack of forethought or knowledge concerning the relevant facts and the real value of the proposed actions. Thus, the process of rehabilitation requires not just the targeting of isolated 'factors' but also the holistic reconstruction of the 'self'.

Goods and risks

According to the GLM, correctional interventions should aim to (a) promote offenders' aspirations and plans for better lives, as well as (b) manage/reduce their risk to the community. This assumption has both normative and pragmatic strands to it. Normatively, the assertion that interventions should promote well-being alongside reduce risk reflects the ethical foundation of the GLM in human rights theory and practices (Laws and Ward, in press). Pragmatically, it is assumed that because criminogenic needs and human needs are causally related (see below), the promotion of adaptive approach goals should also reduce dynamic risk factors. Thus a major aim of correctional reintegration work is to help individuals to construct a life plan that has the basic primary goods, and ways of effectively securing them, built into it and does not involve inflicting harm on others.

Ecological selves

As discussed above, according to the GLM people are multifaceted beings composed of a variety of interconnected biological, social, cultural and psychological systems, and are interdependent to a significant degree. What this entails is that complex animals such as human beings can only flourish within a community that provides emotional support, material resources, education, and even the means of survival. The complexity of human functioning means that an adequate explanation of something as important as crime will require multiple levels of analysis and theoretical perspectives. In particular, the interdependency of human behaviour points to the necessity of adopting an ecological framework.

The fact that human beings are interdependent and that, therefore, a satisfactory understanding of behaviour will always involve an appreciation of the contexts in which they exist, has important implications for therapists when designing reintegration programmes. Thus, according to the GLM, any assessment and intervention should take into account the match between the *characteristics* of the individual and the likely *environment* where he or she will be functioning. Rather than viewing the offender as essentially a self-contained deviancy machine (or bearer of risk – see below) who therefore requires treatment designed to restore or repair or, more frequently, to manage a faulty system, the aim is to locate him or her within a social network. Treatment consistent with the GLM is viewed as furnishing individuals with some of the agency scaffolding and resources required to establish important social bonds and to engage meaningfully with the world.

The nature of risk

Because people are conceptualised to be constituted from, and to be embedded within, complex systems, risk is viewed as multifaceted rather than purely individualistic (Denny 2005). In our view, risk is best viewed in contextual terms rather than conceptualised purely as constituted by individual deviancy. Thus it is to be expected that an adequate risk management plan would need to take into account individuals' particular lifestyles and environments. Even those dynamic risk factors that can be said to be located 'inside' individuals (impulsivity, aggressiveness) are only meaningful in their specific, cultural and situational contexts.

The trouble with psychometric approaches to risk assessment and management is that they have a tendency to identify risk primarily in terms of individuals' deviancy and to view offenders as essentially bearers of risk (Ward and Maruna 2007; Ward and Stewart 2003). By 'bearers of risk' we mean that in some sense risk is seen as inhering within individual offenders, and to a lesser extent their environments. A difficulty with such a static conceptualisation is that it fails to appreciate how risk can be created by correctional interventions and policies that effectively isolate offenders, such as community notification or geographical restrictions (Vess 2009).

The nature of intervention

Finally, according to the GLM, a treatment plan should be explicitly constructed in the form of a good lives conceptualisation or plan.

In other words, it should take into account individuals' strengths, primary goods and relevant environments, and specify exactly what competencies and resources are required to achieve these goods. An important aspect of this process is respecting the individual's capacity to make certain decisions themselves, and in this sense accepting their status as an autonomous individual. This is in direct contrast to previous recommended practice in the treatment of offending behaviours, where therapists were cautioned not to allow offenders to participate in decision-making (see Salter 1988). Using the GLM, we believe that each individual's preference for certain primary goods should be noted and translated into his or her daily routine (for example the kind of works, education and further training, and types of relationships identified and selected to achieve primary goods).

Aetiological assumptions of the GLM

As stated earlier, the aetiological component of a rehabilitation theory flows logically from a theory's basic assumptions, is general in nature, and functions to give correctional workers a cognitive map or general overview of the broad causes of anti-social behaviour.

According to the GLM, goals are usefully construed as primary human goods translated into more concrete forms, and as such are typically the objects of intentions and actions. Goals are the ultimate and intermediate ends of any actions and collectively give shape to people's lives insofar as they create a structure of daily activities that represent what is of fundamental importance to them. In terms of practical identities, goals are typically thematically linked to concrete identities and the various roles and tasks they imply. For example, as a psychologist a person has responsibility for the assessment and treatment of psychological disorders. Each of these domains of professional practice is linked to actions, guided by particular goals, such as conducting an interview competently, interpreting psychological tests, or assisting an individual to overcome his or her fears of intimacy. Alternatively, the practical identity of being someone's romantic partner generates a variety of tasks such as providing emotional support, spending time together, and maintaining a household. In other words, goals are typically clustered together under specific descriptions; these descriptions are ultimately anchored in practical identities (Emmons 1999; Korsgaard 2009).

According to the GLM, there may be a number of distinct problems within the various domains of human functioning that can result in offending behaviour: emotional regulation difficulties, social difficulties, offence supportive beliefs, empathy problems, and problem-solving deficits. Yet, such individuals' general underlying personal motivations/goals are rarely inherently bad. Instead, it is the means used to achieve these goods that are deviant. The value of this understanding is that it helps to focus clinical attention on primary goods, the ultimate underlying motivating factors, and away from an exclusive focus on the psychosocial difficulties with which individual clients are struggling. That is, there are likely to be distortions in the internal and external conditions required to achieve the primary goods in socially acceptable and personally satisfying ways. The GLM guided analysis goes beyond deficit-based etiological theories (theories that focus on what individuals lack) by encouraging clinicians to think clearly about just what it is that the person is *seeking* when committing the offence. This information has direct treatment implications and can provide a powerful way of motivating individuals to engage in therapy; the aim is to help them to secure human goods that are important to them, but to do so in ways that are socially acceptable and also more personally satisfying. The latter point is especially important, as most of the causal factors involve self-defeating attempts to seek personally valued goals and consequences. The GLM can explain why this is so and provide clinicians with a clear understanding of where the problems reside in an individual's life plan.

From the perspective of the GLM there are two routes to the onset of offending, each reflecting individuals' agency: *direct* and *indirect* (Ward and Gannon 2006; Ward and Maruna 2007). The direct pathway is implicated when offending is a primary focus of the (typically implicit) cluster of goals and strategies associated with an individual's life plan. This means that the individual intentionally seeks certain types of goods directly through criminal activity. For example, an individual may lack the relevant competencies and understanding to obtain the good of intimacy with an adult, and furthermore may live in an environment where there are few realistic opportunities for establishing such relationships. Thus, the actions constituting offending are a means to the achievement of a fundamental good.

The indirect route to offending occurs when the pursuit of a good or set of goods creates a ripple effect in the person's personal circumstances and these unanticipated effects increase the pressure to offend. For example, conflict between the goods of relatedness and autonomy might cause the break-up of a valued relationship and subsequent feelings of loneliness and distress. The use of alcohol to alleviate the emotional turmoil could lead to loss of control in specific circumstances and this might increase the risk of offending. These indirect or ripple effects are particularly evident when two practical identities a person is invested in conflict and cause him or her uncertainty about how best to act. An example of this conflict of identities is when an offender values both his roles as a worker and as a husband. The two identities can on occasions clash and in some circumstances the pressure to work longer hours in order to get a job done might interfere with his responsibilities as a partner.

From the standpoint of the GLM, criminogenic needs are conceptualised as internal or external obstacles that frustrate and block the acquisition of primary human goods. We suggest that there are four major types of difficulties often evident in individuals' life plans. In our view these types of problems are overlapping but conceptually distinct. It is also important to note that the real problem resides in the secondary goods rather than the primary ones. In other words, it is the activities or strategies used to obtain certain primary goods that create problems, not the primary goods themselves (that is primary goods are sought by all humans).

First, an individual who has problems with the *means* he or she uses to secure goods may be using inappropriate strategies to achieve the necessary primary goods needed for a good life. Second, an individual's life plan might also suffer from a lack of *scope* with a number of important goods left out of his or her plan for living. Third, some people may also have *conflict* (and a lack of coherence) among the goods being sought and their associated practical identities and therefore experience acute psychological stress and unhappiness (Emmons 1999). Fourth, a final problem is when a person lacks the *capabilities* (knowledge, or skills) to form or effectively implement a life plan in the environment in which he or she lives, or to adjust his or her goals to changing circumstances (for example impulsive decision-making). The problem of capability deficits has both internal and external dimensions. The internal dimension refers to factors such as skill deficits while external dimension points to a lack of environmental opportunities, resources and supports.

In summary, the aetiological commitments of the GLM are general in form and stem from a view of human beings as creatures capable of reflective agency, usually acting under the conceptual constraints of a range of practical identities. That is, we propose that human beings are goal-seeking, culturally embedded animals who utilise a range of strategies to secure important goods from their environments when occupying personally valued social or cultural roles (partners, workers, citizens, playmates, artists, helpers and so on). When the internal or external conditions necessary to achieve valued outcomes associated with practical identities are incomplete or absent, individuals tend to become frustrated and may engage in anti-social behaviour. The etiological commitments serve to orient correctional workers and require supplementation from specific theories to supply more fine-grained explanations of anti-social behaviour and particular types of offences.

Implications of the GLM for practice

A GLM-oriented treatment programme seeks to tailor an intervention plan around an offender's core values and associated practical identities. The good lives plan unfolds from this value centre and incorporates all of the various goods required to function as a reflective and effective agent within specific environments. Where possible, local communities and resources are recruited and the objective is to assist in the building of a better life rather than simply trying to contain risk. For example, an individual's treatment plan could be based on his or her desire to learn a trade (become a mechanic, for example) and establish a romantic relationship. The skills required to become a mechanic, such as mechanical knowledge of engines, effective work habits, at least a reasonable degree of social and communication skills, affective and self-control competencies, may reduce risk while consolidating the offender within a social network. Access to work-mates and hobbies that cohere with his or her interests might further open up opportunities to meet potential partners who are law-abiding and supportive. The result of such a plan will hopefully be a life that is fulfilling, meaningful, ethically acceptable and socially productive (Burnett 2002; Maruna 2001).

We will now briefly describe each of the five phases of a GLM rehabilitation framework (for more detail on GLM-oriented treatment see Laws and Ward, in press; Ward and Maruna 2007; Ward and Stewart 2003).

The first phase when intervening with offenders from the standpoint of the GLM involves the detection of the social, psychological and material phenomena implicated in individuals' offending. This requires a careful analysis of offenders' level of risk, their living circumstances, physical and social problems and psychological capabilities around the time of their offending and stretching into their past as well. Offenders are likely to have multiple problems, such as poverty, substance abuse, lack of accommodation, high levels of impulsiveness and aggressive behaviour, and so on.

In the second phase of the GLM the function of offending (what the individual expected to achieve *via* his offending) is established through the identification of primary goods that are directly or indirectly linked to the criminal actions. In addition, the identification of the overarching good or value around which the other goods are oriented should also be ascertained. This step requires that practitioners identify the practical identities endorsed by offenders and clarify how they are causally related to their offending actions. It is anticipated that the core goods (for example, mastery or caring) will be translated into more concrete values and tasks that directly connect with offenders' general life circumstances and their offence-related actions.

In the third phase of the GLM rehabilitation process, the selection of the practical identities and their overarching good(s) or value(s) is undertaken and made a focus of a plan. As discussed earlier, frequently practical identities are aligned with the primary goods and in a sense simply flesh out the abstractness of the good in question. In effect, practical identities and their goals, strategies and practices provide the detail needed to effectively work with an offender. For example, an individual might nominate knowledge and relatedness as the two most important goods and decide that going to university and establishing a relationship with a woman are means to these ends.

In the fourth phase, a greater level of detail is added to the above developing plan and the selection of secondary goods or values that specify how the primary goods will be translated into ways of living and functioning, is undertaken. In this step identification of the contexts or environments in which the person is likely to be living while in the community during or following treatment is conducted. For example, the practical identity of being a university student (and partner in a relationship) is now examined with respect to a possible environment and the educational, social, psychological and material resources required to make this possible are noted. The GLM is a regulatory and pragmatic model so it is imperative that the probable environments a person will be living in are identified and their potential to provide the required resources to realise the good lives plan ascertained.

In the fifth phase, the practitioner constructs a detailed intervention plan for the offender based on the above considerations and information. The plan will be holistic, specify the internal and external conditions required to successfully implement it, revolving around offenders' core values and their associated practical identities, and the various tasks for correctional practitioners will be carefully detailed. Dynamic risk factors or criminogenic needs are indirectly targeted when cognitive behavioural techniques and social interventions are utilised in the acquisition of offender competencies. Thus, taking into account the kind of life that would be fulfilling and meaningful to the individual (primary goods, secondary goods, and their relationship to ways of living and possible environments), the evaluator notes the capabilities or competencies the individual requires in order to have a reasonable chance of applying the plan. Practical steps are then taken to organise the various actors involved and to put the good lives plan into action. The offender is consulted in all the various phases and in a robust sense he or she drives the content of the plan, if not its form. Furthermore, the practitioner seeks to balance the ethical entitlements of the offender with those of victims and members of the community.

The GLM and the MORM

In this section we briefly discuss the relationship between the GLM and the MORM. The GLM is a broad rehabilitation framework that has the potential to organise and guide all aspects of offender rehabilitation, while the MORM is a specific theory of treatment readiness. The focus of the MORM is on the factors associated with engaging an offender in the treatment process and in this role it can be incorporated within the GLM framework as a useful conceptual model of intervention preparation. The assumptions of the GLM concerning the nature of human beings and the implications of these facts for the onset and treatment of offending related problems arguably underpin the MORM. That is, the basic assumptions of this readiness model about the required person and contextual factors for effective engagement in treatment point to problems in the scope, capacity, means and conflict within offenders' good lives plans (GLP). To be ready for treatment means accepting that it can provide a way of achieving important goals, valued outcomes and their reflection in practical identities that are salient for an offender (see Chapters 1, 2 and 3). The critical task for practitioners is to provide a bridge between what an offender values and needs, his current circumstances (imprisonment, or serving a community sentence), and a possible future life. Providing that bridge is the task of readiness interventions: creating a sense of efficacy, linking past and future lives to valued goals, highlighting the way treatment programmes can be helpful in securing these personal goals, creating a context that scaffolds and supports treatment, and most importantly, treating the offender with respect and listening carefully to his concerns and hopes.

What we are saying is that the GLM contains the necessary general conceptual resources to help practitioners locate the relevant readiness factors in specific individuals. It can do this because of its view that people are inherently value-seeking and, as such, actively pursue and seek to implement important goals by way of their associated GLPs. Individuals' ability to construct and implement adaptive and fulfilling GLPs depends on their possession of the necessary capabilities and an environment that is receptive to their efforts. Readiness interventions depend upon the identification of these (often) implicit GLPs and their associated practical identities, and represent attempts to directly connect them to the process of treatment. Readiness interventions can be viewed as conduits between past and future lives by way of emphasising the things that really matter to offenders and showing how participation in correctional programmes can help them to achieve the things they value (see Chapter 11).

Conclusion

In this chapter we have outlined the basic assumptions, aetiological commitments and practice implications of the GLM. Our aim has been to stress the focus of the GLM on the possibility of better lives for offenders and therefore underline the importance of agency considerations rather than simply reduction of risk factors. In our view, the GLM has the theoretical resources to provide practitioners with a conceptual map to guide all aspects of their clinical work with offenders and also help steer the professional activities of other correctional workers and community volunteers. There is natural resonance between the GLM and readiness concepts because of their common assumptions about the importance of intervening with offenders holistically within their social ecology. Furthermore, the fact that the GLM is based upon identifying offenders' core values and establishing ways of realising them makes it easier to motivate them to engage in treatment programmes. It is easier to persuade individuals to work towards the creation of fulfilling lives rather than simply trying to be less harmful to others.

Chapter 5

The assessment of treatment readiness

Treatment readiness is now widely acknowledged as playing an important role in the process of offender rehabilitation. Understanding the extent to which offenders are treatment ready can help to improve programme selection processes, reduce programme attrition, use programme resources more efficiently, and assist in the development of interventions for those who are considered to not be ready for treatment (Burrowes and Needs 2009; Casey *et al.* 2005; Howells and Day 2003). Most importantly, given that the primary goal of rehabilitation programmes is reduced recidivism, the better the fit between the needs of the individual and the programme(s) to which an offender might be referred, the more likely it is that risk of recidivism can be effectively managed (Ward *et al.* 2004b). Yet despite first being articulated in an offender context by Serin and Kennedy (1997; Serin 1998) more than a decade ago, there have been few attempts to clearly operationalise the readiness construct and develop appropriate measurement tools.

According to Ward *et al.* (2004b), the major obstacle to such development has been a failure to distinguish between the three distinct but related concepts of treatment motivation, responsivity, and readiness (see Chapter 1 for a more detailed discussion of these constructs). As a consequence, researchers have worked within each of these frameworks to develop instruments that in their view assess whether an individual is 'treatment ready'. For example, McMurran and colleagues (McMurran *et al.* 2006, 2008; Sellen *et al.* 2006, 2009) have utilised a motivational framework in adapting the Personal Concerns Inventory (Cox and Klinger 2004a) for use with an offender population. Serin (Serin 1998; Serin and Kennedy 1997; Serin *et al.* 2007) has also adopted a motivational approach, but advocates that in addition to a generic model of readiness, there is a need to develop instruments for unique offender groups (for example, sex offenders for whom denial rates are high even after conviction). Perhaps the most frequently used motivational measures, however, are those derived from the transtheoretical model – the Readiness to Change Questionnaire (RCQ) (Rollnick *et al.* 1992); University of Rhode Island Change Assessment (URICA) (McConnaughy *et al.* 1983, 1989); Stages of Change Readiness and Treatment Eagerness Scale (SOCRATES) (Miller and Tonigan 1996); Violence Risk Scale (VRS) (Wong and Gordon 1999–2003); Violence Risk Scale–Sexual Offender (WRS-SO) (Wong *et al.* 2003) – although there is considerable debate about the suitability of such measures for use with offender populations (see Casey *et al.* 2005; Littell and Girvin 2002). More recently, Casey and colleagues (2007) drew on the multifactor offender readiness model (MORM; Ward *et al.* 2004b) to develop a general screening measure that assesses the internal characteristics of treatment readiness as described in the model. This measure, as well as an adaptation for use with offenders entering violence programmes (see Day *et al.* 2009a), has been found to successfully predict offender engagement in group rehabilitation programmes.

The dearth of theoretical development that surrounds the readiness construct and concomitant lack of clarity regarding definition and measurement poses a dilemma for practitioners. On the one hand, there is an expectation of evidence-based practice which necessitates a clear understanding of 'what works when, where, and for whom' (McGuire 2004: 339), while on the other, little is available in terms of psychometrically sound assessment tools to measure treatment readiness. Assessment is a critical element in identifying an individual's strengths and weaknesses. In fact, Hunsley and Mash (2008) have argued that assessment is the foundation that underpins evidence-based treatment, claiming that 'as the identification of evidence-based treatments rests entirely on the data provided by assessment tools, ignoring the quality of these tools places the whole evidence-based enterprise in jeopardy' (2008: 3). Thus, like treatment, assessments should also be evidence-based, with the selection of assessment tools guided by scientific evidence for the clinical utility of the selected instruments. This can be a difficult task. Both Kazdin (2005) and Sechrest (2005) have pointed out that it is not possible to identify a finite set of studies that establishes the psychometric properties of an instrument. This chapter considers published measures that purport to assess treatment readiness with a particular focus on the extent to which these tools meet the criteria for evidence-based assessment.

What follows is a brief overview of evidence-based assessment and the 'good enough' principle developed by Hunsley and Mash (2005, 2007, 2008; Mash and Hunsley 2005) for clinical assessment. This principle is the basis upon which the authors have developed a rating criteria that can be used to assess the psychometric properties of any particular assessment instrument. While their framework has, to date, been applied predominantly to assessments used in the identification of psychological disorders and the measurement of psychosocial deficits that may accompany such disorders, it is equally valid in a forensic context where there is a heavy reliance on assessment in terms of identifying client needs, focusing interventions and, in an environment where there is considerable political and social pressure for change, evaluating treatment outcomes. This is followed by a review and evaluation of instruments identified from the literature as being suitable for assessing an individual's readiness to enter into offender rehabilitation programmes, with a particular focus on use for the purposes of (a) case conceptualisation and treatment planning and (b) treatment monitoring and evaluation.

Evidence-based assessment (EBA)

The ability to conduct assessments has been identified as a core competency of professional psychologists (Hunsley and Mash 2008) and become a unique and defining feature of their professional expertise (Krishnamurthy *et al.* 2004). Yet despite this critical importance, much less attention has been paid to evidence-based assessments than to statements about evidence-based practice and best practice guidelines. Where attention has been paid, the focus has primarily been on ensuring that practitioners use measures with established reliability and validity (see Chambless and Hollon 1998; Kazdin *et al.* 1986), although these criteria are limited in terms of establishing the full nomothetic or idiographic utility of a measure (McFall 2005). More recently, greater attention has been paid to the development of evidence-based assessment (EBA) protocols and using specific criteria to evaluate some of the tools used more frequently in both research and practice (see, *inter alia*, special issues of *Psychological Assessment*, 2005, 17(2) and *Journal of Clinical Child and Adolescent Psychology*, 2007, 36(1) for more detailed discussions of specific assessment types and measures). One of the more well-developed rating criteria is that of Hunsley and Mash (2005, 2007, 2008), which is outlined below and is used here to evaluate treatment readiness assessments. It is first useful, however, to consider what is meant by evidence-based assessment.

An evidence-based approach to the provision of professional services in most health and human service systems (health, mental health, social work, criminal justice) is now a fundamental principle of best practice (Barlow 2004). What this means from a practical standpoint is that providers need to draw on information from a broad range of sources (such as research data, clinical experience, client preferences) when making decisions about service options (Hunsley and Mash 2005). Given that time constraints and resource limitations are frequently key factors in this decision making-process, the role of assessment becomes critical. Practitioners rely heavily on the accuracy of measurement tools for diagnostic and case conceptualisation purposes, as well as decisions about the course and efficacy of treatment. In fact, Weisz, Chu and Polo (2004) have argued that evidence-based practice is an assessment–intervention dialectic which involves (a) accurate identification of initial treatment targets, (b) selection of the most appropriate evidence-based treatment targets, and (c) periodic assessment of treatment to ascertain whether treatment adjustments are required (that is, assess–treat–reassess– adjust treatment).

Although the term 'evidence-based assessment' has been used in the scientific literature in a number of different ways, the definition used in this chapter is one that includes the standard psychometric indices of reliability and validity but goes beyond these criteria to include a number of utility considerations (see Cohen and Parkman 1998). Utility encompasses such things as treatment utility (the extent to which clinical assessment data contributes to positive treatment outcomes; Nelson-Gray 2003) and diagnostic utility (the extent to which assessment data contribute to the formulation of an accurate and complete diagnosis; Hunsley 2003). It also includes such factors as (a) assessment-related costs, including improvements in clinical decision-making resulting from the assessment; (b) any changes in false positive and false negative rates directly associated with the assessment (based on sensitivity and specificity indices); and (c) the economic and psychological costs associated with such errors (Hunsley and Mash 2005, 2007). In addition to the broad range of population-specific and problem-specific psychometric qualities to be considered for each assessment, establishing an EBA framework is further challenged by other factors, including the vast number of assessment measures and procedures available relative to the number of available treatment options; the many purposes of assessment as compared to treatment; and the iterative nature of the decision-making process (Hunsley *et al.* 2004).

Using these considerations as a guide, Hunsley and Mash (2005, 2007; Mash and Hunsley 2005) have identified three critical aspects that define EBA. First, both the selection of constructs to be assessed and the assessment process should be guided by scientifically supported theories and empirical evidence that establish important facets of a particular disorder or problem, identify the key symptoms or elements to be assessed, and where necessary identify common co-morbid conditions. Assessments should, therefore, be disorder or problem-specific and include emotional and relational problems that may also be experienced by the individual (such as loneliness or anger). Given the focus of assessment is to identify the precise nature of an individual's problem(s), it may also be necessary to adopt a multi-stage or iterative approach whereby the assessment process shifts from general or non-specific for initial assessments and then becomes more problem specific as the assessment focus is refined. That is, EBAs need to be embedded in the purpose of assessment (that is, screening, diagnosis, prognosis, treatment planning, treatment monitoring, and treatment evaluation).

Second, practitioners should opt for instruments that are psycho-metrically strong. In addition to evidence of reliability, validity and clinical utility, measures should also have appropriate norms for norm-referenced interpretation and/or replicated supporting evidence regarding the accuracy (sensitivity, specificity, predictive power and so on) of cut-off scores used for criterion-referenced interpretation (Hunsley and Mash 2005, 2007; Mash and Hunsley 2005). This also extends to individual characteristics, with a need for EBAs to be sensitive to an individual's age, gender, race and ethnicity, as well as specific cultural factors. Both the psychometric properties and individual characteristics should be evident irrespective of the purpose for which an assessment tool is used (screening, diagnosis, prognosis, case conceptualization, treatment formulation, treatment monitoring, treatment evaluation). That said, not all psychometric properties apply to all assessment purposes. While group validity statistics (for example, sensitivity, specificity, positive and negative predictive power) are relevant to diagnosis and prognosis (see Hsu 2002), these statistics are much less relevant when assessment is used for treatment monitoring or evaluation purposes. Finally, assessment is inherently a decision-making task, irrespective of the psychometric strength of any assessment tool (Hunsley and Mash 2005, 2007; Mash and Hunsley 2005). It is the practitioner who iteratively formulates and tests hypotheses, a process frequently undertaken with incomplete or inconsistent data. As with evidence-based treatment, an evidence-based approach to assessment should, therefore, evaluate the accuracy and utility of the decision-making process. This would include a review of (potential) data synthesis errors or errors in test interpretation, the financial costs associated with the total assessment process, and the impact of assessment on clinical outcomes (see Doss 2005 for a guide to conducting such an evaluation).

In order to provide an operational definition of these criteria, Hunsley and Mash (2005, 2007, 2008; Mash and Hunsley 2005) have taken into account a range of issues that impact upon the decisions made by practitioners in their choice of measures and how best to integrate assessment outcomes into service provision as a whole. While psychometric strength is, of course, an important factor in the choice of measure, systemic considerations – most notably time constraints and resource limitations – highlight the need for assessments that are brief, clear, clinically feasible and user-friendly (Hunsley and Mash 2008); that is, measures that are 'good enough to get the job done' (2008: 5). The rationale for adopting a 'good enough' position is the absence of any commonly accepted guidelines that stipulate a sufficient level of scientific evidence to warrant use of a particular measure (see Kazdin 2005; Sechrest 2005). In an effort to find a balance between setting criteria that is either too stringent (and rendering EBA a clinically worthless exercise) or too lenient (and thereby undermining the notion of EBA), the good enough principle has been operationalised using rating criteria that can assess specific categories of psychometric properties with obvious clinical relevance, with each category rated as being *less than adequate* (measure did not meet the minimum set criteria), *adequate* (measure meets minimum level of scientific vigour), *good* (measure generally possesses solid scientific support), *excellent* (measure has extensive, high-quality support evidence), *unavailable* (research on measure unavailable or not yet published), or *not applicable* (particular psychometric property not relevant to measure under consideration).

Assessment purposes

Although there are many reasons why assessments are conducted, Hunsley and Mash (2008: 6) have identified seven purposes that underpin most assessments: (a) diagnosis (determining the nature and/ or cause(s) of presenting problems, which may or may not involve the use of a formal diagnostic and categorisation system); (b) screening (identifying those who have or are at risk for a particular problem and who might be helped by further assessment or intervention); (c) prognosis and other predictions (generating predictions about the course of the problem(s) if left untreated, recommendations for possible course of action to be considered, and the likely impact on that course of the problem); (d) case conceptualisation/formulation (developing a comprehensive and clinically relevant understanding of the patient, generating hypotheses regarding critical aspects of the patient's psychosocial functioning and contexts that are likely to influence the patient's adjustment); (e) treatment design and planning (selecting/developing and implementing interventions designed to address the patient's problems by focusing on elements identified in the diagnostic evaluation and the case conceptualisation); (f) treatment monitoring (tracking changes in symptoms, functioning, psychological characteristics, intermediate treatment goals, and/or variables determined to cause or maintain the problem); and (g) treatment evaluation (determining the effectiveness, social validity, consumer satisfaction, and/or cost-effectiveness of the intervention). In the view of Hunsley and Mash, these can be further summarised into three domains for the purposes of undertaking EBAs: (a) diagnosis; (b) case conceptualisation and treatment planning (as these tend to rely on the same data); and (c) treatment monitoring and treatment evaluation (as these tend to use the same assessment data). Of these, (b) and (c) are the most relevant in terms of understanding the readiness construct.

Psychometric properties and rating criteria

Assessment tools can be either idiographic (assess unique aspects of an individual's experience) or nomothetic (assess constructs assumed relevant to all individuals). While it is sometimes difficult or irrelevant to apply psychometric properties to idiographic measures designed to assess individual change (such as self-monitoring forms) or treatment outcomes (such as treatment attainment scales), Hunsley and Mash (2007, 2008) have argued that where this is the case, EBA should examine the extent to which measurement items and instructions are consistent across assessment occasions. With respect to nomothetic instruments, the authors have argued that the most important psychometric properties in terms of establishing an EBA framework are as follows: norms, internal consistency, inter-rater reliability, test-retest reliability, content validity, construct validity, validity generalisation, and clinical utility (see Table 5.1 for a brief description of each category). These categories are applied to both the specific assessment purpose (for example case conceptualisation and treatment planning) and in the context of a specific disorder or condition (such as depression).

Hunsley and Mash's (2007, 2008) rating criteria for each of the psychometric categories is provided in Tables 5.2 and 5.3. The authors point out that while it might be preferable for practitioners to consider only those measures that meet their criteria for 'good' as a minimum standard this may not always be possible, principally because measure development is an ongoing process. Inclusion of the 'adequate' criteria allows for an evaluation of (a) more recently developed measures and (b) measures where the research evidence across all psychometric categories is not yet available. Both these factors are relevant in establishing an EBA framework for treatment readiness given how few measurement tools are available and how little previous work has been undertaken in the area.

As noted above, the rating criteria will be used to assess the psychometric properties of published measures that purport to assess treatment readiness in two domains: first, case conceptualisation and treatment planning, where the emphasis is generally identifying an individual's level of motivation to change, beliefs about whether the individual believes change is possible, and any barriers to change (what has been referred to as 'the will' and 'the way'; see Ward *et al.* 2004b); and second, treatment monitoring and evaluation that typically involves an assessment of the extent to which clients engaged in the treatment process, shifts in motivational states, changes to and/or replacement of maladaptive behaviours, and goal attainment. Previous attempts at establishing EBAs have done so using measures that have been developed specific for one or both of these purposes (see Hunsley and Mash 2008). However, given that the measurement of treatment readiness in an offender context is a relatively new endeavour, the evaluation process will differ a little from that previously used. Rather than examining an array of tools in the context of each assessment purposes and offering an evaluation, what follows is a description of the most commonly used measure and an evaluation of each in terms of the assessment purpose. The rationale for taking this approach is that compared to the assessment of psychological disorders and psychosocial deficits, there are far fewer measures that purport to assess treatment readiness. Moreover,

Table 5.1 Psychometric properties for EBA framework.

Category	Criteria for use
Norms	For standardised, nomothetically-based instruments, norms and criterion-based cut-off scores are necessary to enable the accurate interpretation of individual test scores. Samples should be truly representative of the sample population from which the individual is drawn in terms of demographic (e.g. age, sex) and other important characteristics (e.g. clinical versus non-clinical or offender versus non-offender samples). Used to determine pre- and post-treatment functioning and evaluate whether any change is clinically meaningful. Ratings of 'adequate' require data from a single large clinical sample; 'good' requires normative data from multiple samples (including population specific samples); while 'excellent' requires data from large representative samples.
Internal consistency	All items that purport to measure a single construct (e.g. treatment readiness) should contribute in a consistent way to the data obtained for that measure (items that reflect the same construct should yield similar results). While internal consistency can be reported as the average inter-item correlation, average item-total correlation, split-half reliability, the most commonly used measure is Cronbach's alpha (α).
Inter-rater reliability	Similar results should be obtained when a measure is used or scored by a clinician or researcher. Inter-rater (or inter-observer) reliability should be established outside of the study for which the results are reported (e.g. in a pilot study).
Test-retest reliability	The same results should be obtained if the test is administered to the same sample on two different occasions (i.e. assumes no substantial change in the construct under investigation between the two occasions). Two important caveats when considering test-retest reliability: (1) the time between measurement needs to be sufficient to ensure the outcome is not influenced by temporal factors (e.g. too short a period may result in practice effects); (2) some constructs are not expected to show temporal stability (e.g. measures of state-like variables).

Table 5.1 continues opposite

Table 5.1 continued

Category	Criteria for use
Content validity	Items should reflect the content domain of the construct purportedly measured by an instrument (items should represent the various aspects or facets of the construct an instrument was designed to measure) and the degree to which a test is a representative sample of the content of whatever objectives or specifications the test was originally designed to measure. To investigate the degree of match, test developers often enlist well-trained colleagues to make judgements about the degree to which the test items matched the test objectives or specifications.
Construct validity	A relationship should exist between a theoretical construct and any instrument that purports to measure that construct. A measure has strong construct validity if it has both convergent and discriminant validity. Convergent validity shows an acceptable level of agreement between different instruments that that purport to measure the same construct (e.g. scores on two instruments that purport to measure depression are shown to be highly correlated). Discriminant (or divergent) validity tests whether constructs that should not be related are, in fact, unrelated.
Validity generalisation	Evidence for validity generalisation is dependent upon a body of accumulated research supporting the use of a particular instrument across both situations and populations (the predictor or criterion generalises across studies and will continue to show similar parameters when the situation changes).
Clinical utility	Refers to the ease and efficiency of using an assessment tool and the (clinical) relevance and meaningfulness of the information it provides. Utility generally comprises: availability and ease of use; administration time; 'learnability' and clinician's qualifications; format; scoring and information derived; meaningful and relevant information obtained.

Table 5.2 Norms and reliability criteria.

Norms	
Adequate	Measures of central tendency and distributions for the total score (and subscores if relevant) based on a large relevant clinical sample are available.
Good	Measures of central tendency and distributions for the total score (and subscores if relevant) based on several large relevant samples (must include data from clinical and non-clinical samples) are available.
Excellent	Measures of central tendency and distributions for the total score (and subscores if relevant) based on one or more representative samples (must include data from both clinical and non-clinical samples) are available.
Internal consistency	
Adequate	Preponderance of evidence indicates α values of .70–.79.
Good	Preponderance of evidence indicates α values of .80–.89.
Excellent	Preponderance of evidence indicates α values of ≥ .90.
Inter-rater reliability	
Adequate	Preponderance of evidence indicates κ values of .60–.74; preponderance of evidence indicates Pearson correlation or interclass correlation values of .70–.79.
Good	Preponderance of evidence indicates κ values of .75–.84; preponderance of evidence indicates Pearson correlation or interclass correlation values of .80–.89.
Excellent	Preponderance of evidence indicates κ values ≥ .85; preponderance of evidence indicates Pearson correlation or interclass correlation values of ≥ .90.
Test-retest reliability	
Adequate	Preponderance of evidence indicates test-retest correlations of at least .70 over a period of several days to several weeks.
Good	Preponderance of evidence indicates test-retest correlations of at least .70 over a period of several months.
Excellent	Preponderance of evidence indicates test-retest correlations of at least .70 over a period of a year or longer.

Source: Hunsley and Marsh (2008: 8).

no clear distinction has been made in the literature regarding the purpose of each measure (other than to assess readiness). For these reasons, it is more useful to review the elements of each measure and then evaluate each in terms of the two assessment categories. Copies of all measures reviewed are contained in the Appendix.

Treatment readiness assessment tools

Stages of change measures

Given the centrality of motivation to the treatment readiness construct, and in the absence of any offender-specific assessment tools, it is not surprising that there has been a heavy reliance of measures based on the transtheoretical model (TTM) of change (Prochaska and DiClemente 1984, 1986). According to the TTM, behaviour change is thought to occur in a series of identifiable stages, the number of which differs between measures but generally includes some variation of pre-contemplation (no wish to change/no recognition of a problem), contemplation (intention to change problem behaviour within the next six months); preparation (intention to take immediate action, usually measured as within the next month); action (characterised by specific, overt modifications within the past six months); maintenance (relapse prevention); and termination (change process is complete/no further need to prevent relapse). An intrinsic component of this stage construct is its developmental, recursive nature (Begun *et al.* 2001), which typically involves between three and seven 'cycles' before long-term maintenance of the desired change is achieved (Prochaska *et al.* 1992). Moves towards maintenance are periodically interrupted by spiralling back to previous stages, which is subsequently followed by forward progress. Relapse is not seen as failure, but a predictable pattern in the change process. This allows any relapse to be reframed, viewed as a learning opportunity, and made available for refining future change and maintenance.

One of the most widely used of the stages of change measures is the University of Rhode Island Change Assessment (URICA) (McConnaughy *et al.* 1983, 1989). Comprising of four stages (precontemplation, contemplation, action, maintenance), this 32-item measure was originally designed to assess changes in smoking behaviour but has since been used for a broad range of health-related and addictive behaviours (such as excessive alcohol and drug use; see Brown *et al.* 2000; Davidson *et al.* 1991) as well as mental health and

Table 5.3 Validity and utility criteria.

Content validity

Adequate   The test developers clearly defined the domain of the construct being assessed and assured that selected items were clearly representative of the entire set of facets included in the domain.

Good   In addition to the criteria for an adequate rating, all elements of the instrument (e.g. instructions, items) were evaluated by judges (experts or pilot research participants).

Excellent   In addition to the criteria used for a good rating, multiple groups of judges were employed and quantitative ratings were used by all the judges.

Construct validity

Adequate   Some independently replicated evidence of construct validity (e.g. predictive validity, concurrent validity, and convergent and discriminant validity).

Good   Preponderance of independently replicated evidence across multiple types of validity (e.g. predictive validity, concurrent validity, and convergent and discriminant validity) is indicative of construct validity.

Excellent   In addition to the criteria for a good rating, evidence of incremental validity with respect to other clinical data.

Validity generalisation

Adequate   Some evidence supports the use of this instrument with either (a) more than one specific group (based on socio-demographic characteristics such as age, gender and ethnicity) or (b) in multiple contexts (home, school, primary care settings, in-patient settings).

Good   Preponderance of evidence supports the use of this instrument with either (a) more than one specific group (based on socio-demographic characteristics such as age, gender and ethnicity) or (b) in multiple contexts (home, school, primary care settings, in-patient settings).

Excellent   Preponderance of evidence supports the use of this instrument with (a) more than one specific group (based on socio-demographic characteristics such as age, gender and ethnicity) and (b) across multiple contexts (home, school, primary care settings, in-patient settings).

Table 5.3 continues opposite

Table 5.3 continued

Treatment sensitivity

Adequate   Some evidence of sensitivity to change over the course of
               treatment.

Good   Preponderance of independently replicated evidence indicates
               sensitivity to change over the course of treatment.

Excellent   In addition to the criteria for a good rating, evidence of
               sensitivity to change across different types of treatment.

Clinical utility

Adequate   Taking into account practical considerations (e.g. costs,
               ease of administration, availability of administration and
               scoring instructions, duration of assessment, availability of
               relevant cut-off scores, acceptability to patients) the resulting
               assessment data are likely to be clinically useful.

Good   In addition to the criteria for an adequate rating, there
               is some published evidence that the use of the resulting
               assessment data confers a demonstrable clinical benefit (e.g.
               better treatment outcome, lower treatment attrition rates,
               greater patient satisfaction with service).

Excellent   In addition to the criteria for an adequate rating, there is
               independently replicated published evidence that the use of
               the resulting assessment data confers a demonstrable clinical
               benefit.

Source: Hunsley and Mash (2008: 9)

psychotherapy (see McConnaughy *et al.* 1989; Petrocelli 2002). This breadth has been possible because responses are made to general questions about the individual's 'problem' (for example, 'It might be worthwhile to work on some of my problems') rather than specific issues. Attitudinal differences that characterise each of the four stages of change are assessed, with items used (a) to ascertain a stage 'profile' of the individual (as originally proposed by the developers); (b) a continuous score of readiness (Project MATCH Research Group 1997, 1998); or (c) to identify motivational subtypes (DiClemente and Hughes 1990; McConnaughy *et al.* 1983). In the offender context, the URICA has been used with specific populations, for example with offenders with drug use problems (see El-Bassel *et al.* 1998) and adapted to assess problem-specific stages of change (such as intimate partner/domestic violence; see Levesque *et al.* 2000).

Another of the stage measures, the Readiness to Change Questionnaire (RCQ) (Rollnick *et al.* 1992) is a 12-item measure consisting of three stages (precontemplation, contemplation, action). Developed along the same lines as the URICA (in fact, some items are direct adaptations, with the word 'problem' changed to 'drinking'), its primary purpose is a brief measure for excessive alcohol use in those who may not identify as problem drinkers or those with low levels of dependence, who are identified opportunistically in medical or other settings (that is, it is intended for harmful and hazardous drinkers not seeking treatment from specialist facilities). The Readiness to Change Questionnaire [Treatment Version] (RCQ-TV) (Heather *et al.* 1999) is a revision of the original measure, which can be used to assess problem drinkers prior to treatment entry. A 15-item instrument, it differs from the RCQ in that specific reference is made to total abstinence in addition to reduced drinking. The authors argued that this distinction is appropriate as total abstention is more likely to be a selected goal in treatment populations (whereas it can be seen as a disincentive in those referring only to cut down on alcohol use). Like the URICA, the RCQ has been used to assess treatment readiness in offender populations. For example, Williamson and colleagues (2003) used a modified version of the RCQ to assess violent offenders referred to an anger management programme (by changing the word 'drinking to 'anger'; for example, 'Sometimes I think I should try and cut down on my drinking' was rephrased as 'Sometimes I think I should try and control my anger'; 2003: 297). Tests of predictive validity revealed that the instrument correctly identified those offenders for whom the programme was successful in reducing scores on measures of anger experience and anger control. The authors suggested that the measure could help optimise programme outcomes by identifying those most suitable to participate as well as helping to facilitate staged-matched interventions.

The Stages of Change Readiness and Treatment Eagerness Scale (SOCRATES) (Miller and Tonigan 1996) is another problem-specific (alcohol) measure of behaviour change. Developed in parallel with other stages of change measures (such as URICA), the 19-item instrument is used to allocate clients presenting for alcohol-related treatment to one of three stages: recognition, taking steps, and asmbivalence. Miller and Tonigan claim that unlike measures such as URICA, the SOCRATES subscales represent 'continuously distributed motivational processes that may underlie stages of change' (1996: 84) but note that it does not assess all possible motivational vectors. A recent adaptation by Mitchell *et al.* (2005) produced a 14-item measure for military personnel seeking treatment for alcohol and drug problems. While the factor structure was shown to replicate the original measure, five of the 19 items were omitted. The authors explained this in terms of population sample differences; that is, the military sample were younger, more ethnically diverse, more likely to be fully employed, presented with substance problems much earlier, and therefore experienced many fewer physical symptoms associated with substance abuse, and the study included participants with co-morbid drug and alcohol problems.

The first measure to incorporate treatment readiness into an assessment of offender risk, the Violence Risk Scale (VRS) (Wong and Gordon 1999–2003), and more recently the Violence Risk Scale–Sex Offender version (VRS-SO) (Wong *et al.* 2003), is used to identify who to treat (high-risk/need offenders), what to treat (identify dynamic risk factors), how to treat (matching therapeutic approaches to specific stage of change), and whether there have been post-treatment improvements (see Wong and Gordon 2006; Wong *et al.* 2007). In other words, the VRS and VRS-SO assess risk, criminogenic need, client responsivity, and treatment change using a single assessment process. The VRS comprises six static and 20 dynamic variables while the VRS-SO has seven static and 17 dynamic variables. The former is derived from and theoretically underpinned by the psychology of criminal conduct (Andrews and Bonta 2003) while the latter is modelled closely on the VRS, also relying on other sources related specifically to sexual offending (for example Hanson and Harris 2000; Proulx *et al.* 1997; Ward and Hudson 1998). For the purposes of risk assessment, all variables are rated on a four-point scale (0, 1, 2, 3) using file information and a semi-structured interview. Dynamic variables identified as treatment targets (rated 2 or 3) are then assessed for treatment readiness using a qualitative guide (see Wong and Gordon 1999–2003 for detailed stage descriptors for each dynamic variable). Allocation to one of the five stages of change (precontemplation, contemplation, preparation, action, maintenance) is based on information drawn from the file review and interview regarding the offender's attitudes, behaviour and affect. A forward progression through the stages (except precontemplation to contemplation) is considered improvement (the VRS translates forward progress from one stage to the next as a quantitative risk reduction of 0.5).

Personal concerns inventory–offender adaptation (PCI-OA)

The Personal Concerns Inventory–Offender Adaptation (PCI-OA)

(McMurran *et al.* 2006, 2008; Sellen *et al.* 2006, 2009) takes a different approach to motivation from that described in the transtheoretical model by adopting a theory of motivation in which goal-striving plays a central role (see Klinger and Cox 2004a). An adaptation of Cox and Klinger's (2002) Personal Concerns Inventory (PCI), the PCI-OA examines the latent processes or ('current concerns') that underpin any active goal pursuit. This exploration of current concerns involves both the conscious and subconscious cognitive and affective processes that are in operation up to the point where an individual either attains his or her goal(s) or gives up the goal pursuit. By way of example, Sellen *et al.* (2009) explain how alcohol may be a valued goal (and problem drinking understood within an overall goal framework). First, alcohol use is selected as a goal because of its rewarding properties (for example the pharmacological effect on emotions). The incentive value for continued use is influenced by various factors including individual difference characteristics (the biochemical responsivity to alcohol, personality traits), social factors (parental models, social norms), and context (the availability of similarly rewarding, non-drug alternatives). Over time, this incentive value may change. For example, excessive use may lead to addiction and/or changes in individual circumstances (job loss or family breakdown).

The PCI-OA requires offenders to describe their current concerns in the 12 life areas from the PCI (self changes; employment and finance; partner, family and relatives; education and training; home and household matters; substance use; friends and acquaintances; health and medical matters; hobbies, pastimes and recreation; love, intimacy and sexual; spiritual matters; other areas) as well as two additional areas that are offender-specific (my offending behaviour; current living arrangements). As with the PCI, each area is rated in terms of value, attainability, imminence and controllability (Cox and Klinger 2002). The PCI-OA also requires that offenders to rate how (a) offending and (b) being in prison helps or interferes with the attainment of their goals. Responses have been shown to fall along three dimensions. The first two, *adaptive motivation* and *maladaptive motivation*, are consistent with the PCI. An adaptive motivational profile is characterised by high levels of perceived likelihood regarding goal attainments, expectations of happiness when goals are attained, and commitment to goal strivings. A maladaptive motivational profile, on the other hand, is characterised by having goals that are seen as unimportant, expecting little happiness at goal achievements, and having low commitment to goals. The PCI-OA has also been found to have a third factor – *lack of direction* – which appears to reflect unhappiness in the face of goal achievement, difficulty in knowing how to achieve goals, and a perception that prison and offending may be helpful in terms of goal achievements. Scores on each of the indices can then be calculated. An adaptive motivation (AM) index is calculated by subtracting the sum of variables with negative loadings from the sum of variables with positive loadings, and the mean then calculated. The maladaptive motivation (MM) index is calculated by subtracting the sum of variables with positive loadings from the sum of variables with negative loadings, and calculating the mean for that subscale. Finally, lack of direction (LoD) is calculated by subtracting the sum of the rating scales with positive loadings from the sum of the scale with a negative loading.

Treatment readiness measures

Although Serin and Kennedy (1997; Serin 1998) developed what was perhaps the first offender-specific assessment of treatment readiness, there has been little reference in the literature to their semi-structured interview outside that published by Canadian Corrections (see Chapter 2). Williamson *et al.* (2003) adapted the interview schedule to be used as a brief (11-item) questionnaire – the Serin Treatment Readiness Scale (STRS) – and while moderately high correlations were noted between this measure and their Anger Readiness to Change Questionnaire (ARCQ, adapted from Rollnick *et al.* 1992), no other psychometric properties were reported. More recently, Serin, Mailloux and Kennedy (2007) have developed a clinical rating scale for offender readiness: the Treatment Readiness Clinical Rating Scale (TRCRS). The general premise that underpins this measure is similar to that espoused in the MORM (Ward *et al.* 2004); that is, treatment readiness can be influenced by a range of internal and external factors (such as treatment setting, individual offender characteristics, treatment intensity, motivational issues). Serin *et al.* have also taken the position that any treatment response is incremental in nature, a reflection of general treatability issues (that is, readiness and participation) which in turn provides an indication of the overall treatment effect (the treatment gains and the generalisation of new knowledge and skills to new situations).

Given the proposition that treatment readiness and interpersonal style are related and serve to influence programme performance (see Serin and Kennedy 1997), the 16-item measure developed by Serin *et al.* (2007) comprises eight items that reflect these two domains. The reported factor analysis confirmed the existence of each domain as an independent, albeit correlated, subscale. Items are representative of each domain (for example, problem recognition and treatment goals reflect the treatment readiness domain; pro-criminal views and denial reflect interpersonal style), with responses made using a four-point Likert scale. Unfortunately, the authors have not provided any further information relating to item content or how scores on the measure might be calculated and subsequently used to assess levels of treatment readiness. They do note, however, that unpublished research has shown that the domains differentiate offenders with respect to programme attrition, recidivism and types of sexual offenders. The measure has also be included in the evaluation framework of a motivational primer for violent offenders (see Blanchette and Moser 2006).

The Corrections Victoria Treatment Readiness Questionnaire (CVTRQ) (Casey *et al.* 2007) is a generic screening measure that can be used to assess readiness for treatment prior to programme entry. While not a test of the model *per se*, item content is derived from the internal factors identified in Ward *et al.*'s (2004b) multifactor offender readiness model on treatment readiness (for example, beliefs about treatment, past experiences of programmes, offender goals). An attempt to distinguish treatment readiness from treatment motivation and responsivity, the MORM subscribes to the definition of readiness proposed by Howells and Day (2003) as 'the presence of characteristics (states or dispositions) within either the client or the therapeutic situation, which are likely to promote engagement in therapy and which, thereby, are likely to enhance therapeutic change' (Ward *et al.* 2004b: 650). To be ready for treatment, the individual needs to be motivated (wants to, has the will to), has the ability to respond appropriately (perceives he or she can), finds it relevant and meaningful (can engage), and has the capacities (i.e., is able) to successfully enter the rehabilitation programme. Readiness is, therefore, perceived as more inclusive than either motivation or responsivity and is, in fact, thought to encompass both these constructs.

The 20-item CVTRQ consists of four subscales: attitudes and motivation (attitudes and beliefs about programmes and the desire to change); emotional reactions (emotional responses to the individual's offending behaviour); offending beliefs (beliefs about personal responsibility for offending behaviour); and efficacy (perceived ability to participate in treatment programmes). Responses are made using a five-point scale, with higher scores indicating higher levels of readiness (scores can range from 20 to 100). Initial ROC analysis suggested a cut-off score of ≥ 72, which provides a sensitivity of 69.49 and specificity of 59.38 (which represents a positive predictive value of 61.2 per cent and negative predictive value of 67.9 per cent). In the absence of large-scale predictive validity studies, the authors suggest that cut-off scores might reasonably fall between 68 and 74. The choice of cut-off will ultimately depend on a cost–benefit analysis. If the main aim is to maximise the number of clients ready for treatment programmes, then choosing a cut-off that maximises sensitivity is generally preferable (but will lead to the inclusion into the programme of more clients who are not treatment ready). Conversely, maximising specificity will ensure that most of those included in the programme are, in fact, treatment ready (although this may result in lack of programme access for those individuals who are indeed ready to change). Validation of the measure also revealed that the attitudes and motivation subscale was most strongly related to overall treatment engagement (the outcome variable in the study). While suggesting that this aspect of readiness is likely to be particularly important, the profile of scores across subscales is likely to reveal those aspects of readiness that are salient for an individual. Interventions that target low readiness can therefore be targeted towards specific deficits identified by the measure.

Finally, the Violence Treatment Readiness Questionnaire (VTRQ) (Day *et al.* 2009a) is an adaptation of the CVTRQ that can be used to screen violent offenders prior to programme allocation. The only modification to the original measure was to change item wording to reflect violence rather offending in general (for example, 'I have not offended for some time now' was replaced with 'I have not acted violently for some time now'). As with the general measure, a moderately high correlation was found between readiness as measured by the VTRQ and self-reported treatment engagement. In fact, this relationship was stronger than that found for other measures of readiness used in the study to assess convergent validity, namely the RCQ (Rollnick *et al.* 1992) and STRS (Williamson *et al.* 2003). The finding that post-treatment readiness scores were significantly higher than pre-treatment scores illustrates the dynamic nature of the construct, increasing over the course of programme participation. While it may not be surprising that by the end of treatment participants can demonstrate changes in their attitudes and motivation, emotional reactions to their offences, offending beliefs and efficacy, it does point to an additional use of the VTRQ as a measure of change in interventions that are designed to increase problem awareness and motivation prior to entry in structured treatment programmes.

Overall evaluation: case conceptualisation and treatment planning

Perhaps the most important point to be made when considering the suitability of readiness measures for the purposes of case formulation and treatment planning is the need to utilise more than a single measure in order to obtain accurate and meaningful information (see Hunsley and Mash 2008; Serin *et al.* 2007). For example, measures based on the transtheoretical model (Prochaska and DiClemente 1984, 1986), while suitable for determining an offender's motivational state, are less suitable for establishing treatment readiness (see Casey *et al.* 2005). Similarly, the PCI-OA (McMurran *et al.* 2008a; Sellen *et al.* 2006, 2009) enables the practitioner to assess motivation and determine whether there is a fit between an offender's goals and their criminogenic need(s), but there is no provision in the instrument to directly assess readiness for treatment. This latter issue is addressed in the CVTRQ (Casey *et al.* 2007) and VTRQ (Day *et al.* 2009a), but even these measures need to be used in conjunction with, for example, a measure of motivation, to ensure that the offender's readiness is not a function of external pressure to enter treatment (such as for parole purposes). The biggest difficulty in adopting an EBA approach is the limited number of measures from which to choose and the paucity of evidence regarding their psychometric properties. This highlights the need for practitioners to ensure that the measures selected are both relevant to the task at hand and psychometrically sound. That said, the majority of measures described herein are available at no cost and require little or no training for administration (the PCI-OA is perhaps the most difficult); the stages of change measures, VCTRQ and VTRQ, take only a few minutes to complete.

While the URICA (McConnaughy *et al.* 1983) is one of the most widely used measures of motivational readiness and displays adequate levels of clinical utility, it has poor validity generalisation with respect to an offending context. The major limitation is a failure to clearly define 'problem' behaviours; first, some offenders may not perceive their behaviour as problematic, and second, even when behaviours are acknowledged as being cause for concern, if the offender presents with more than one problem (for example poly-substance abuse, co-morbid diagnosis), difficulties may arise in terms of question interpretation and subsequent responses. Another frequently used stage of change measure is the RCQ (Rollnick *et al.* 1992) and, more recently, the RCQ-TV (Heather *et al.* 1999). Although the psychometric properties are slightly stronger than the URICA (see

Table 3.4) and the measure has been adapted for offender populations (see McMurran *et al.* 1998; Williamson *et al.* 2003), there appears to be some confusion about which of the RCQ measures is most appropriate. The original RCQ instrument was developed to assess motivation to change among excessive alcohol consumers identified opportunistically in medical settings and is the one most commonly adapted for offender populations (McMurran *et al.* 1998; Williamson *et al.* 2003). A decision to use this measure at the case conceptualisation and treatment planning stage, whether to assess for alcohol or drug use or adapting it for use as an offence-specific measure, needs to be informed by the offender's beliefs about the problem behaviour. In other words, it is important to determine whether it is the offender who has self-identified the behaviour as problematic or whether it is the practitioner's assessment of that behaviour. For example, if an offender presents with a criminogenic need relating to anger and/or violence and recognises that his or her behaviour is problematic, it would be more useful to adapt the treatment version of the RCQ, as it includes reference to abstaining from the problematic behaviour. On the other hand, if in the process of case conceptualisation the practitioner identifies substance use as problematic but the offender does not, it may be more appropriate to use (or adapt) the original RCQ.

On face value, the integration of stages of change, risk/need assessment, and treatment outcomes in the VRS (Wong and Gordon 1999–2003, 2006) and VRS-SO (Wong *et al.* 2003) would seem to provide a broad (multi-method) approach to assessment. In terms of case conceptualisation and treatment planning, static variables can provide an empirical-actuarial assessment of risk while the dynamic variables identify areas of criminogenic need that should be the target for intervention(s). Readiness can also be (qualitatively) assessed prior to treatment. The limitation of the instrument in terms of assessing treatment readiness, from an EBA perspective at least, is the absence of any psychometric evaluation of the readiness component of the measure. Thus while both the VRS and VRS-SO have been shown to be psychometrically sound (see Olver *et al.* 2007; Wong *et al.* 2007; Wong and Gordon 2006), it is not possible to consider readiness as an independent property of the measure other than to note that it has adequate content validity and validity generalisation. The qualitative nature of interpretation may also be problematic, particularly when relying on responses to a semi-structured interview.

As the limitations of using stages of change measures to assess treatment readiness have been discussed in more detail elsewhere

(Casey *et al.* 2005; Littell and Girvin 2002; Tierney and McCabe 2001), an extensive critique will not be given in this chapter. In brief, however, the main issues to consider are as follows. First, factors that might influence an individual's motivation to change may differ markedly between a prison and non-prison environment. An incarcerated offender may have little internal motivation to change their behaviour, but the external motivators might be such that the advantages of participating in a treatment programme far outweigh the disadvantages. Second, there is considerable difficulty in monitoring any change in criminal behaviour where the offender is incarcerated. Criminal offending, particularly in a prison environment, will not only occur less frequently, but when it does occur, is typically less likely to be observed. Moreover, the artificial environment in which offenders live may contribute to any reduction in frequency, even a temporary remission of offending behaviour. Third, there is a tendency for offender rehabilitation programmes to adopt a 'one size fits all' approach, which is inconsistent with evidence from the clinical arena that suggests stage-matched treatments result in more successful outcomes. Finally, and perhaps most important from an EBA perspective, allocation can differ as a function of the scoring method used. The simplest interpretation is placing the respondent in the highest scoring stage (which can be problematic when the individual scores are equally high in more than one stage). It is possible to calculate readiness to change composite scores by summing the contemplation, action and maintenance scores and then subtracting the precontemplation score. The Italian Composite scores are calculated by subtracting the sum of the precontemplation and contemplation scores from the sum of the action and maintenance scores, while the committed action composite scores are calculated by subtracting contemplation scores from the action scores (see McMurran *et al.* 2006).

Despite problems with stages of change measures, if the purpose of assessment is confined to motivation to change problematic substance use, the SOCRATES (Miller and Tonigan 1996; Mitchell *et al.* 2005) measure is psychometrically much stronger than either the URICA or RCQ. It provides information on three dimensions of motivation, namely problem recognition (acknowledgement that that there is a problem related to drugs or alcohol); ambivalence (uncertainty/openness to reflection as to whether substance use is a problem); and taking steps (whether steps have already been taken to change drinking or drug-related behaviours). The narrower focus on motivation rather than on stages of change also serves to increase its utility; that is, rather than measuring the stage constructs as conceived by Prochaska and DiClemente (1983, 1986), it explains the 'continuously distributed motivational processes that may underlie stages of change' (Miller and Tonigan 1996: 84). In an offending context, the SOCRATES measure has been shown to reliably predict later substance use (see Prendergast *et al.* 2009) but not substance-related offending (Nochajsk and Stasiewic 2005; Prendergast *et al.* 2009).

Looking next at the PCI-OA (Sellen *et al.* 2009), its utility would seem to be in understanding the concerns offenders may have and identifying positive goals rather than being a direct assessment of whether to enter either offence-specific or generalist programmes. Moreover, while the authors claim that the similarity in factor structure between this and Klinger and Cox's (2004a) original instrument (adaptive and maladaptive motivation subscales) and this adaptation supports the structural validity, the poor psychometric properties of the lack of direction (LoD) subscale ($\alpha = .36$) undermines this claim. In order to meet EBA criteria one would expect at least adequate levels of internal consistency – only the adaptive motivation subscale meets this criterion – for specific populations or offence types (Hunsley and Mash 2008). A further limiting factor (in terms of EBA) is that while the authors provide a method for calculating scores for each of the indices, no cut-off scores are provided. Nor is there provision in the scoring to accommodate high or low scores on both the adaptive motivation and maladaptive motivation. An offender who scores high on both motivational scales can have the same score as someone who has scored low on both. Interpretation is left to the practitioner, which could in turn reduce its clinical utility. The strongest argument for using the measure is at the case conceptualisation stage where information about the offender's goals can be considered in the context of overall risk assessment and identified criminogenic and non-criminogenic need.

For the purposes of screening offenders prior to treatment entry, the CVTRQ (Casey *et al.* 2007) and VTRQ (Day *et al.* 2009a) both display adequate levels of reliability, validity (including generalisation validity) and clinical utility. The inclusion of cut-off scores means that when used in conjunction with an offender's risk/needs profile, practitioners can make a decision about treatment referral that is based on empirical evidence of the relationship between readiness and engagement in the treatment process (that is, predictive validity). Where an offender is not treatment ready, scores on any of the four components (attitudes and motivation; emotional reactions; offending beliefs; efficacy) provide specific targets for improving readiness. What

Table 5.4 Ratings of instruments for case conceptualisation and treatment planning.

Instrument	Norms	Internal consistency	Inter-rater reliability	Test-retest reliability	Content validity	Construct validity	Validity generalisation	Clinical utility
URICA	+	++	NA	U	U	++	−	+
RCQ/RCQ-TV	+	++	−	+	+++	+	−	+
SOCRATES	+++	+++	NA	+++	+++	+	−	+
PCI-OA	−	+	U	U	+	+	U	−
TRCRS	+	++	U	U	++	+	U	−
VRS/VRS-SO	U	U	U	U	+	U	+	U
CVTRQ/VTRQ	+	++	U	U	+	+	++	++

URICA = University of Rhode Island Change Assessment; RCQ = Readiness to Change Questionnaire; SOCRATES = Stages of Change Readiness and Treatment Eagerness Scale; PCI-OA = Personal Concerns Inventory – Offender Adaptation; TRCRS = Treatment Readiness Clinical Rating Scale; VRS = Violence Risk Scale; CVTRQ = Corrections Victoria Treatment Readiness Questionnaire; VTRQ = Violence Treatment Readiness Questionnaire.

+ = Adequate; ++ = Good; +++ = Excellent; NA = Not applicable; U = Unavailable; − = Less than adequate.

this means at the case conceptualisation and treatment planning stages is that practitioners can adopt the approach advocated by Weisz *et al.* (2004) of treat–reassess–adjust treatment. For example, offenders low in treatment readiness can receive an intervention designed to increase readiness (such as motivational interviewing), have their level of readiness reassessed, and when a sufficient level of change is noted be moved to a criminogenic needs programme. Consistent with the multi-method approach of EBA, using this measure to determine treatment referral might be done in conjunction with (a) an assessment of the individual's motivation to change (such as SOCRATES, for substance use) to ensure that there is a correlation between motivation and treatment readiness; and (b) an assessment of the individual's needs or goals using, for example, the PCI (Klinger and Cox 2004a), the PCI-OA (Sellen *et al.* 2006, 2009), or the Good Lives Model (Ward and Stewart 2003).

Overall evaluation: treatment monitoring and evaluation

Assessments during treatment and follow-up are necessary to determine the effectiveness of any intervention and whether the changes noted immediately following treatment are sustained over time. As noted above, the provision of programmes to offenders who are treatment ready is not only a better use of scarce resources, it is also likely to result in sustained treatment outcomes (as evidenced by reductions in recidivism). The choice of instrument used for the purposes of treatment monitoring and evaluation will depend on whether the practitioner wants to assess improvements in treatment readiness (following specific interventions to increase readiness) or whether the goal is to evaluate the effectiveness of an offence-specific programme (for example the relationship between treatment readiness, therapeutic alliance and behavioural change). Another important consideration for assessment is that like motivation, readiness is dynamic in nature. An offender who is treatment ready at the commencement of a programme may wax and wane over the course of the programme (as a result, for example, of shifts in motivation, changing attitudes towards treatment, levels of engagement with programme content, beliefs about self-efficacy, external pressure, therapeutic alliance).

The stages of change measures are most useful for monitoring progress in treatment designed to improve readiness (such as motivational interviewing). Of the measures available, the two with most evidence of treatment sensitivity are SOCRATES (Miller and Tonigan 1996) and URICA (McConnaughy *et al.* 1983, 1989). While SOCRATES would be more strongly recommended for offenders with substance abuse disorders (given its stronger psychometric properties), the URICA may be more appropriate for other offence types (particularly if the 'problem behaviour' is clearly identifiable). Both the VRS (Wong and Gordon 1999–2003) and VRS-SO (Wong *et al.* 2003) enable the practitioner to monitor the extent to which any newly acquired positive attitudes and coping skills are stable, sustainable, and generalisable. Forward progression in treatment is subsequently used to redefine risk by at the completion of treatment (using an algorithm). Despite the lack of psychometric evidence for the states of change component of this measure, outcome studies have shown that offenders assigned to treatment on the basis of their VRS or VRS-OS scores do have better outcomes in terms of reductions in recidivism rates (see, for example, Wong *et al.* 2003, 2007, 2005).

Although the psychometric properties of the PCI-OA (Sellen *et al.* 2009) are not strong, Sellen and her colleagues have noted modest changes over the course of treatment in adaptive motivation (with corresponding reductions in the maladaptive motivation and lack of direction subscales). Given the higher level of sensitivity to change noted in the PCI (Klinger and Cox 2004a), this measure is perhaps preferable to the PCI-OA for assessing whether treatment has resulted in a downward shift in personal concerns, at least until further validation of the PCI-OA is undertaken. Finally, in addition to screening offenders for programme suitability, the CVTRQ (Casey *et al.* 2007) and VTRQ (Day *et al.* 2009a) can be used for both treatment monitoring and outcome evaluations. For example, cut-off scores can be used to assess changes following treatment designed to improve readiness (such as experiential and drama therapy, motivational interviewing). In terms of treatment monitoring, Ward *et al.* (2004b) have argued that engagement in treatment is an intermediate goal before change in criminogenic need takes place. Therefore, an assessment of the relationship between treatment readiness and treatment engagement midway through a programme would enable practitioners to monitor treatment efficacy.

Conclusions and future directions

As noted at the beginning of this chapter, despite the importance of treatment readiness to the rehabilitative process, there remains a need

Table 5.5 Ratings of instruments for treatment monitoring and evaluation.

Instrument	Norms	Internal consistency	Inter-rater reliability	Test-retest reliability	Content validity	Construct validity	Validity generalisation	Treatment sensitivity	Clinical utility
URICA	+	++	NA	U	U	++	-	+	+
SOCRATES	+++	+++	NA	+++	+++	+	-	++	+
VRS/VRS-SO	U	U	U	U	+	U	+	U	U
PCI-OA	-	+	U	U	+	+	U	-	-
CVTRQ/VTRS	+	++	U	U	+	+	++	+	+

URICA = University of Rhode Island Change Assessment; SOCRATES = Stages of Change Readiness and Treatment Eagerness Scale; VRS = Violence Risk Scale; PCI-OA = Personal Concerns Inventory-Offender Adaptation; CVTRQ = Corrections Victoria Treatment Readiness Questionnaire; VTRQ = Violence Treatment Readiness Questionnaire.

+ = Adequate; ++ = Good; +++ = Excellent; NA = Not applicable; U = Unavailable; - = Less than adequate for theoretical advancement in the area. While this is important from an evidence-based approach to assessment, it is equally important in terms of gaining a better understanding of the construct and how it can (or should) be measured. Readiness is a complex and dynamic phenomenon: an individual is ready for something. In the case of offender treatment, he or she is ready to engage in a process (treatment) that will bring about behavioural change (non-offending). This highlights two important considerations in terms of assessment. First, readiness can change over time. Someone who is ready for treatment prior to the commencement of a rehabilitation programme may, for a vast number of reasons, shift along the readiness continuum throughout the treatment process. It may be, for example, that readiness issues (such as anxiety about self-disclosure in a group settings) are resolved in the early stages of a treatment programme. For others, their experiences of the treatment in the early sessions may entrench and reinforce low levels of readiness (beliefs that correctional treatment isn't confidential, or isn't effective, for example). Second, its complexity necessitates multi-method assessment. The measures described herein all provide information about the individual but none provides the practitioner with a comprehensive assessment of all facets of readiness. There is a limit to the extent to which self-report measures of the type described in this chapter can provide a comprehensive assessment of an individual's preparedness and ability to engage in treatment. Psychometric assessments are one part of a broader assessment of readiness, which should take into consideration an individual's level of risk and presenting needs. There is, however, an urgent need to undertake and publish validation studies using the measures already available, as these measures offer the practitioner a way of making decisions that are both informed and reliable. In a forensic context it is critical that practitioners are able to publicly defend their clinical decision-making. The research literature as it currently stands is an important first step, but if evidence-based assessment does underpin evidence-based treatments, then scientific evidence should guide the selection of readiness instruments in the same way as it should guide any other form of clinical assessment.

Part Two

Readiness and Offenders

Chapter 6

Interpersonal violence: the need for individualised services

It is widely accepted that one of the most important initial tasks in violent offender treatment programmes is finding a way to engage participants in a therapeutic process. This is seen as a necessary, and perhaps even sufficient, condition for change to take place. In Chapter 12, Christina Kozar reviews evidence to suggest that at least a quarter of the therapeutic change observed can be directly attributed to the nature of the relationship formed between the client and the treatment provider. Kozar notes that clients who do not experience a collaborative purposeful therapeutic relationship tend to either leave treatment or do not make as many gains as other clients, and this would appear to be particularly true for many violent offenders who are referred to rehabilitation programmes (Ross *et al.* 2008).

Many violent offenders do not readily view their aggression and violence as problematic, and participants in violent offender treatment commonly (if not typically) experience serious, complex problems, personality disorders, and possibly outright mental illness, which potentially leaves them unreceptive to intervention and likely to drop out of or not complete programmes. This is a serious issue, given evidence to suggest that the risk of reoffending is increased following the non-completion of violent offender treatment programmes. In their work Dowden, Blanchette and Serin (1999) have shown that programme drop-outs have the highest rate of violent reoffending (40 per cent), compared with both untreated (17 per cent) and treated (5 per cent) groups. A more recent review of offender treatment non-completion across a wide range of offender treatment programmes produced similar findings (McMurran and Theodosi 2007). High attrition rates are commonly reported in evaluations of programmes for violent offenders, particularly when programmes are offered in the community. Among court mandated domestic violence offender programmes, for example, non-completion rates of up to 75 per cent have been reported (Buttell and Carney 2008), although the completion rate of approximately 55 per cent for 16-week group-based programmes reported by Gondolf (2008) is probably more typical. Such findings underscore the importance of considering the nature of treatment readiness in violent offenders, such that appropriate placement into rehabilitation programmes takes place.

A number of the factors are likely to influence the ways in which violent offenders engage with rehabilitation programmes. These are described elsewhere in this book. For example, attitudes and beliefs about offending and violence that potentially undermine readiness are described in Chapter 3. Many violent offenders present with difficulties in regulating their emotions, notably anger, and in the treatment context this may also impact on readiness (Chapter 3). In addition, some violent offenders will also have long-term difficulties, sometimes associated with personality disorders (Chapter 9), that make the task of programme delivery particularly challenging. The aim of this chapter, however, is not to repeat this material, but to consider the need to match the needs of the individual offender to the particular type of programme being offered. Too often correctional agencies make referrals to programmes on the basis of offences, and fail to adequately consider the heterogeneity that exists in offender groups. This can result in the delivery of standardised programmes that can be seen as irrelevant or unnecessary by participants. As such, even if motivation exists to change aggressive and violent behaviour, the lack of an appropriate programme might inhibit readiness. Day and Howells (2008) describe the problem as follows:

> It is tempting (and sometimes administratively convenient), in setting up treatment programmes for violent (or other) offenders, to define the problem topographically and to use topographic descriptions to allocate offenders to programmes. Thus 'sex offenders' would be directed to a sex offender programme, 'violent offenders' to a violence programme, and so on. The dangers of such an approach, although these can be offset by practical advantages, lie in the implicit assumption that individuals in the offender group share features and needs that go beyond the fact that they have all engaged in violent acts. (2008: 17)

In the past decade evidence has increasingly demonstrated that violent offenders are indeed heterogeneous in terms of their needs and the causal influences on their offending behaviour. Serin (2004), for example, has suggested that violent offenders are sufficiently heterogeneous that endeavours to distinguish among types of offenders should be strongly encouraged and that current strategies to assign all violent offenders to anger management programmes is both inefficient and ill-advised. Similarly, in his comprehensive review of treatment outcomes for violence programmes, McGuire (2008) concludes that different sub-groups may be differentially responsive to existing treatments. The argument put forward in this chapter is that offering programmes that are more closely aligned with the needs of participants (or 'functional' approaches to treatment allocation, see Sturmey 2007), is likely to lead to higher levels of engagement, participation, completion and ultimately reduction in risk. Indeed, as a group, violent offenders can be considered particularly heterogenous in relation not only to their offences, but also to a range of other factors that include the triggers of their aggression, the role that emotional arousal plays, and gender differences. These are discussed below.

Offence type

Nowhere is the heterogeneity of violent offenders more obvious than in relation to the nature of the offence. Sexual violence, for example, is widely acknowledged to require different understandings from general violence.[1] Sexual offences are sometimes classified as violent offences, and for some offenders (for example, those who commit serious violent acts that have a sexual component) the decision whether to allocate a sexual offender or a violent offender rehabilitation programme is not always easy to make. Whichever choice is made, the offender may regard the referral as inappropriate to his or her own circumstances, and be reluctant to engage or participate. Violence that occurs within families or intimate relationships also has a number of features that potentially distinguish it from other forms of violent offending. It typically occurs, for example, behind closed doors, where the only witnesses are victims, and as a result the facts of the offence are often difficult to establish. Even after conviction, offenders commonly dispute the evidence that is presented to the police and/or the courts in relation to the frequency and intensity

[1]Readiness in sexual offenders is discussed separately in the next chapter.

of their violence, the reliability of victim statements, and the extent to which they consider themselves personally responsible. Mandated referral to a domestic violence treatment programme is thus often seen as further evidence that they have been treated either unfairly or unjustly (O'Leary et al. 2009).

In interviews with men who had just begun a community-based domestic violence programme, O'Leary et al. (2009) reported that many men expressed a sense of injustice about being there, because they believed, at the very least, that their partners were equally responsible for the circumstances that led to their order to attend the programme. One participant spoke of attending the programme 'under duress'. He described it as follows: 'to be perfectly frank, I'm unfortunately in the situation where I don't think I'm suitable for the course. I'm not innocent in relation to the few areas where I've crossed the line but what I am completely shocked at is the system where the other party is not brought to account' (2009: 170). When men were asked about the court or correctional services ordering them to attend the programme, it was not uncommon for men to be unclear about this process. Many men commented that they felt the length of the programme was excessive, with one man commenting that he had been put on bonds that had not lasted as long as the programme. There was some apprehension from men about content and the fact that they would be in a group with other men. The following quote highlights one man's confusion about the referral process and programme: 'Just a bit confused I suppose, no one told me what its all about, I've waited about 6 months and then I find out it is 24 weeks I have to come or something, but I am curious as well, yeah, more than anything else, yeah. Yeah, I haven't got that I shouldn't be here attitude ... Just don't know what to expect' (2009: 175). Most men in this study, however, did not completely dismiss the potential for benefits to arise from their attendance at the group, sometimes even in the face of claims of innocence and unfairness from the mandatory order.

There has been a great deal of discussion concerning the extent to which mentally disordered offenders have specific risk factors that differentiate them from general offender groups (see Howells et al. 2004a). The co-occurrence of mental disorder and violent behaviour is widely acknowledged, but the nature of the causal links (if any exist) between the two classes of phenomena remains controversial and uncertain, despite research efforts over several decades. Bonta, Hanson and Law (1998) conducted a meta-analysis of studies predicting recidivism in mentally disordered offenders and found that broadly similar factors predicted reoffending in the mentally disordered as in non-disordered offenders. However, there are also a number of risk factors for violence that may be specific to disordered offenders. First, there is some evidence to support the inclusion of the role of psychotic symptoms and substance abuse as criminogenic, at least for some patients. Particular psychotic symptoms such as paranoia (Grossman *et al.* 1995), and delusions involving personal targets (Nestor *et al.* 1995), have been associated with violent behaviour. There have also been suggestions that experiences involving a loss of self-control (for example, thought insertion) may lead to a loss of constraint on behaviour. Link and Stueve (1994) reported that patients who felt threatened by others and were unable to have control over their own thoughts were twice as likely to have been violent than those who reported other psychotic symptoms. Swanson, Borum and Swartz (1996) reported that a combination of substance abuse and these particular symptoms very strongly predicted future violence.

Qualitative research (for example, Chambers *et al.* 2008) has further suggested that a number of different causal pathways to violent offending can be identified, and that violent offences may be best conceptualised in terms of individual goals with respect to the offending (approach versus avoidance) and the manner in which the individual attempts to achieve these goals (passive versus active; see Ward *et al.* 2004a; Yates and Kingston 2006). Chambers (2006) identified three separate pathways to violent offending which she referred to as 'honour offences' (following a perceived threat to status or safety, characterised by situational violent reactions to perceived threats), 'punishment offences' (concerning either revenge or retribution towards a victim perceived to have committed a norm violation), and 'denial offences' (involving extreme emotion occurring under conditions of extreme stress). It follows that offenders in each of these three pathways will benefit from quite different therapeutic responses, and should begin treatment with some understanding about the how the programme might be relevant to their offending, if they are to be considered 'ready' for treatment.

Hostile and instrumental aggression

One of the most enduring distinctions made between different forms of violent behaviour has been between hostile and instrumental forms of aggression (McEllistrem 2004). Whereas hostile aggression comprises a triggering event (typically in the form of a frustration), an internal state of negative emotional arousal, and an impulse to hurt or harm the provoking agent, instrumental aggression is intended to secure an environmental reward and, as such, negative emotional arousal is less likely to be present as an antecedent. Some robberies clearly illustrate violence that is instrumental in nature, while some though not all homicides appear to be predominantly anger-mediated forms of violence (Howells 2008). A wide variety of terms have been used in the literature to describe what is essentially the same distinction; these include angry, affective, hostile, reactive, hot-blooded versus non-angry, predatory, proactive, planned, cold-blooded and so on (see McEllistrem 2004). Offenders who engage in hostile aggression are typically seen as being in need of interventions that develop more effective self-regulation of anger and other negative affective states (Cavell and Malcolm 2007), while instrumental aggressors have different and poorly understood treatment needs.

There are a number of problematic features of the angry versus instrumental distinction (Bushman and Anderson 2001; Duggan and Howard 2009). The first is that the distinction is most appropriately applied to acts than to actors. A violent individual may engage in both forms of violence, though a particular type of offence may still predominate in his or her history. Second, the distinction between the two forms is often difficult to make in practice (Barratt and Slaughter 1998; Bushman and Anderson 2001). Third, hostile aggression appears to be wrongly confounded with impulsivity, and instrumental aggression with planned violence. Many crimes of violence indicate that angry reactions to a provocation can be carefully rehearsed and nurtured over time until a planned retaliation, delayed revenge, is enacted. While some clinicians might readily equate instrumental violence with 'cold' psychopathic characteristics, Patrick's (2006) analysis suggests a more complex picture of the role of angry emotion in psychopathy (see Howells 2009).

Current neurobiological and developmental studies of violence appear to concur and to support the importance of the angry–instrumental distinction. In a recent review of the neurobiology of violence published by the Royal Society (Hodgins et al. 2008), Rutter (2008) concludes that violence is heterogeneous and that angry, instrumental and sadistic forms of violence should be distinguished. Blair's work on brain systems (2004, 2008) also suggests that there are different neuro-anatomical pathways for angry and instrumental violence. Blair observed different developmental pathways to violence that are broadly consistent with these categorisations. Once again, this research suggests that matching the needs of the offender with the type of intervention offered is likely to be important – and that if a mismatch occurs, then levels of readiness are likely to be low.

Gender differences

The angry–instrumental distinction does not exhaust work suggesting the heterogeneity of violent offenders. Work on gender differences suggests that males and females differ in the pattern of and antecedents for aggression and violence (Archer 2000, 2004; Campbell 2006; Graves 2006). Women may have a stronger association between aggression and internalising conditions such as depression; a greater inhibition of aggression as a result of socialisation; and a stronger association of aggression with physical and sexual victimisation and subsequent post-traumatic stress reactions. Such gender difference may be best explained by improved acquisition of self-regulatory behaviours in females rather than by instigatory differences (see Campbell 2006), and suggest that a violent offender programme for women would require a different focus from that adopted in programmes developed for men. Murdoch, Vess and Ward (in press), in a qualitative investigation of the processes underlying the violence perpetrated by women offenders, have suggested that the psychological context in which violence occurs can be characterised by substance abuse, poor emotional management, poly-victimisation, lack of life goals, poor educational attainment, poor social support networks, and dysfunctional coping styles. They conclude that women offenders who are convicted of violent offences tend to have numerous and long-standing needs that require specific individualised approaches to rehabilitation, which should adopt a different focus from interventions that have been designed for male offenders.

Treatment readiness in violent offenders

The heterogeneity of violent offender groups has major implications for how treatment is delivered. If violent offenders are functionally heterogeneous then it makes little sense to allocate all violent offenders to the same programme, unless the programme were so structured and were sufficiently flexible that session content and therapeutic objectives could be individualised in some way. In practice, however, violent offender treatment programmes tend to be highly structured and manualised, with relatively little opportunity to adapt programme content to individual needs (Polaschek and Collie 2004). It is perhaps unsurprising then that programme facilitators commonly report encountering hostility, resistance and non-compliance from their clients – especially in the early stages of intervention. Renwick and colleagues (1997) have pointed to the therapeutic pessimism felt both by clients and therapists in institutional settings and to enduring problems of low motivation, treatment resistance and avoidance in violent offenders. They note the resentful, distrustful and even combative style of some participants in therapeutic groups. In addition, programme facilitators can experience strong reactions to participants who are frightening or intimidating. In their focus groups with programme facilitators, Kozar and Day (2009) encountered many instances of situations in which facilitators thought that they were going to be attacked, or had direct and indirect threats made towards them (for example, one client asked a facilitator if she was worried that anyone might hit her in a group; another facilitator described how she sat with her heart pounding and feeling very disturbed because a client was being hostile). This can lead facilitators to be manipulated, both overtly and covertly, such that they deviate from treatment plans. Kozar's interviews with programme facilitators further suggest that this may lead some to avoid dealing directly with violence, or become overly reactive or punitive. Murphy and Baxter (1997) have also pointed to the need to consider the influence of situational and contextual factors on readiness to change in domestically violent men, including the interpersonal dynamics of the relationship in which the violence occurs, and the impact of changes in living arrangements for the individuals involved (such as separation, reunification).

Existing research on readiness with violent offenders has tended to focus on identifying and responding to individual difference factors. Howells and Day (2003), in their analysis of treatment readiness in offenders referred to anger management programmes, identified seven potential impediments to therapeutic engagement. These included: the complexity of the cases presenting with anger problems; the setting in which anger management is conducted; existing client inferences about their anger 'problem'; the influence of coerced or mandatory treatment; inadequate analysis of the context of personal goals within which the anger problem occurs; and gender and cultural issues. Similar themes have been picked up in the domestic violence literature. For example, Gilchrist (2009) has identified ten potential implicit theories held by domestically violent men, each of which potentially undermine the extent to which perpetrators see their behaviour as problematic (including: 'women are dangerous';

'the need for control'; 'women are objects'; 'entitlement/respect'; 'sex drives are uncontrollable'; 'real man'). Others have applied the transtheoretical model (TTM) of change to violent offenders, a model that places emphasis on problem awareness, self-efficacy and motivation to change (see Casey *et al.* 2005). This work suggests that many offenders who are referred to violent offender programmes can be classified as being in the early stages of change, or as low in treatment readiness. Indeed, the task of engaging such participants often becomes the primary goal of programme providers.

Responding to low levels of readiness in violent offenders

Novaco, Ramm and Black (2001) have provided accounts of how programmes might be modified to meet the needs of those with low levels of readiness, including, for example, by introducing a more extended pre-intervention assessment, a preparatory phase to develop necessary skills, and an extended, more intensive programme. Others have suggested that reduction of 'resistance' may be undertaken during individual pre-programme therapy sessions (for example Preston 2000), or at the beginning of a group programme. For instance, the Canadian Intensive Programme for Violent Offenders (Preston and Murphy 1997) begins with a 'two-week motivational module that addresses client interaction, commitment and trust using techniques such as a cost-benefit analysis of programme completion. This motivational module enables suitable foundations for group work to commence, with the implementation of rules of conduct for the offenders in the group' (Chambers *et al.* 2008: 281). Another alternative is to offer individual treatment, utilising motivational interviewing techniques (these are described in Chapter 10).

Day and Carson (2009) have suggested that one of the major therapeutic tasks in violence perpetrator programmes is to reach a shared understanding with the client about the nature, extent and seriousness of their violence. While general counselling techniques can be used to develop an affective bond (through the development of rapport and trust), and treatment goals and tasks can be set in the process of developing change plans, it is less clear whether the defining feature of the therapeutic alliance – collaboration – should be a goal in interventions for violent men, given the tendency of some to claim that their behaviour was not serious or that their victims provoked or deserved the violence. There is a choice that each practitioner makes between confronting, persuading, cajoling and motivating clients into some form of agreement with the basic goal of non-violence, and beginning work from the offender's own frame of reference. The former is associated with a didactic, educational approach to group work, the latter with a more therapeutic approach. Thigpen and colleagues (2007) suggest that the provider should act as a model and demonstrate anti-criminal expressions of behaviour, and that the effective practitioner must be 'consistent' and 'unerring' in communicating pro-social and high moral values. At the same time, highly discrepant therapist–client values are likely to adversely affect treatment outcomes by impairing the development of a strong relational bond.

Less direct consideration has been given to the impact of external or systemic factors on low levels of treatment readiness. Day *et al.* (2009b) have observed that a major contributing factor to low levels of readiness in domestically violent men is the inconsistency and delay in the criminal justice and referral pathways for mandated domestic violence offenders. For example, court referral and administration by correctional services to intervention programmes can take place after a significant time delay (sometimes years) since the offence. There may also be a need, at least in some violent offender programmes, for the criminal justice system to reinforce the link between the charges and attendance at a behaviour change programme, and to reinforce and clarify the legally mandated nature of programme attendance. In addition, Babcock, Green and Robie (2004) in their meta-analytic review of domestic violence programmes found that the most effective programmes incorporated 'retention techniques' for use with those who may be reluctant to attend community base programmes. These included reminder phone calls and follow-ups, as well as the use of what they referred to as 'emotion-focused' interventions to improve emotional awareness and expression, empathy and communication skills.

Conclusion

Levels of treatment readiness, particularly in relation to problem recognition and motivation to seek help, are likely to be particularly low in violent offenders who are referred to offender rehabilitation programmes. Part of this may be attributable to personal beliefs about offending which rationalise and justify violence. However, low levels of readiness may also be a function of referrals to programmes that are not perceived as being likely to address the particular needs of individual offenders. In this chapter we have focused on the match between the needs of the individual and the content of the programme as an important determinant of engagement in violent offender treatment programmes. The balance between programme content that allows facilitators to respect individual differences while maintaining acceptable levels of programme integrity is a delicate one to maintain, but nonetheless likely to be critical in engaging this group of offenders in any process of behaviour change.

Chapter 7

Sex offenders: understanding low readiness

There have been a variety of laws passed since the early 1990s to protect the public from the perceived threat posed by sexual offenders. These laws allow for special sanctions such as indefinite civil commitment, preventive detention, continued detention, extended community supervision, registration and community notification for those convicted of sexual crimes. There has also been an expansion and refinement in the treatment approaches taken with sex offenders in an effort to reduce the risk of reoffending. Mixed empirical findings regarding the effectiveness of treatment suggest that some but not all sex offenders achieve the desired benefits of treatment (Hanson *et al.* 2002; Marques *et al.* 2005). Despite advances that have been made, sex offenders are often difficult to engage in treatment, perhaps especially so in response to the involuntary and potentially coercive treatment or supervision programmes that have been legally mandated. This chapter examines specific factors that may contribute to this difficulty, and offers suggestions to improve treatment readiness with this challenging population.

The framework adopted here is the multifactor offender readiness model (MORM) (Ward *et al.* 2004b). As presented in earlier chapters, this model asserts that treatment readiness is a function of both internal and external factors. The factors internal to the person are cognitive, affective, volitional, behavioural, and identity based. The external or contextual factors depend on circumstances, such as an adversarial legal process and coercive treatment; opportunities for treatment, such as the availability of specific programmes; resources, such as the availability of adequately trained and qualified staff, cultural sensitivity and a positive therapeutic milieu; interpersonal supports for the offender; and programme characteristics, such as the type of treatment and its timing. This model suggests that an offender will be more ready to change offending behaviour when he or she has these personal characteristics to a greater degree, and when he or she occupies an environment that can effect and support such change. Rather than being a static quality of the individual or a progression through various stages, readiness for change also fluctuates over time, depending on variations in these internal and external factors.

Internal readiness conditions

Cognitive factors

Sex offenders can exhibit a variety of attitudes, beliefs and thinking styles that interfere with treatment readiness. A common feature among sex offenders is denial of their offending. Studies cited by Yates (2009) have reported complete or partial denial in between 50 per cent and 87 per cent of sex offenders (Barbaree 1991; Maletsky 1991; Sefarbi 1990), and that denial is unrelated to actuarially-measured risk to reoffend (Simourd and Malcolm 1998). Although denial has not been found in the meta-analyses of Hanson and his colleagues to be empirically associated with higher rates of sexual recidivism (Hanson and Bussiere 1998; Hanson and Morton-Bourgon 2004, 2005), more recent evidence suggests that denial may predict recidivism for some types of offenders. Nunes et al. (2007) found that denial was associated with increased sexual recidivism among low-risk and incest offenders and decreased recidivism among high-risk offenders. Regardless of the relationship with reoffence risk, the targeting of denial and minimisation remains an emphasis within treatment programmes for sex offenders (see for example Langton et al. 2008). Many sex offender treatment programmes will not admit offenders who deny their offending, and denial continues to be considered a serious obstacle to treatment participation and progress (ATSA 2005; Levensen and Macgowan 2004; Lund 2000; Schneider and Wright 2001; Wright and Schneider 2004).

In order to understand denial in sex offenders and how we might constructively deal with its impact on treatment readiness, it is necessary to be clear about what denial means, and perhaps more importantly, what function it serves for the individual. Different types of cognitive processes have been labelled as denial in the professional literature, ranging from complete denial of committing an offence to not accepting responsibility, minimising the seriousness of the offending or the harm done to the victim, and various thinking errors (Marshall *et al.* 1999; Lund 2000). One study by Winn (1996) described seven different overlapping positions that may be considered forms of denial: denial of facts, denial of awareness, denial of impact, denial of responsibility, denial of grooming oneself and the environment, denial of deviant sexual arousal and inappropriate sexualisation of problems, and denial of denial. Levenson and Macgowan (2004) subsequently noted that denial may sometimes refer to a complete refutation of the facts related to an offence, but may also represent a continuum that includes minimising the impact of the offending on victims, and refusing to acknowledge the severity or repetitive nature of their offending behaviour.

Beyond what denial *is*, it is useful to consider what denial *does*. Denial serves a protective function, described as a form of self-preservation (Winn 1996) or a self-protective strategy (Kear-Colwell and Pollock 1997). Yates (2009) suggests that denial represents a normal cognitive process that all people use to maintain self-esteem, and that sex offenders may be particularly invested in some forms of denial in light of the personal, social and economic costs to individuals who admit to sexual offending.

One way to consider denial in sex offenders is by way of the concept of a defence mechanism (Levenson and Macgowan 2004). Denial is defined in the DSM-IV-TR (American Psychiatric Association 1994) as a defence mechanism in which 'the individual deals with emotional conflict or internal or external stressors by refusing to acknowledge some painful aspect of external reality or subjective experience that would be apparent to others' (1994: 811). Defence mechanisms are considered automatic psychological processes that protect the individual against anxiety and from the awareness of internal or external dangers or stressors, often outside of the individual's conscious awareness. This introduces the question of whether denial is a conscious misrepresentation of something the individual knows to be otherwise or a distortion of reality of which the individual is unaware, or incompletely aware. Yates (2009) notes that the view of cognitive distortions as constituting denial arises from the assumption that these are nearly always deliberate and conscious distortions, as suggested earlier by Marshall *et al.* (1999). However, Yates provides various examples from the research literature of the misperceptions and misinterpretations that sex offenders are prone to make, such that they may not always be intentionally distorting or denying the truth. The implication is that denial and minimisation by sex offenders is not always deliberate.

Regardless of whether denial and related cognitive distortions are deliberate or largely unconscious, some studies have attempted to empirically address the assumption that there is a significant relationship between denial, treatment engagement and treatment progress for sex offenders. Levenson and Macgowan (2004) found that treatment progress was correlated with higher levels of treatment engagement and lower levels of denial. They use the ATSA definition of denial as the failure of sexual abusers to accept responsibility for their offences, and conclude that their findings support the standards of practice that maintain that admitting to a sex crime is a necessary condition for successful treatment. However, these authors note that it is unclear whether denial causes an inability or unwillingness to engage in treatment, or whether treatment creates a willingness to let go of denial. This appears to be a crucial distinction. If engagement decreases denial, and decreased denial is important for treatment progress, then readiness to engage in treatment becomes an important goal, prior to or even instead of overcoming denial. This becomes particularly salient in situations where denial of sexual offending is a criteria used to exclude sex offenders from treatment.

Yates (2009) points out that although denial and engagement in combination accounted for a significant proportion of the variance in treatment progess in the Levenson and Macgowan (2004) study, engagement was a stronger predictor than denial. She also notes that treatment progress was measured through therapist ratings that included admission of offending, presenting a potential methodological confound.

Is overcoming denial necessary for treatment progress and reduction of risk for sexual reoffending? Earlier positions on this issue considered the confrontation and elimination of denial as an explicit requirement of effective treatment (for example, Salter 1988). More recent researchers continue to support this premise (Levenson and Macgowan 2004). Noting that offender accountability is considered a central goal by almost all cognitive behavioural treatment programmes, Wright and Schneider (2004) have empirically investigated treatment progress as a function of denial and offender explanations of accountability using the Facets of Sexual Offender Denial (FoSOD), a self-report measure designed to assess various aspects of denial throughout the treatment process with child victim sex offenders. These authors describe three processes of denial: refutation, minimisation and depersonalisation. Refutation is a form of absolute, full, or categorical denial of sexual offending. Minimisation represents partial acknowledgement that something about his or her behaviour is problematic or potentially harmful. Depersonalisation, considered the most entrenched form of denial, is the rejection of the possibility that the offender is the kind of person who could commit a sexual offence. While an offender engaged in depersonalisation may acknowledge his (or her) involvement in a sexual offence and accepts responsibility for these behaviours, there remains an inability to recognise predispositions likely to influence future behaviour, and therefore denial of risk for future offending. Wright and Schneider found that their measure showed significant reductions in denial only for those who progressed in treatment, but also that reductions in denial continued through more advanced levels of treatment. Conversely, denial scores changed little for those who did not advance in treatment. Wright and Schneider consider their findings consistent with the view that denial consists of cognitive processes that function to maintain distorted thinking and to excuse the offenders' responsibility for their behaviour throughout treatment. Their results are presented as suggesting that denial is a dynamic factor inversely related to the treatment goal of accepting responsibility, and the reduction of denial is therefore central to treatment progress.

Others have taken the position that focusing on denial is not so essential, at least not initially, and certainly not through aggressive confrontation. Recognising that denial is a form of self-preservation allows the clinician to address the offender in ways that do not rely on direct confrontation and the activation of defences that often result (Cooper 2005; Kear-Colwell and Pollock 1997; Winn 1996). Marshall and colleagues (Marshall 1994; Marshall et al. 2006; Mann and Marshall 2009) have observed that effective therapeutic approaches reduce denial, and that denial may be dealt with clinically in different ways. They suggest that it is important to distinguish between offenders' cognitions that are related to risk (and therefore important to focus on in treatment), and those that are not. *Post-hoc* rationalisations and minimisations that occur after the offence are not necessarily causally related to the offending process. As denial and minimisation are not generally associated with risk of sexual recidivism, their reduction or elimination should not be a primary goal of treatment. Vigorously confronting denial and minimisation, especially early in treatment without an adequate therapeutic alliance, is likely to decrease rather than increase readiness. But according to Mann and Marshall

(2009) there are cognitive phenomena that *are* important for risk, and therefore are relevant when it comes to discussing the issue of treatment effectiveness. These occur prior to and during the offence, and are likely to reflect underlying schemas.

Schemas and readiness

The various forms of denial that have been described in the professional literature appear similar to the broader category of cognitive distortions that have been identified with sex offenders (Abel *et al.* 1984). Cognitive distortions have more recently been conceptualised as implicit theories (Ward 2000; Ward and Keenan 1999). All of these cognitive phenomena might be productively considered within the concept of schema (Baker and Beech 2004; Mann and Beech 2003; Mann and Shingler 2006; Thakker *et al.* 2007; Yates 2009). Schemas are defined as cognitive structures that serve to influence and direct the processing of incoming stimuli by simplifying and classifying the information based on previous experiences (Beck 1964, 1967). Thus they originate from early life experiences, and are organised around various themes for understanding the self, others and the world. The content of schemas may or may not be available to conscious awareness, and can include rules, attitudes, self-verbalisations, beliefs and assumptions. From this perspective, denial and other cognitive distortions are seen as products of underlying schemas. Schemas are theorised to be stable and enduring, and they are activated by the presence of situational cues, particularly ambiguous or threatening cues, as perceived through the filter of the schema.

The treatment process can be seen as presenting a variety of ambiguous or threatening cues that will activate the existing schemas of the offender, especially treatment that is vigorously confrontational or insensitive to an offender's defences. Consideration of schemas may therefore offer a productive way to approach denial and other cognitive factors that impede treatment readiness. Mann and Shingler (2006) recommend the use of 'life maps' or 'life histories' to identify recurring thinking patterns and the previous experiences that have shaped these patterns. Recognising the work of Young (1990) on early maladaptive schemas, the goal of intervention is not to change schemas, as this is unlikely to be successful in the time-limited and structured group programmes that constitute most sex offender treatment. This collaborative and supportive approach attempts to allow the offender to understand and recognise the underlying schemas that influence his or her interpretation of and response to events, by explaining the concept of schemas and helping offenders recognise their own schemas in action. This approach is likely to more effectively support the development of a positive therapeutic alliance, thereby improving treatment readiness.

Finally, a cognitive factor that may strongly influence sex offenders' treatment readiness has been identified in the general treatment outcome research as client expectations (Arnkoff *et al.* 2002; Garfield 1994; Kirsch 1990). Ward *et al.* (2004b) note that expectancies can come from previous experiences of treatment, the experience of the assessment process, the reputation of the treatment programme and perceptions about treatment staff. To the degree that these expectancies are based on positive prior experiences, treatment readiness might be improved, or at least not further compromised. However, it will be important to consider the individual offender's perceptions of previous assessment and treatment experiences. Adversarial legal process and coercive treatment conditions may contribute to the formation of negative and defensive expectancies by offenders. Concerns about confidentiality and the uses of information disclosed in treatment can become significant barriers to treatment readiness. These contextual factors, considered in more detail later in this chapter, may lead to negative expectations and related fears that what the offender says may be subsequently used against him, such as evaluations for extended supervision or involuntary civil commitment following his prison term.

Affective factors

Affect is typically considered a broad term that includes emotions, moods and feelings (Berkowitz 1999; Power and Dalgeish 1999 from Howells and Day 2006). In ways similar to Howells and Day in their approach to affective determinants of treatment engagement with violent offenders, the affective reactions of sex offenders are likely to have a major influence on their treatment readiness. Strong emotions have been found to play a role in the offence pathways for at least some sex offenders (Howells *et al.* 2004b; Polaschek *et al.* 2001; Proulx *et al.* 1996; Ward *et al.* 2006), so that access to and experience of these emotions may be essential to the eventual modification of these pathways. A relationship between schemas, as discussed earlier, and affect has been noted by Serran *et al.* (2003), who observed that offence-related cognitive schemas are typically only activated by particular emotional states. Yet some offenders have trouble accessing and indentifying various affective states. An extreme example of this may be the profound affective deficits exhibited by psychopaths, which may also relate to difficulties engaging in or benefiting from treatment.

Readiness for treatment in sex offenders may be related to affect in several ways. One hypothesis is that sex offenders (and treatment clients in general) are often motivated to engage in treatment to reduce distress, meaning that some level of negative affect is necessary initially to prompt the desire for treatment. Beutler, Clarkin and Bongar (2000), for example, have argued that treatments for depression achieve their best outcomes among those with moderate to high initial levels of distress. Yet if there is no appreciable *a priori* distress, as may be the case when a sex offender's denial or other defence mechanisms are working effectively, there is little to stimulate treatment readiness. In fact, the prospect of engaging in treatment, with the attendant requirement to admit and disclose distressing offence-related information, may be far more distressing than the offender's usual affective state.

Some sex offenders may lack the ability, which could be viewed as a skill, to access and identify different emotional states. Such individuals may never have had much practice at this process, and have grown up and always lived in family or cultural environments where expressing feelings (other than anger, perhaps) was not modelled or rewarded. These individuals may actually require help to acquire the skills of affect recognition and expression. In our view, these types of skills are likely to be most easily acquired within the context of a safe and supportive therapeutic environment, as addressed below.

For other sex offenders, offending may have provided a mechanism for emotional regulation (see Day 2009; Howells *et al.* 2004b; Ward and Hudson 1998). Proulx, McKibben and Lusignan (1996) found that negative moods and conflicts were associated with 'overwhelming' deviant fantasies and increased masturbatory activity for both rapists and child molesters. Negative mood and interpersonal conflict may be a common experience for offenders in many sex offender treatment programmes. If this occurs early in the treatment process, it might result in an increase in the very cognitions and behaviours that the programme is intended to reduce. Howells, Day and Wright (2004b) note that reciprocal determinism between behaviour and the environment helps us to understand how some individuals, including sex offenders, are extraordinarily skilled at creating negative and punishing environments for themselves, which in turn produces negative affective experiences. Anyone who has worked in a correctional treatment programme for sex offenders will be familiar with those offenders who, under the rules and procedures of that structured and scrutinised environment, consistently create a conflictual dynamic and the associated negative affect both for themselves and others. Howells *et al.* suggest that life skills training to assist offenders to develop the skills that make life and relationships more rewarding may have an important role to play, along with a specific focus on improved recognition and regulation of emotions. Affective skills training and acceptance-based approaches such as mindfulness training to allow accurate experiencing and labelling emotional states should result in improved engagement in therapy (Day 2009; Howells and Day 2006). This could be particularly useful in the early stages of treatment to facilitate a secure therapeutic alliance, prior to more direct and forceful confrontation of behaviour and defences that may rupture the alliance and decrease treatment readiness.

A particularly salient affective factor for treatment readiness with sex offenders is likely to be the impact of guilt and shame in response to acknowledgement of their offending. Proeve and Howells (2002, 2006) note that evaluation of the self distinguishes guilt from shame. Individuals experiencing guilt tend to focus more on specific behaviours, but do not tend to make the global negative evaluations of self associated with shame. Shame involves the judgement of self as inferior or bad and can also involve the perception of being negatively judged by others as defective in some respect. Sexual offending may be considered a 'quintessential shame-eliciting form of behaviour' (Proeve and Howells 2006: 128).

Shame and guilt may have different impacts on treatment readiness. The action tendencies associated with guilt are thought to include confession, apologising, and attempting to repair the damage inflicted by guilt-inducing behaviours (Barrett 1995; Frijda 1986). These actions may be conducive to increased levels of self-disclosure and to treatment engagement. Shame, on the other hand, is associated with action tendencies to hide the self from others, and therefore is associated with a weaker therapeutic alliance and lower levels of treatment readiness. Effective treatment with sex offenders may require a movement from shame towards guilt, away from a focus of 'who I am' towards a focus on 'what I have done'. Confrontation in therapy, particularly without adequate preparation regarding the role of confrontation in the therapeutic process, is likely to be experienced as an attack on the self, and actually increase levels of shame. Educating offenders about the differences between shame and guilt, and explicitly focusing on the behaviours of offending rather than the self of the offender, may help to minimise defensive resistance and facilitate treatment engagement.

The relationship between shame, cognitive distortions, empathy deficits and self-esteem has been recently addressed by Marshall and his colleagues (Marshall *et al.* 2009). Citing evidence that many sex offenders suffer from low self-esteem, these authors note that such individuals appear reluctant to attempt novel behaviours, an inherent element of treatment. Denial and cognitive distortions in such cases function to protect an offender's already low self-image. This is to be expected, and is an understandable response to the offender's situation and experiences in the judicial and correctional systems, rather than necessarily indicating a defect in character. Empathy is positively associated with guilt and negatively associated with shame. Integrating these concepts, Marshall *et al.* propose that shame, cognitive distortions, and lack of victim empathy serve to avoid further erosion of self-esteem. Such offenders will typically be difficult to engage in treatment (that is, will have low treatment readiness) unless efforts are made to overcome these interrelated problems. In an earlier work, Marshall and colleagues (1997) recommend procedures for enhancing self-esteem that have demonstrated effectiveness with sex offenders and caution against vigorously challenging or aggressively confronting offenders too early in treatment. Early stages of treatment should focus on engagement and motivation, with goals of enhancing the offender's self-esteem, reducing his shame, and teaching him basic coping behaviours. These authors further note that treating the offender respectfully and demonstrating empathy and warmth have also been shown to facilitate treatment-induced changes with sex offenders, features of the therapist that are addressed in more detail below under external readiness factors (for discussion of this issue see Chapter 3). They also caution that not all offenders will have low self-esteem or struggle with guilt or shame, and therefore it is important to take into account offenders' unique personality factors.

Personal identity factors

Another set of internal factors that will have a strong ongoing effect on treatment readiness relate to the offender's personal identity. Sex offenders with features of personality disorders and psychopathy may present some of the most overt challenges to treatment readiness and the development of an effective therapeutic alliance. Although findings have been mixed, some studies have reported that almost 90 per cent of their samples exhibit features of at least one personality disorder (Berger *et al.* 1999). In a recent study, Craissati, Webb and Keen (2008) reported that in their sample of 103 sex offenders who completed the MCMI-III, 73 per cent presented with personality dysfunction and 37 per cent reported personality dysfunction sufficient to warrant possible personality disorder diagnoses. Psychopathy has also been reported in significant proportions of sex offenders, although in higher percentages of rapists than child molesters and incest offenders (Forth and Kroner 1995, cited in Craissati *et al.* 2008). Furthermore, personality disorders have been associated with treatment attrition for sex offenders (Abel *et al.* 1988; Craissati and Beech 2001), and psychopathy in particular poses a variety of challenges to effective treatment. Problems with treatment readiness in high-risk offenders with personality disorders have been specifically identified (Howells and Day 2007).

In the multifactor offender readiness model (MORM), Ward *et al.* (2004b) have spoken of personal identity in terms of the pursuit of primary human goods in ways that will shape an individual's sense of mastery, self-esteem, perception of autonomy and control (see Chapters 3 and 10). The perspective taken here is concerned with personal identity in terms of the offender's sense of self, which relates back to the concept of schemas. Much has been written in the general clinical and psychotherapy literature about self-schemas and their role in the treatment process, especially in the field of personality disorders. While some sex offenders may present characteristics that are consistent with various aspects of personality disorder, the consideration of self-schemas may be more broadly useful in understanding important features of treatment readiness and resistance to change. Livesley (2003) has delineated a sequence of phases for the treatment process in managing personality disorders that comprises safety, containment, control and regulation, exploration, and finally integration and synthesis. His description of the process of change emphasises the role of the therapeutic relationship in leading to increased self-knowledge, problem recognition, and the acquisition of alternative behaviours.

A key to facilitating this process is an appreciation of the individual's self-states. Drawing from Horowitz (1998), self-states are defined as states of mind consisting of conscious and unconscious experiences with associated patterns of behaviour, which can last for short or long periods of time. Self-states are important for understanding the structure of self-experience and the flow of interpersonal behaviour.

They are structured and initiated by underlying core schemas, which are activated by different (usually interpersonal) events or mood changes. Livesley (2003) states that most people experience several self-states, which sometimes conflict. Once activated, the schema can arouse strong emotions and other schemas that help to maintain the self-state. Resulting behaviours can often evoke reactions from others that are perceived as confirming and reinforcing the underlying schema, which makes for a repetitive cycle that is difficult to modify. Livesley also argues that the most general schema is the person's overall conception of the self, sometimes referred to as the theory of the self, and that more abstract schemata are difficult to change.

As noted earlier, the relationship between self-concept and underlying schemas has been taken up by Young (1990, 1999), who identifies a set of distinct early maladaptive schemas that result in recurrent dysfunctional patterns of behaviour that are self-perpetuating and resistant to change. These early maladaptive schemas are organised into five broad domains, which are hypothesised to correspond to developmental needs of childhood that were not met. These are disconnection and rejection, impaired autonomy and performance, impaired limits, other-directedness, and overvigilance and inhibition. Space constraints do not allow for a detailed analysis and application of these maladaptive schemas in this chapter, but it appears that several may be relevant to the sense of self often experienced by sex offenders. These include disconnection and rejection expectations regarding abandonment, mistrust, emotional deprivation, defectiveness, shame, and alienation, which may be particularly relevant among child molesters. Deficiencies related to impaired limits, including entitlement, grandiosity and insufficient self-control or self-discipline, may be particularly relevant for rapists.

A consistent observation by those who address the nature of self-concept or identity from a schema perspective is that self-schemas are difficult to change (Beck et al. 2004; Livesley 2003; Young 1999). Leahy (2001) considers resistance in cognitive therapy to be based in part on the need for self-consistency or self-verification. According to this principle, people are driven to achieve balance and consistency in their beliefs and roles, to maintain control. Part of this process involves self-verification, whereby individuals seek out and attend to information that verifies their self-concept, regardless of whether that self-concept is positive or negative (Swann et al. 1992).

Another source of resistance that will reduce treatment readiness is schema avoidance. Young (1999) notes that when early maladaptive schemas are triggered, the associated affective experiences can be intense and unpleasant. Therefore, individuals develop several types of both volitional and automatic processes for avoiding the activation of these schemas, including cognitive, affective and behavioural avoidance techniques. Livesley (2003) states that modifying schemas and associated maladaptive patterns of behaviour is an important part of the change process in treatment, and requires identification and recognition of these patterns. However, schema avoidance may hinder recognition and acceptance, and often occurs when a schema is identified before the individual is ready, or when the therapeutic alliance is in a compromised state.

More recently, Livesley (2007) has advocated for the relevance of an integrated approach to the treatment of personality disordered offenders. The defining features of personality disorder that he or she presents appear similar to some of the features that describe many sex offenders: failure to achieve stable and integrated representations of self and others; failure in the capacity for intimacy; and failure in adaptive functioning in the social group as indicated by failure to develop the capacity for pro-social behaviour and cooperative relationships. Livesley argues that interventions need to be directed towards personality pathology *per se*, because it directly affects compliance and the ability to respond to interventions. This position suggests that it will not be sufficient to apply interventions found to be effective with non-personality disordered offenders while neglecting the personality disorder component. Livesley recommends an integrated and multifaceted approach tailored to the needs of individual offenders, with an emphasis on facilitating the development of more integrated and coherent personality functioning. Citing the work of Piper and Joyce (2001), he notes that the best results occur when treatment is individually tailored and the patient and therapist agree on a specific treatment contract. The common elements of treatment for personality disordered offenders, and by extension all offenders, are based on the therapeutic relationship, with attention given to maintaining a stable therapeutic process.

Behavioural factors

In the multifactor offender readiness model of Ward *et al.* (2004b), three types of behavioural factors that influence treatment readiness are distinguished, and are proposed as occurring in a temporal sequence. First, current behaviour must be identified as a problem. Then, help must be sought for the problematic behaviour. Finally, offenders must have competencies to participate in the treatment process. We have already noted that denial of offending behaviour, or denial that it is a problem, may be common among sex offenders. We would argue that this does not preclude the engagement of sex offenders in a therapeutic process that eventually leads to behaviour change in the area of sexual offending. From the perspective of the Good Lives Model, the goals of treatment are the securing of primary goods in more pro-social and less harmful ways than the offender has behaved in the past (see Chapter 4). Ward *et al.* (2004b) have argued that to be ready for treatment, the individual must recognise a need to change: that is, that their offending creates problems for themselves and others. If this is defined more broadly, at least initially, than an exclusive focus on sexual offending, it is more likely that a need for change in the offender's life will be recognised and accepted. This implies that an offender may be ready to work on a particular problem, but not the one that the therapist views as relevant and central to offending. This approach calls for there to be a collaboration between the offender and the service provider to identify treatment aims that will help the offender meet broader personal goals. To do this, both the offender and the therapist have to be ready for a treatment process that identifies and works towards the meaningful life goals of the offender rather than exclusively avoidance goals to reduce risk. This issue is taken up further in the external readiness factors section later in this chapter.

Volitional factors

Volition refers to an intention to pursue certain goals, and is closely associated with what is often termed motivation in the offender treatment literature. Yet despite its long history in the field of offender rehabilitation, the construct of motivation has been criticised as ambiguous (Drieschner *et al.* 2004) or even unnecessary (Draycott 2007b). Ward *et al.* (2004b) conceptualise volitional factors, including motivation, to involve the formation of an intent to pursue certain goals and the development and implementation of a plan to achieve these goals. The goals must therefore be relevant and valued by the offender if he or she is to be motivated to pursue them, including the goals of treatment. Other aspects of volition include the belief that one is capable of exercising choice and can directly control important personal outcomes. In the context of offender rehabilitation, this includes the ability to consent to treatment, to make decisions based on the costs and benefits to oneself, and to make decisions without coercion.

Motivation for treatment is not best conceptualised as a static trait of the individual, but rather as a fluctuating state dependent on dynamic factors (Drieschner *et al.* 2004) and the relevance of the goals to the individual at a given point in time. Barrett, Wilson and Long (2003) have specifically addressed motivation to change in sex offenders, and found that motivational measures varied over the course of treatment. They also noted that motivation is dynamic and may be impacted by internal, external and alliance issues. Their study highlighted the influence of environmental determinants on motivation. Motivation and other aspects of treatment readiness may therefore be as much a function of external factors as internal factors.

External readiness conditions

Circumstance factors

One of the defining features of sex offender rehabilitation in the criminal justice context is the degree of coercion that compels offenders into treatment (Vess 2009). Treatment is often mandated, and relatively few offenders seek help with their sexual offending and its related problems voluntarily, particularly in correctional settings. However, it has been argued that the experience of coercion is not entirely a function of whether treatment is mandated; furthermore, Day, Tucker and Howells (2004) have distinguished coerced treatment from pressured treatment. Rehabilitation activities are pressured in the sense that the decision of whether to undertake a programme is influenced by negative consequences for non-participation. This is a common element of treatment programmes that will be seen as favourable, or even necessary, by parole boards when making decisions about release from prison, for example, although participation in the programmes will not be mandated in a formal sense. In a recent meta-analysis of offender coercion in treatment, Parhar and colleagues examined 129 studies of various offender rehabilitation programmes (Parhar *et al.* 2008). To avoid the false dichotomy of mandated versus voluntary treatment, these researchers created five levels, ranging from mandated involuntary to non-mandated voluntary programmes across both custody and community settings. The strongest effect sizes were found for voluntary treatment without coercion, and the weakest effect sizes were found for mandated treatment. Furthermore, treatment setting had a significant effect, whereby mandated treatment had no effect on recidivism when the programme was delivered in a custodial setting. The authors suggest that custodial settings may increase the perception of forced treatment, with negative consequences for treatment responsiveness.

Day *et al.* (2004) point out that coercion and pressure are not simple objective facts, but rather have more to do with the offender's subjective experience regarding freedom of choice. However, a significant problem is that a number of sex offenders appear unlikely to choose treatment voluntarily. Grubin and Thornton (1994), for example, found that 41 per cent of sex offenders in the UK said that they would only participate in treatment in order to gain parole. Consistent with these findings, Burdon and Gallagher (2002) concluded that coercion remains the only effective means of protecting society from sex offenders. These authors also noted that while coercion increases treatment retention, it does not necessarily improve treatment outcome, although they cite trends in the research findings that suggest treatment can transform the perception of coercion and lead to better outcomes. If most sex offenders come to treatment because it is mandated or coerced, which can have negative effects on treatment compliance and ultimate outcomes, an important question arises: what can be done to modify the subjective experience of coercion and improve treatment readiness?

Coercion is experienced when treatment is not congruent with the individual's personal goals and there is a subsequent perceived misalignment between programme goals and desired outcomes. One challenge is therefore to help the offender to identify with and invest in (that is internalise) the goals of the treatment programme. Meeting this challenge will depend largely on several interrelated external conditions, including resource factors, location factors, opportunity factors and programme factors.

Resource factors

Engaging coerced offenders in treatment is a task that requires high levels of therapeutic skill (Day *et al.* 2004). Thus one of the crucial resources for enhancing treatment readiness with sex offenders is the availability of adequately trained and effective staff. Sex offenders have reported that they assessed the quality of the treatment programme based on their perception of the therapists' competence, and that they relied on their perception of the therapists to determine whether or not to get involved in therapy (Drapeau 2005). It is only relatively recently that greater attention has been paid to the skills and qualities necessary to be an effective sex offender therapist (Beech and Hamilton-Giachritsis 2005; Harkins and Beech 2007). Marshall and colleagues have written extensively about the therapeutic process with sex offenders (Marshall 2005; Marshall *et al.* 2005; Serran *et al.* 2003). They recommend that a non-confrontational approach, where confrontation is defined as a harsh challenging of clients that seems likely be perceived by the client as denigrating, is adopted by clinicians. While distorted and dysfunctional perceptions, beliefs, attitudes and schemas of sex offenders need to be challenged in treatment, the critical issue is how to do this effectively without diminishing treatment readiness. Research has revealed that therapist qualities of warmth, empathy, respect, rewarding, and directive are all related positively to indices of beneficial change in treatment (Marshall 2005). While unqualified support of sex offenders in treatment is not called for, directive and supportive therapists can help clients recognise problems and consider the benefits of behaviour change. Referring back to the internal readiness factors discussed earlier, rather than seeing offenders as resistant to treatment, therapists should conceptualise minimisation, denial and avoidance as a desire to avoid shame and to protect self-esteem. Pushing against these defences is unlikely to enhance treatment readiness and more likely to impede treatment progress. Rather, resistance should be seen as a signal to switch therapeutic strategies rather than as a reason to attempt to coerce the client into accepting the therapist's position (Serran *et al.* 2003).

Much of the currently available therapy for sex offenders occurs within a group treatment format, and therefore sex offender therapists need to be properly trained and qualified in group process skills. The importance of group leadership in producing cohesiveness, appropriate group norms, and the instillation of hope have long been recognised for running effective groups and producing therapeutic change (Yalom 1995; Yalom and Lieberman 1971). Highly cohesive groups are associated with positive outcomes, and qualities such as leader support have a clear effect on cohesion, expressiveness and other positive group process indicators in sex offender treatment groups, as reported by Beech and Hamilton-Giachritsis (2005). These researchers suggest that group therapy skills are particularly important for engaging sex offenders in treatment, given the coercive circumstances of many programmes. Under these conditions, it is particularly important for programmes to select and train their treatment staff well.

Programme factors

Other therapist qualities associated with treatment engagement and a positive treatment outcome include humour and flexibility. However, Marshall and colleagues (Marshall *et al.* 2005) have noted that flexibility is often constrained by the overly detailed treatment manuals of many sex offender treatment programmes. Flexibility refers to the need for therapists to adapt their strategies to each client's particular characteristics, throughout the treatment process (Marshall 2005). Marshall *et al.* (2005) consider strict adherence to detailed manuals a mistake, as they discourage the flexibility and sensitivity required by the therapist to promote effective engagement in therapy.

Flexibility extends to the identification of treatment goals. It has already been noted in the section on internal factors above that treatment readiness will be influenced by the degree to which treatment appears to encompass goals that are personally relevant and valued by the individual. If the treatment programme, and by extension the therapists, insist that the offender pursue goals that are defined by the programme as important rather than those identified by the offender, poor treatment readiness is likely to result. This is especially salient in mandated treatment settings where subjective perception of coercion is likely to be inherently high. In one author's experience (JV) in California's Sexually Violent Predator treatment programme, many of the offenders committed for treatment considered themselves more as political prisoners than legitimate treatment clients, and efforts to engage them in treatment to pursue risk reduction goals defined by the programme were fraught with difficulties. Sometimes this low state of treatment readiness could be gradually overcome through the skilful therapeutic work of highly trained and experienced staff, but there was often an enduring lack of perceived alignment between the goals of the programme and the goals of the offender.

Marshall *et al.* (2005) summarise five general concerns about current treatment approaches with sex offenders as follows:

(a) there is an excessive emphasis on negative issues in both targets of treatment and language used by treatment providers,

(b) there is a failure to explicitly encourage optimism in clients and encourage their belief in their capacity to change, (c) there is a general absence of an explicit attempt to work collaboratively with clients, (d) the role and influence of the therapist has been all but neglected, and (e) there have been few attempts to provide clients with goals that will result in them leading a more fulfilling and prosocial life. (2005: 107)

It is argued that as more of these concerns are addressed in treatment programme design and function, treatment readiness and treatment effectiveness will improve. Movement away from earlier positions that advocated that the therapist must impose the goals of treatment (see Salter 1988) towards more collaboration – a practice in which the therapist works with the client to define together the nature of the client's problems and to agree on a process for working together – has been recommended as an approach to apply from the initial contact with the client (Marshall *et al.* 2005). Attention to these concerns may also help to reduce the attrition rate from many programmes, reported as high as 30–50 per cent, as predictors of treatment attrition are seen as indicators for programme improvement rather than shortcomings in the offenders (Beyko and Wong 2005).

Opportunity, location and support factors

There are three brief points to make regarding these external readiness factors. One is the need for the availability of treatment in a variety of settings in order to fully address the needs of sex offenders. Although the risk principle of the risk–need–responsivity model suggests that treatment resources should be applied to higher-risk offenders, this can result in an imbalance and potential misdirecting of scarce resources. As an example, the State of California releases over 700 sex offenders a month from its prison system, but less than 1 per cent are committed as 'sexually violent predators' (Vess *et al.* 2004; Vess 2005). The cost of treating this small minority of offenders in a high-security facility exceeds $100,000 per offender each year, over the course of an indefinite length of treatment from which few offenders have been recommended for release to the community. In light of findings cited earlier in this chapter that mandated treatment in custodial settings has demonstrated negligible effects on recidivism, we might question whether this balance in the distribution of treatment opportunity resources is optimal.

A related issue under opportunity factors is the limited opportunity for offenders to practise and demonstrate improvement in the dynamic risk factors known to be associated with risk of sexual reoffending while they are incarcerated in a custodial setting. It is often difficult or impossible to create the conditions that offenders will face in their lives outside the institution, and it is difficult to extrapolate current risk assessment measures from the custodial setting to the anticipated functioning of the individual once released to the community. Treatment and assessment and reduction of risk can therefore struggle to reach any semblance of ecological validity. This may be a limiting factor in the effectiveness of custodial treatment opportunities, and mitigate against the trend towards longer prison sentences and post-sentence detention that has developed in recent years (Vess 2008, 2009).

The third issue under this topic is related to support, which is often influenced by opportunity and location. The readiness of an offender to enter and stay in treatment is likely to be a function of the degree of support available to him or her. Yet many offenders are imprisoned in facilities far from family and friendship networks, particularly in large correctional systems that routinely move offenders across different facilities. Others will have been rejected by family and friends in response to their sexual offending or continued criminality. In these circumstances, the presence of supportive clinicians, prison officers and custodial or community corrections staff who support and facilitate engagement in treatment will be particularly important. Yet not all custodial and supervision staff, or even all clinical staff, will have positive and supportive attitudes towards sex offenders. This lack of consistent and overt support is likely to diminish treatment readiness.

Summary and conclusion

This chapter has reviewed the internal and external treatment readiness factors as they apply to sex offenders. It is proposed that treatment readiness can be improved by understanding both the general principles of treatment readiness presented throughout this book, as well as the particular features of sex offender treatment covered here. To facilitate treatment readiness, efforts can focus on modifying the client, modifying the treatment, or modifying the setting. Modifying the client will involve recognising and adapting to the needs, defences and schemas presented by individual sex offenders. Readiness may be enhanced by meeting the client with a clear understanding of these individual differences at the start of treatment, as well as throughout treatment, as readiness is a dynamic feature that will fluctuate throughout the treatment process in response to internal and external factors. Modifying the treatment may involve greater flexibility in defining the goals of treatment, and allowing therapists to adapt their approach to meet the needs and characteristics of individual clients (see Chapter 10). Having well-trained and experienced staff who facilitate effective treatment groups and a positive therapeutic environment is essential to developing and maintaining treatment readiness. Creating an appropriate social climate in which to conduct effective therapy may present one of the biggest challenges to treatment readiness, particularly in the current environment of many custodial settings. Although, it is heartening to note that the development of prisons that are more treatment focused and supportive has begun in some jurisdictions (Laws and Ward, in press). Facilitating the opportunity for offenders to participate in supervised leave programmes and community-based treatment programmes may further promote treatment readiness and treatment effectiveness in the transition from custody to community. Greater attention to the factors that promote treatment readiness is considered necessary if we are to continue to make progress in reducing recidivism and assisting offenders to achieve better lives.

Chapter 8

Substance use and readiness

Substance use is regarded as a pervasive problem in many countries. In addition to the direct and indirect economic costs, there are negative social (e.g. family dysfunction, unemployment) and health (e.g. HIV-AIDS) consequences associated with use. Of particular concern is the well-documented association between substance use and crime (Graycar 2001; Hiller *et al.* 1999; Makkai 2000), the frequency and severity of which has been directly linked to substance use levels (Anglin *et al.* 1999; Chaiken and Chaiken 1990; Makkai and Payne 2003). While alcohol is frequently implicated in offending, particularly crimes involving violence, it is the widespread use of illicit substances that is cause of widespread concern. For example, between 60 and 80 per cent of arrestees test positive to at least one illicit substance (Kouri *et al.* 1997; Milner *et al.* 2004; Prendergast and Maugh 1994), while for incarcerated offenders, approximately two-thirds of first-time male and three-quarters of first-time female prisoners report a history of problematic drug use in the six months prior to incarceration (Makkai and Payne 2003). These figures rise to 80 per cent in males and 90 per cent of females for second and subsequent incarcerations (Department of Justice 2002). Approximately 55 per cent of females (Johnson 2004) and 52 per cent of males (Makkai and Payne 2003) meet the criteria for substance dependence while in prison, around 55 per cent of offenders relapse into drug use within one month of release from incarceration, while some 75 per cent of offenders have reported using substances during their incarceration (Nurco *et al.* 1991).

The typical criminal justice response to the drugs/crime nexus has been the implementation of a broad range of initiatives, the intensity of which differs according to where interventions are offered. At the lower end, a range of police-based interventions target first or second-time offenders detected as being in possession of minor amounts of illicit drugs (such as cannabis or prescription drugs) and/or drug implements. These interventions are low intensity and typically involve an educational component, ranging from on-the-spot written material, through telephone-based education sessions, to meetings with a specialist drug counsellor (Wundersitz 2007). Court-based drug diversion initiatives sit at the intermediate level and target offenders charged with crimes at the lesser end of the severity spectrum (for example property, driving and good order offences) that are directly linked to the use of illicit drugs (although eligibility criteria can differ across jurisdictions). Treatment in diversion programmes is often relatively short term (three to four months) and most often undertaken at the pre-sentence stage. More serious offences are dealt with in formal drug courts, the first of which was established in the US around two decades ago, and which now exist in most western jurisdictions (Payne 2006). Drug courts deal with repeat offenders whose criminal behaviour (excluding violent or sexual offences) is directly connected to long-term drug dependency (usually heroin and amphetamines), and for whom the likely sanction is a term of imprisonment (potential participants must be eligible for bail or release). Treatment programmes usually last for 12 months, during which time the offender undergoes regular drug treatment as well as being provided with support in areas such as accommodation, financial advice and health care (Wundersitz 2007). Frequent and regular random urinalysis is mandatory and offenders who persistently fail this component or repeatedly fail to comply with other conditions set down by the court may be terminated from the programme and sanctioned with a short term of imprisonment.

Prison-based treatment programmes are at the uppermost end of the criminal justice continuum, with incarcerated substance users representing that sub-group of the criminal population whose offences are serious enough or whose offending is sufficiently repetitive to justify imprisonment. In terms of treatment options, most correctional agencies offer opiate replacement therapy (although this is not as extensive in the USA as in other countries) in addition to a range rehabilitation programmes that are psycho-educational or psychologically based. An influential treatment paradigm (again, outside the USA) is that of offender rehabilitation, namely the risk–needs–responsivity model, which is based on work conducted by Canadian researchers (see Andrews and Bonta 2006). This approach advocates that interventions should be targeted towards higher-risk offenders (risk principle), aimed at changing those areas of need that are functionally related to offending (needs principle), and delivered in ways responsive to the individual (responsivity principle). Risk is typically assessed using actuarial instruments, and treatment approaches are often cognitive behavioural in orientation.

The issue of being ready for treatment is an important consideration at any of the above junctures. It may not be practical or appropriate to assess readiness at the earliest stages of intervention (for example, police diversion), but once an individual's behaviour has reached the critical point of being arrested and/or charged with a criminal offence, it is relatively easy for the individual to become entrenched in a drugs/crime cycle that can ultimately lead to a term of imprisonment. The criminal behaviour of those offenders who are sentenced to prison is likely to be more serious and/or more entrenched than in those who are diverted, and if behaviour change is to be successful a comprehensive assessment of the offender's readiness to change (and identification of factors that might compromise that readiness) is likely to be important. As noted in Chapter 4, this assessment needs to be sufficiently broad, using multiple methods and sources. It should also take into account a number of factors with the potential to impact on an individual's level of readiness for treatment. Some of these factors are addressed in this chapter.

Physiological considerations

A starting point in any discussion of behaviour change in substance-using offenders is the role of addiction and dependence. While there is no laboratory test for dependence, it has been operationally defined in the DSM-IV-R as a pathological condition manifested by three or more of seven criteria. Two of these – tolerance and withdrawal – indicate neurologic adaptation (that is, physiological dependence). Physiologic adaptation on its own, however, is neither necessary nor sufficient for a diagnosis of substance dependence. Diagnosis requires that the individual show a compulsive desire for and use of a particular substance or substances, even in the face of adverse consequences (American Psychiatric Association 1994). The propensity for addiction is also thought to have a genetic component, with published heritability estimates of 0.34 for males dependent on heroin, 0.55 for males dependent on alcohol (Tsuang et al. 1996), and 0.52 for females dependent on marijuana (Kendler and Prescott 1998).

These figures are comparable to the heritability for such disorders as Type 1 diabetes (0.30–0.55; Kyvik *et al.* 1995) and adult onset asthma (0.36–0.70; McLellan *et al.* 2000).

Drugs of dependence have an effect on the brain circuitry involved in controlling motivated and learned behaviours (Koob and Bloom 1998). Drugs such as alcohol, cocaine and opiates all have significant effects on the dopamine system, albeit through different mechanisms. Cocaine increases synaptic dopamine by blocking re-uptake into pre-synaptic neurons, amphetamines produce an increase in the pre-synaptic release of dopamine, while opiates and alcohol disinhibit dopamine neurons leading to an increase in firing rate. Given the dopamine system is a reward system associated with feelings of euphoria, many drugs of dependence (including cocaine and opiates) act to produce supranormal stimulation of the reward circuitry. The combined actions of the neuroanatomy and neuropharmacology also produce an immediate and profound desire for re-administration which, at a particular dose, frequency and chronicity, produces enduring (possibly permanent) pathophysiologic changes to the reward circuitry, neurochemical levels, and the stress response system (Kreek and Koob 1998). The exact amount required to make such changes is unknown.

Dependence can be understood as a chronic, relapsing condition due to the integration of the dopamine reward circuitry and the motivational emotional, and memory centres within the limbic system (Childress *et al.* 1999). This interconnectedness is responsible for the substance user not only experiencing the pleasures of reward but also learning specific signals for reward and to respond in an anticipatory way (McLellan *et al.* 2000). The repeated pairing of substance use with an object (needle), person (drug-using friend), or even an emotional state (anger, depression) can result in rapid and entrenched learning. This process helps to explain how a previously substance-dependent individual who has been abstinent for a long period will experience significant, conditioned physiological reactions (withdrawal, craving) when encountering the conditioned object, person or emotional experience previously associated with substance use (Childress *et al.* 1999).

As noted above, chronic substance use can result in neuroanatomical and neurochemical damage leading to impairment across a number of cognitive domains (Aharonovich *et al.* 2006). While there are generalised cognitive deficits across all classes of addictive substances (most notably decision-making deficits), subtle differences have been noted for specific substances due to distinct modes of action (Rogers and Robbins 2001). Chronic users of cocaine, for example, show deficits in attention, decision-making and problem-solving (Cunha *et al*. 2004; Tucker *et al*. 2004), while those with alcohol abuse disorders have been shown to have problems acquiring new coping behaviours, learning and retaining new material, and engaging with therapeutic interventions (Fals-Stewart 1993; McCrady and Smith 1986; Alterman and Hall 1989). Chronic marijuana misuse is associated with impaired memory as well as deficits in attention, abstraction and executive functioning (Aharonovich *et al*. 2008; Lamers *et al*. 2006), while MDMA (Ecstasy) use has dosed-related long-term deficits in verbal memory, processing speed, and planning and problem-solving (Hanson *et al*. 2008).

Cognitive impairments may contribute to substance abuse and dependence in at least two ways. First, the various cognitive deficits can increase the likelihood of drug-seeking behaviour. For example, decision-making deficits may lead substance-dependent individuals to persist with risky behaviour even in the face of known negative consequences (labelled 'myopia for the future'; Clarke and Robbins 2002). Research by Bechara and colleagues (Bechara and Damasio 2002; Bechara *et al*. 2002) has shown that prolonged substance use can result in users (a) becoming insensitive to future consequences regardless of the emotional valence, (b) showing learned feedback about reward but not punishment guided by long-term decision-making, or (c) becoming hypersensitive to reward but hyposensitive to punishment. Second, persistent use can interfere with the individual's capacity to participate in rehabilitation programmes with an educative and cognitive emphasis which, in turn, can lead to poor retention and high relapse rates. Adequate cognitive function is a requirement for many of the activities in substance-use programmes. It is therefore reasonable to assume that cognitively impaired substance users participating in cognitively oriented treatment may encounter difficulties since many treatment modalities require the verbal, memory and learning skills that are often impaired as a result of chronic use.

Offending pathways

The process by which an individual becomes involved in substance use may also influence decisions about the need to change either their offending behaviour or their substance use. Although clear evidence exists for a relationship between substance use and crime, a direct causal link has yet to be established. From the considerable debate that has taken place, three possible explanations have emerged: (a) drug use leads to crime; (b) crime leads to drug use; and (c) any relationship between drugs and crime can be explained by a set of common causes (Gorman and White 1995). With respect to the proposition that drugs lead to crime, Goldstein (1985) has identified three ways this might occur. First, the pharmacological model posits that intoxication (disinhibition, poor judgement, cognitive-perceptual distortions) and its by-products (withdrawal, enhancement of psychopathological disorders, sleep deprivation) can lead to crime (either while under the influence or as a consequence of substance use). Second, the economic motivation model assumes that drug users commit crime (theft, burglary, drug dealing) to generate income to support their addiction. Third, the systemic model proposes an intrinsic link between the system of drug distribution and violent crime (such as 'turf wars', physical assaults related to the collection of drug debts, robbery of dealers or buyers).

According to the second proposition, crime leads to substance use because individuals involved in deviant behaviour are more likely than non-deviant individuals to find themselves in situations where substance use is condoned and/or encouraged. It is the involvement in this type of subculture that provides a context for substance use (Collins and Messerschmidt 1993; White 1990). It has also been suggested that deviant individuals may use drugs in order to self-medicate or to provide an excuse for their deviant behaviour (Collins 1993; Khantzian 1985). Finally, the common cause explanation argues no direct causal link between drugs and crime but proposes instead that the two are related through common causes (for example, childhood abuse, early school failure, family problems, temperamental traits, anti-social personality disorder, neighbourhood disorganisation; see White *et al.* 1993; White and Gorman 2000). Subcultural norms have also been implicated in this explanation as substance use and crime can help individuals achieve membership and status within the subculture (Gorman and White 1995).

Heterogeneity in the substance-using population

An important consideration when making decisions about treatment, and by extension treatment readiness, is the complex and heterogeneous nature of substance use and dependence and the impact that this has on the individual offender presenting for treatment. Dependence occurs as a function of the interaction between physical

(physical adaptation to the substance), psychological (reasons for substance use), and social factors (availability of drugs and drug-using lifestyle), all of which are strongly influenced by personal and environmental factors (Gowing *et al* 2001). Consequently, substance users can differ markedly in terms of their age; the length and severity of their substance use; the presence of co-morbid conditions; the extent, type and severity of offending; their levels of psychosocial functioning; the motivations for and functions of substance use; their social status; and their treatment history. Importantly, they will also differ in terms of their level of motivation to change (or modify) their substance use, the extent to which they can engage in the treatment process, and the length of time any changes gained in treatment can be sustained (Simpson *et al*. 1997).

An example of this heterogeneity is evident in German and Sterk's (2002) study of crack cocaine users. Based on in-depth interviews with active users, the authors identified four sub-groups: stable users; tempted users; grappling users; and immersed users. The most salient dimensions differentiating each typology were the level of protective strategies used by individuals to avoid negative consequences, and the frequency of use (which was directly related to daily life structure and access to crack cocaine). Recently, Wittchen and colleagues (Wittchen *et al*. 2009) reported on a longitudinal study investigating the relationship between sustained cannabis use and mental health problems. While a large proportion of participants (59 per cent) were identified as 'unproblematic users', 14.4 per cent had 'primary alcohol use disorder', 17.9 per cent had 'delinquent cannabis/alcohol DSM-IV abuse', while the remaining 8.5 per cent had 'cannabis use disorder with multiple problems'. The probability of unmet treatment needs was highest for those falling into the category of primary alcohol disorder or multiple problems. Finally, a substantial body of research also points to the heterogeneity in alcohol abuse and dependence as a function of genetic predisposition (see Maher *et al*. 2002; van der Zwaluw and Engels 2009), culture (Bau *et al*. 2001; Delva *et al*. 2005), sex (Oxford *et al*. 2003), deviant peer influence (Li *et al*. 2002; Wiesner *et al*. 2008), and co-morbid mental health problems (Maher *et al*. 2002; Shumway and Cuffel 1996).

Compulsory and coerced treatment

While use of the criminal justice system to direct offenders to treatment is commonplace in the US, its use has been the subject of fierce international debate (Klag *et al.* 2005; Wild 2006; Wild *et al.* 2002). Critics opposing coerced or compulsory treatment have argued that individuals who are forced into treatment are less motivated (Brecht *et al.* 1993) and show greater treatment resistance (Shearer and Ogan 2002), which subsequently compromises positive therapeutic and legal outcomes. Other research has shown reductions in both drug use and crime in mandated or legally coerced clients that is similar to (and in some instances better than) voluntary clients (Farabee *et al.* 1998; Hiller *et al.* 1998; Marlowe 2001). Ethical concerns inevitably arise in any discussion of mandated or coerced treatment. There is a need to ensure that treatment does not supplant basic civil or human rights in meeting the larger societal goal of reducing the risk substance users pose to others (Kleinig 2004). While the issue of coercion and its relationship to treatment readiness has been articulated in Chapter 2, there are some issues specific to substance-using offenders that require further comment.

Policies supporting the use of coerced treatment rest on three main assumptions: (1) substance use and crime are so highly correlated that a reduction in the former will result in a concomitant reduction in the latter; (2) because the treatment substance use has been found to reduce criminal behaviour, at least part of that behaviour is related to substance use; and (3) even substance-using offenders who do not perceive they have a substance-use problem have been shown to benefit from treatment (Prendergast *et al.* 2009). There is a strong body of evidence that supports all three assumptions (for example, Allen *et al.* 2001; Anglin and Perrochet 1998; Dowden and Blanchette 2002; Wild *et al.* 2002). The extent to which coerced clients and those who do not recognise or acknowledge problematic substance use can become engaged in the therapeutic process and have positive gains that are comparable to voluntary clients depends to a large extent on whether the individual *perceives* the treatment as coerced. This is an important consideration, particularly as much of the coercion literature fails to distinguish between objective, external or legal sources of coercion (courts, prisons, parole boards) and the individual's subjective experience (Prendergast *et al.* 2008).

There is also an assumption that criminal justice clients undergoing coerced or mandated treatment do so against their will. A study by Farabee, Prendergast and Anglin (1998) revealed that most of the clients interviewed reported that they would have entered treatment in the absence of pressure from the criminal justice system. Specific to the issue of readiness to change and coerced treatment, Gregoire and Burke (2004) used the Readiness to Change Questionnaire (Rollnick *et al.* 1992) to assess mandated and non-mandated substance users presenting as outpatient clients. A significantly higher proportion of the mandated group reported being in either the action stage or the contemplation stage. Better outcomes for mandated as compared to non-mandated treatment participants remained even when prior treatment and addiction severity were controlled. Gender differences were also noted, with females being more likely to be in the action stage, independent of either severity of substance-use or legal coercion.

Sex differences

Although it is widely acknowledged that the aetiology and subsequent rehabilitation needs of male and female offenders are different, much less is known about the specific needs of females presenting with substance-use problems. While this may be a product of the considerable imbalance between the male and female offending populations, there has been a not unsubstantial increase in the number of female offenders incarcerated for substance-related offences over the past decade. For many of these women, offending is directly related to their involvement in drug-related crimes. Substance use is also more likely to precede the offending behaviour of females than it does for males (Makkai and Payne 2003). For example, in one Australian study of police detainees (Milner *et al.* 2004), two-thirds of respondents reported having used illegal drugs prior to or within the same year as their first offence. This suggests that for a substantial proportion of female offenders, substance use plays a critical role in the aetiology of their offending behaviour.

The origins of female substance-use would appear to be embedded in the psychosocial problems and traumatic life events that women frequently experience. Female offenders with substance-use histories are more likely to have employment, mental health (depression, anxiety, bipolar affective disorder, psychosexual disorders, eating disorders, post-traumatic stress disorder) and family problems (family dysfunction, lack of adequate role models) than their male counterparts. They are also more likely than males to have required help for emotional problems at a younger age and to have attempted suicide (Brady and Ashley 2005). Females are also significantly more likely to exhibit recent physical, emotional or sexual abuse (Gentilello *et al.* 2000) and report more problems related to physical and sexual abuse and domestic violence victimisation than males (Green *et al.*

2000). The physiological effects of substance use also display gender differences, with females tending to report more physical problems and be more vulnerable to the physiological effects of substance use (Wasilow-Mueller and Erickson 2001). Gender differences have also been noted in the reasons why females initiate substance use. For example, they are more likely to use substances to alleviate either physical or emotional pain (Corcoran and Corcoran 2001; Langan and Pelissier 2001) and more likely to have been initiated into both substance use and anti-social behaviour by male partners (Henderson *et al.* 1994).

It is noteworthy that the gender differences described above frequently mirror those of female substance users who are non-offenders. Perhaps more importantly, given the much harsher societal response to females with substance-use problems as compared to males (Van der Walde *et al.* 2002), these problems also parallel gender differences found within the non-offending female populations (Brady and Ashley 2005). On a more positive note, despite the extent and complexity of the problems experienced by females with substance-abuse histories, there would seem to be a 'gender paradox' at work: first, women are no more likely than males to relapse following treatment, and second, they are much more likely than men to engage in treatment (Fiorentine *et al.* 1997).

Co-morbidity

Substance use disorders frequently co-occur with a range of other mental health and behavioural disorders. Large epidemiological studies in the US, for example, report lifetime prevalence rates for co-morbid substance disorders and mood disorders (26 per cent), anxiety disorders (28 per cent), psychotic thought disorders (7 per cent), and anti-social personality disorder (18 per cent) (Kessler *et al.* 1997; Regier *et al.* 1990). Reiger and colleagues also noted that more than half of those identified as meeting the criteria for a drug disorder also had a mental disorder of some type. The figures are similar in clinical populations for patients seeking treatment for substance use and co-morbid mood disorder (41 per cent), anxiety disorder (26 per cent), post-traumatic stress disorder (25 per cent), severe (psychotic) mental disorder (17 per cent) and borderline personality disorder (17 per cent) (McGovern *et al.* 2006).

Recent research indicates gender differences in the pattern of co-morbid conditions and temporal onset, in both general and clinical populations. For example, females with substance-use disorders report higher rates of anxiety, depression, eating disorders and borderline personality disorder, while males report higher rates of anti-social personality disorder (Zlotnick *et al.* 2008). Gender differences in temporal onset show that as compared to males, females tend to have primary psychiatric disorders that antedate the onset of substance-use disorders. This would indicate a difference in the aetiological relationship of substance use and co-morbid disorders from that found for males (Kessler 2004). The relationship between addiction, trauma, and post-traumatic stress disorder is also stronger in females. This is particularly so for female victims of childhood abuse as well as those exposed to violence in adulthood (Kendler *et al.* 2000).

Rates of co-occurring substance use and psychiatric disorders in male (Swartz and Lurigio 1999) and female offenders (Abram *et al.* 2003) are similar to those found in the general and clinical population. For example, it has been reported that female offenders undergoing substance-use treatment are twice to three times more likely to meet the diagnostic for major depression, post-traumatic stress disorder, borderline personality disorder, or any affective, anxiety, or psychotic disorder (Zlotnick *et al.* 2008). Anti-social personality disorder is more prevalent in male offenders. As compared to their male counterparts, female offenders report more severe substance-use histories and more frequent co-morbidity prior to incarceration (Messina *et al.* 2006) and lifetime prevalence for depression, anxiety, and psychosis (Messina *et al.* 2003).

The combination of a substance-use disorder and co-occurring psychiatric condition has a detrimental impact on treatment engagement and therapeutic outcomes due to the complex interaction of the two problems (DiClemente *et al.* 2008). For example, individuals with a dual diagnosis that includes substance-use disorder have been found to not adhere with medication regimes, to experience symptom exacerbation, and have frequent episodes of rehospitalisation, poor social adjustment, and poor prognosis (Drake *et al.* 1996). Treatment is also characterised by a lack of therapeutic engagement, low levels of motivation to change, and frequent relapse. The more severe the substance-use problem and co-morbid psychiatric condition, the greater the likelihood that dysfunctional thought processes, impaired decision-making capabilities, and poor insight will impair the ability to either recognise or seek out and participate in treatment.

Treatment considerations

The above discussion highlights the heterogeneous nature of the substance-using population. Given this heterogeneity, it is important that treatment providers endeavour to match services to individual need, taking into account levels of motivation and readiness to change when making decisions about treatment type and intensity. One of the first considerations in determining an individual's treatment needs is their level of motivation to change. Motivation is at the core of successful behavioural change, although many substance-using offenders can present as being ambivalent about their substance use and the need to change (although even ambivalent clients can benefit for treatment if they remain in treatment). Motivation reflects the degree of interest or concern an individual has about the need for change, their goals or intentions, the need for them to take responsibility, the capacity to sustain change that is made, and the need to have adequate incentives to change (DiClemente *et al.* 2004). Perhaps the most influential model of motivational tasks and intentional behaviour change is Prochaska and DiClemente's (1984) transtheoretical model, described in Chapter 4. A staged model of change, it includes pre-action (pre-contemplation, contemplation, preparation), action, and maintenance stages. Pre-action tasks are preparatory: for example, acknowledging that substance use is problematic, creating goals, formulating intention, planning of and commitment to change. The action stage is where behaviour change is initiated (ceasing or reducing substance use) while the maintenance stage involves sustaining any change over time.

According to DiClemente (2005), forward movement through these stages can only occur if stage-specific tasks are sufficiently well accomplished. The model also posits that behavioural change is likely to occur only after the individual has 'recycled' through the stages several times. The activities and experiences used to complete the various tasks and facilitate progress through the stages are referred to as Processes of Change. These processes, which include both cognitive/experiential (consciousness raising, self re-evaluation, environmental re-evaluation, emotional arousal) and behavioural activities and strategies (self-liberation, stimulus control, counter conditioning, contingency management, and helping relationships), are relevant to the tasks required at each of the different stages in order that the task goals of each stage be met, that forward movement through the stage process occurs, and that behavioural change outcomes are achieved (Prochaska *et al.* 1992).

For problematic substance use, motivation and intention are critical components of treatment readiness. Increased motivation has been positively associated with treatment engagement, attempts to stop substance use, reduced alcohol consumption, treatment retention, sustained abstinence, and more positive life outcomes (Joe *et al*. 1998; Project MATCH Research Group 1997). This highlights the importance of assessing motivation to change in conjunction with an assessment of treatment readiness. The most frequently used measures have been described in Chapter 4. Of these, the University of Rhode Island Change Assessment (URICA) (McConnaughy *et al*. 1983, 1989) has versions designed specifically for alcohol and drug use (see Appendix). In addition to the original 32-item scales, both have shorter versions that can also be used to assess change over time (that is, pre- and post-treatment). Rehabilitation efforts can then be targeted at the individual's location in this cycle. For example, education programmes aimed at improving motivation may be most appropriately aimed at those offenders who are reluctant to enter more formal treatment programmes. An alternative strategy is the use of motivational enhancement techniques (such as motivational interviewing; MI) which might be used to engage the individual in the sorts of cognitive (for example, psycho-education) and experiential (for example, drama therapy) activities that might promote preparation for change. Described more fully in Chapter 10, MI is a collaborative process whereby the therapist helps identify the potential for change within the client and facilitates the change process. Readiness for change can be increased when MI serves to enhance engagement and reduce reactance. This is especially pertinent with offenders, with whom engagement in change is often difficult to achieve.

Matching services to the pre-treatment characteristics of the client is perhaps the simplest form of adapting treatment to the needs of the individual. For example, tailoring services to the specific needs of females, youths or minorities is a basic approach to adapting treatment for the client. Similarly, a history of negative outcomes in previous treatment episodes might lead a programme to prescribe a higher dosage or greater variety of services for a new client than would ordinarily be provided to new admissions. This, too, is a simple form of adapting treatment to the needs of the individual. At a more sophisticated level of adaptive programming, the nature and intensity of services is continuously readjusted as a consequence of the client's ongoing performance in treatment. For example, if a client fell below an effective threshold for engagement in treatment (such as missing a predetermined number of scheduled counselling appointments), he or she might be reassigned to a motivational enhancement intervention or might be encouraged to try a different and more desired form of treatment.

The notion of matching client needs to treatment intensity has informed two of the largest substance-use treatment evaluations undertaken: Project MATCH (Project MATCH, 1997) and Project REFORM (Wexler et al. 1991). Project MATCH was an eight-year multi-site study conducted in the US that was designed to test the assumption that treatment outcomes could be improved by carefully matching individuals to therapeutic approaches for alcohol abuse/ dependence, based on their personal characteristics. While positive gains were only noted for those identified as having lower levels psychological distress, this may have been a function of the intensity of programmes offered, all of which would fall into the category of low intensity under current best practice guidelines (such as 12-step programmes, 12-session CBT-based coping skills, and brief motivation enhancement). Individuals with higher levels of distress are more likely to benefit from more intense treatments. This is noted by Wexler, Blackmore and Lipton (1991) when writing about Project REFORM. In their view, prisoners assessed as having 'moderate' level substance-use problems should be assigned to non-residential programmes (reside in mainstream but undertake programme) whereas those offenders with severe or chronic substance-use problems should be directed to isolated, residential treatment programmes.

Although there are few published accounts of good practice in offender substance-use programming, an analysis of Project REFORM (Wexler et al. 1991) suggests the following principles and guidelines for programmes in correctional systems that seek to reduce recidivism.

- Assist the offender to identify personal impediments to recover.

- Provide the offender with incentives, positive or otherwise, to participate in recovery programmes.

- Separate participants from the general prison population as soon as possible.

- Reinforce pro-social behaviours rather than attempt to directly reduce the frequency of negative behaviour.

- Establish clear, unambiguous rules and consequences for breaking such rules.

- Establish clear behavioural contingencies.

- Employ ex-offenders/ex-addict staff to serve as role models.

- Maintain treatment integrity, autonomy, flexibility, openness, and fiscal and political support.

- Establish continuity of intervention, from the outset of custody to its termination.

- Establish programme evaluation systems and analyse cost-effectiveness.

The US National Institute on Drug Abuse also specifies the following principles of effective programming:

- No single treatment is appropriate for all individuals.

- Treatment needs to be readily available.

- Effective treatment attends to multiple needs of the individual, not just his or her drug use.

- An individual's treatment and service plans must be assessed continually and modified as necessary to ensure that the plan meets the person's changing needs.

- Remaining in treatment for an adequate period of time is critical for treatment effectiveness (minimum of three months).

- Counselling (individual and group) and other behavioural therapies are critical components of effective treatment for addiction.

- Medications are an important element of treatment for many patients, especially when combined with other behavioural therapies.

- Addicted or drug-abusing individuals with co-existing mental disorders should have both disorders treated in an integrated way.

- Medical detoxification is only the first stage of addiction treatment and by itself does not change long-term drug use.

- Treatment does not need to be voluntary to be effective.

- Possible drug use during treatment must be monitored continuously.

- Treatment programmes should provide assessment for HIV/AIDS, hepatitis B and C, tuberculosis and other infectious diseases, and counselling to help patients to modify or change behaviours that place them at risk of infection.

- Recovery from drug addiction can be a long-term process and frequently requires multiple episodes of treatment.

Conclusion

Given the chronic, relapsing nature of substance-use disorders, individuals who present for treatment (whether voluntarily or in response to some level of coercion) might not be motivated to change and, therefore, are unlikely to be treatment ready. While this may be the case, there is evidence to support the proposition that once in treatment, the experience of the therapeutic process can result in positive gains irrespective of motivation levels. There are, however, a number of factors internal and external to the individual that have the potential to negatively impact on treatment outcomes, even in those who wish to participate. Chronic substance use can, for example, result in physiological change that increases the likelihood of treatment failure (for example, through relapse or an inability to participate fully in the treatment process due to cognitive deficits). The heterogeneity of substance-use problems is also a potential impediment to treatment success. Finally, the presence of a co-occurring psychiatric disorders may result in the individual being differentially motivated with respect to each condition to the extent that neither is adequately addressed. This all suggests that treating substance-use problems in a criminal justice context is likely to be particularly challenging, and highlights the need to carefully assess those who are referred to programmes to ensure that they are both able and willing to undertake a process of behaviour change. The framework for understanding treatment readiness in this book offers a structure by which offenders can be assessed and a rationale for offering comprehensive assessments. There is a need to ensure that the scope of any assessment is sufficiently broad to enable treatment to be matched to the needs and characteristics of the individual presenting for treatment.

Chapter 9

Readiness and treatment engagement in personality disordered offenders: towards a clinical strategy[1]

In the decade since the advent of the millennium, therapeutic and rehabilitative interventions for offenders have proliferated in many jurisdictions and the confidence of forensic and clinical practitioners appears to have grown. Proliferation and confidence are likely to be a product, in part, of the substantial evidence base that has become available, indicating that treatment and rehabilitation programmes can indeed have an impact in changing important outcomes, such as recidivism, and suggesting that positive outcomes are associated with particular features of programmes, such as attention to the 'risk, needs and responsivity principles' (Andrews and Bonta, 2006; Hollin and Palmer, 2006, Ward and Maruna 2007). The growth in confidence has had a number of positive effects. One of the latter has been the emergence of healthy conceptual and empirical critiques of the What Works movement (Ward and Maruna 2007), another has been the development of what might be termed a positive psychology perspective on the goals of treatment and rehabilitation, with an emphasis on 'good lives' (Ward and Brown 2004).

A third effect has been an expansion of the field to accommodate other populations. While What Works programmes developed mainly in criminal justice systems, many offenders, particularly high-risk offenders, are to be found within forensic mental health services.

[1]We would like to thank Matthew Tonkin, Allison Tennant, Lawrence Jones, Mary McMurran and Kerry Sheldon for their contributions to my thinking and the NIHR (CLAHRC) programme for supporting work in the Institute of Mental Health, Nottingham University.

Typically offending behaviours such as violence or sexual offending occur in the context of the presence of a mental disorder, and admission to the health system under mental health legislation is seen as preferable to admission to the criminal justice system (McMurran *et al.* 2008a). There is some evidence that the criminogenic needs (and hence treatment targets) for mentally disordered and non-mentally disordered offenders overlap substantially and that the causal influence of mental disorder *per se* for serious offending is somewhat uncertain (Duggan and Howard 2009; Howells, in press). It would follow from the latter that what have become established types of offender rehabilitation programmes are also likely to be necessary in forensic mental health services, though progress in implementing and evaluating such programmes in forensic mental health systems has been slow (Howells *et al.* 2005; McMurran *et al.* 2008a).

It is likely that distinct problems arise, or will arise, as interventions develop for the mentally disordered offender. The features of disorders themselves have the capacity to impair the individual's ability to benefit from programmes and there is a consequent need to adapt such programmes to accommodate the characteristics of the mentally disordered person, as would be suggested by the responsivity principle (Andrews and Bonta 2006).

One increasingly recognised area in which all treatment programmes may be deficient is that of insufficient attention to responsivity. It has been proposed in this book that an important dimension of responsivity is the readiness of the person for the programme and the readiness of the programme itself for the particular population to which it is to be delivered. The assumption here is that low readiness produces low engagement, which in turn influences non-completion of treatment and ultimately poor treatment outcomes. Certainly, there is evidence for non-completion of programmes in offender populations, particularly in community programmes, where between a third and a half of starters fail to complete. There is less evidence available as to completion rates in mentally disordered populations, though engagement problems appear to be common for people with schizophrenia, particularly when substance misuse is also present (Tait *et al.* 2002). Hodge and Renwick (2002) have described extensive problems of motivation and engagement in mentally disordered offenders and these have been explored by Sainsbury, Krishnan and Evans (2004).

Such problems may be accentuated for the personality disordered offender (PDO). The PDO has, in the past, been seen as falling into the gaps between mental health and criminal justice services. Personality disorder itself has been neglected within mental health services and it is only in the past decade that there has been a considerable increase in clinical and academic interest in personality disorder, particularly in the links between personality disorder and risk of violence (Duggan and Howard 2009; McMurran and Howard 2009). In the United Kingdom, increased interest has stimulated the rapid development of new clinical assessment and therapeutic services, particularly for those whose personality disorder is seen as severe and whose ensuing risk is deemed to be very high. The Dangerous and Severe Personality Disorder (DSPD) programme, for example, an initiative of the UK government, has given rise to a range of high security and community services for this population (see Howells *et al.* 2007, for an overview).

It was acknowledged from the outset of the DSPD programme that these patients would pose particular challenges to services and this has proven to be the case, though the units created have now been in operation for more than five years. Patients with severe personality disorders and high risk fall at the extremes of dimensions of mental disorder and of offending and thus might be anticipated to be particularly difficult to engage. This population includes a significant group who meet the criteria for psychopathy (Sheldon and Krishnan 2009). Hemphill and Hart (2002) have reviewed evidence that individuals with psychopathic traits resist the role of being a mental health patient and that their treatment engagement is low. Difficulty in forming a therapeutic relationship with therapists, need for control and dominance, and impulsivity in the treatment environment may all work against treatment engagement in such individuals (Hemphill and Hart 2002; Howells and Day 2007).

It is important that readiness factors are seen as both intrapersonal and situational (see the MORM model, Chapter 1). Thus there is a need to investigate the situational context of admission to a hospital as well as the social and environmental aspects of the treatment environment. Typically, for example, DSPD patients have been transferred to a high secure hospital setting from a prison where they have either failed to complete mainstream offender programmes or been perceived as unlikely to be able to cope with them, often because of personality disorder traits. For DSPD patients, they may have been transferred from prison under the Mental Health Act and against their will, late in their sentence, when they may have been anticipating release into the community. It might be expected that such circumstances would, at least initially, enhance resentment, resistance to treatment and perceptions of unfair coercion.

Treatment completion in the personality disordered

McMurran, Huband and Overton (submitted) have conducted a systematic review of completion of therapy in people with personality disorder and also of correlates of non-completion (drop-out). McMurran *et al.* found three categories of readiness factor to be present in published studies: patient characteristics, need factors and environmental factors. The authors reported a median non-completion rate of 37 per cent in studies of PDOs, pointing out that this figure was higher than that (20.5 per cent) reported in a recent review of RCTs of psychological treatments for people with PD (Duggan *et al.* 2007) but slightly lower than that found (47 per cent) in a meta-analysis of drop-outs from general psychotherapy. As McMurran *et al.* suggest, non-completion rates for PDOs may be comparable to those for other psychological disorders but the rate is nevertheless substantial and likely to have a number of adverse consequences. What is unclear is whether criminological characteristics and psychological disorder interact when they are co-morbidly present within the individual. Do PDOs have particularly poor completion rates? A factor likely to confound answers to the latter question is the likelihood that such patients/offenders will often be found in secure forensic mental health or prison institutions where there are often strong pressures, even perceived obligations, to attend therapy sessions and to complete treatment, whereas many personality disordered people who are not serious offenders are likely to be treated in a community setting where the patient can more easily drop out.

Treatment programmes for the personality disordered offender, particularly where the PDO is deemed to present a high risk (Howells *et al.* 2007) are likely to involve a high degree of coercion (Day *et al.* 2004). In the DSPD population, for example, offenders in prison may be involuntarily transferred to a high-security forensic mental health service under the Mental Health Act in England and Wales, in order to receive treatment. While studies of recidivism in the past have reported mixed results in terms of the impact of coercion on outcomes such as reduction in recidivism, Parhar *et al.*'s (2008) comprehensive meta-analysis provides evidence that mandated treatment is more likely to be ineffective, particularly when treatment is located in a custodial as opposed to a community setting.

Individuals diagnosed with anti-social personality disorder (ASPD), in particular, have typically been seen as problematic to treat, with a resulting rejection of them by mental health services (Duggan 2009). Duggan identifies several 'attitudinal barriers' to treatment of ASPD, including perceptions by clinicians that those with ASPD may be difficult to work with because of traits of rule-breaking, egocentricity and defensiveness, and also the 'lukewarm' commitment of such people to interventions and therapies. It is reasonable to conclude that the negative perceptions, expectations and pessimism of clinicians and services, although often based realistically on previous experience of working with such populations, nevertheless may sometimes constitute a situational factor impairing readiness to engage in patients and offenders. One implication is that measurement of, and development of interventions to modify, such expectations are important tasks for the future (discussed below).

One noteworthy feature of previous studies of low engagement has been the pejorative way in which low engagement has been described. The patient may be described as 'resistant' or 'unmotivated'. Such descriptions tend to pathologise the person and to ignore the possibility that non-engagement may be a product of legitimate and rational concerns and of problems being in the treatment environment rather than within the person (see Chapter 1).

It is apparent from the above discussion that a host of readiness and engagement issues arise in relation to PDOs and that these may be even more marked for those admitted to high-secure services of the DSPD type. The failure to engage in such services also has large potential economic costs, in that treatments have been developed that are often labour and resource intensive. Such an investment of resources is vitiated should patients fail to become engaged in treatment or drop out from it.

Conceptions of readiness

Utilising Howells and Day's (2003) analysis of impediments to therapeutic engagement in patients with anger problems, Ward et al. (2004b) define treatment readiness as 'the presence of characteristics (states or dispositions) within either the client or the therapeutic situation, which are likely to promote engagement in therapy and which, thereby, are likely to enhance therapeutic change'. Ward et al. suggest that these factors can reside within the person, the context, or within the therapy or therapeutic environment, and outline a number of internal and external factors that are likely to influence the extent to which an individual approaches and ultimately engages with the treatment being offered. In the readiness model (the MORM) outlined by these researchers, internal readiness factors fall within particular domains: cognitive, affective, identity-related, volitional (motivational) and behavioural skills. The cognitive domain, for example, includes personal beliefs about the nature of the problem, therapy expectations and self-efficacy beliefs, while the affective domain includes excessively high or excessively low subjective distress. Volitional factors refer to the personal goals of the patient, which may be either consistent or inconsistent with the goals of the treatment offered. External readiness factors include lack of social support (staff, family and friends) for engagement in treatment, responsivity failures in the treatment programme itself, and poor therapeutic climate within the treatment setting. There may also be wider influences that affect the degree to which patients engage with treatments, associated with, for example, the organisation of care, the roles ascribed to different professional groups, the impact of national and local-level policies, and other organisational factors.

Howells and Tennant (2007) have suggested that the MORM model, when applied in a personality disorder service, directs the clinician to ask a series of straightforward questions:

- How does the patient perceive the therapeutic programme?
- Does the patient believe he or she is capable of change?
- How does the patient perceive the therapeutic staff and the system?
- What expectancies has the patient acquired, for example from previous exposure to therapy?
- What is the patient's affective state?
- What emotional reactions does he/she have to their offending and other related problems?
- What are the personal goals of the patient?
- Are personal goals congruent with the goals of the programme?
- What is the self-identity of the patient and is it compatible with treatment?
- Does the patient have the behavioural and cognitive skills required by the programme?
- Does the patient have the capacity to form a therapeutic alliance?

- What support is given by staff and other patients for therapeutic engagement?

- What support is given by relatives and friends for therapeutic engagement?

- How does the patient perceive coercion into treatment?

- Has the programme been adapted for the (DSPD) population?

- Is the climate of the service supportive of engagement, therapy and of change?

External readiness conditions

External readiness factors are important to consider in treatment services for the PDO. A high proportion of personality disordered offenders will be found within the prison system or within secure forensic mental services (McMurran *et al.* 2008). While PDOs are likely to have many needs in common with offenders (particularly violent and sexual offenders) who have not been diagnosed as having a personality disorder, they will also have distinctive needs that may require adaptations of the content of programmes and of their style of delivery (Tennant and Howells 2010). To implement a sex offending programme with PD sex offenders in exactly the same way as would be done with non-PD sex offenders would infringe the Responsivity Principle and be an instance of low programme readiness (Jones 2010). This latter problem may be diminished in part by the high probability that many offenders in mainstream offender programmes in prison settings would prove to be diagnosable as having a PD, were they to be clinically assessed. To this end, future research is needed, evaluating the level of PD in those attending mainstream non-PD programmes in the criminal justice system, to determine whether and how they might differ from those already diagnosed as personality disordered.

It is possible that features of institutional life, particularly in prisons, work against engagement in therapeutic programmes in some cases and that the services are thus 'unready'. The provision of therapy is typically not a primary goal for prison systems. Even where therapeutic goals are acknowledged as important, for example in specialist therapeutic prisons, they are secondary to the custodial and deterrence functions of imprisonment. PDO services located within prisons face the challenge of maintaining a therapeutic rather than a custodial regime and the effort required is necessarily greater than it is within high-security mental health services, where understanding the individual, the need for treatment enabling patients to improve their well-being, and social adjustment have historically been core, high-priority goals. It must be acknowledged, however, that in the past mental health services have also struggled to prevent institutional environments from becoming 'toxic' (Davies 2004). Hodge and Renwick (2002) and Ginsburg *et al.* (2001) have identified a range of organisational factors that can impede readiness, including perceived lack of safety, poor facilities, security versus therapy disputes, adversarial staff–service user relationships, pejorative labelling of those in treatment and reinforcement of non-engagement within the informal institutional culture.

The identification and measurement of features of settings and organisations that might impede engagement in treatment is an important task for the future. Within both mental health and correctional settings the construct of therapeutic climate has become an important one. The most relevant body of scientific work for understanding, measuring and modifying negative environments and milieux is that on social climate, pioneered for over 30 years by Rudolph Moos (see Timko and Moos 2004) in a range of service settings, including health, mental health and correctional institutions. One of Moos's most important contributions has been the Ward Atmosphere Scale (available in different versions for different settings; Moos 1997). In recent years the Moos scales have been subject to critiques (for an overview see Schalast *et al.* 2008) that suggest problems with item content being outdated, and the time and effort required for completion being too great for repeated clinical use; and criticise the low internal consistency of some scales, and discrepancies between the scales and the factor structure of the measure (Rossberg and Friis 2003). In response to such criticisms, Norbert Schalast at the University of Essen in Germany has developed a new climate measure, specifically designed for use in forensic psychiatric wards. This is a 15-item instrument (named EssenCES: Essen Climate Evaluation Schema). The measure has three factor-analytically supported scales: Therapeutic Hold, Patients' Cohesion and Mutual Support, and Experienced Safety. The Therapeutic Hold scale assesses perceptions of the extent to which the climate is supportive of patients' therapeutic needs; the Patient Cohesion scale assesses whether mutual support of a kind typically seen as characteristic of therapeutic communities is present; and the Safety scale assesses tension and perceived threat of aggression and violence.

In a recent validation of EssenCES, Schalast and colleagues collected data in 17 forensic mental hospitals in Germany. High internal consistencies were found for the scales and good support for the expected factor structure. Convergent validity was demonstrated in terms of correlations with related measures, including job satisfaction in staff and perceived therapeutic milieu (Schalast et al. 2008). Since this initial validation study, EssenCES has been translated into a number of different languages, including Japanese, Dutch, Finnish and English. The English translation of EssenCES has been used in English high- security settings, particularly in high secure services for PDOs (Howells et al. 2009). In this latter study, internal consistencies, factor structures and correlations with measures of ward experience, climate and milieu were broadly similar to those reported by Schalast et al. (2008) in their German sample. EssenCES has considerable face validity as a method for operationalising environmental readiness factors in that perceived supportiveness of therapy by staff and fellow patients in the setting, as measured by EssenCES, are likely predictors of engagement (Ward et al. 2004b). Nevertheless, there is a clear need to test directly the hypothesis that levels of engagement will be higher in wards and units with more positive therapeutic climates. A comparison of climate in prison as opposed to health service units would also provide an opportunity to test the hypothesis (above) that environmental support for engagement is likely to be lower in prison settings. Therapeutic climate is a dynamic rather than a static factor and likely to change over time, thus a measure such as EssenCES could be used as a dependent measure in pre–post comparisons for service changes or initiatives to improve engagement in treatment in PDO or other groups. Initiatives may take the form of increased staff training, changes in unit philosophies and methods of working or even improvements in the physical design and layout of buildings.

Assessing MORM characteristics in a personality disordered offender population

The Multifactor Offender Readiness Model (MORM) provides a useful framework for conceptualising and classifying potential impediments to engagement and has influenced recent studies with offender populations, where psychometric measures have been developed derived in part from the MORM (see Chapter 5). An alternative approach, particularly suited to assessing long-stay personality disordered offenders in clinical health settings, is to use routinely collected clinical interview material (often extensively available in such intensive services) to classify reasons proffered by patients themselves as to reasons for not engaging in or failing to complete treatment. In a recent preliminary study of this sort Sheldon, Howells and Patel (submitted) studied clinical interview material in this way and devised a brief manual based on the MORM to be used by raters. In this case the patients were severely personality disordered and high-risk in-patients in a high security hospital. The rating system is shown below, adapted from Sheldon, Howells and Patel.

Multifactor Offender Readiness Rating Manual: internal and external factors

Internal readiness factors influencing treatment completion and engagement

Cognitive factors: These include appraisals and beliefs about the treatment on offer, for example its relevance and likely effectiveness, beliefs about the therapists, the criminal justice or health system and about self-efficacy (perceived ability to meet the requirements of the programme). *Examples*: 'I don't trust the staff'; 'You can't do treatment in places like this'; 'These programmes don't work'; 'It wouldn't be any use to me'; 'I will never get out so there is no point'; 'I struggle in groups'; 'It's too complicated'; 'I won't be able to do the homework' 'I am not attending because I don't like the other group members'. As the cognitive factor is likely to be a common one, we also indicated which of the following cognitive domains applied: (a) self-efficacy belief (b) negative staff evaluation (c) negative patient evaluation (d) negative programme evaluation (e) negative outcome expectation (f) negative system evaluation (of unit or forensic service).

Affective factors: This includes the level of general distress of the patient but also specific emotional reactions to previous offending that might lead to low engagement (for example, shame). Therefore, any statements indicating that emotional arousal, or its absence, has contributed to low engagement would be categorised as affective. *Examples*: 'I was in too much of a state'; 'He was overwhelmed with fear about telling others about his past'; 'I was too disturbed to be able to participate'; 'I felt too self-conscious to participate'; 'I am frightened of other participants and their reactions'. It is of note that some of the descriptions that would count as 'affective' may also qualify as 'cognitive' or 'behavioural'. For example, 'I couldn't cope' could reflect self-efficacy beliefs, emotion or a lack of group skills. In general, an emotional state must be indicated as an antecedent to drop-out: for example, sadness, fear, anger, distress, guilt, shame or their opposites.

Volitional factors: This comprises the personal goals being pursued by the patient, the location of offending behaviour within the goal system of the patient, that is, the functions it serves for them (see Daffern *et al.* 2007), the effectiveness of strategies for achieving personal goals and the congruence of personal goals with the explicit or implicit goals of the therapeutic programme being offered. Generally this would include any indication that a person is not engaging or dropping out because they have other priorities (other goals they are pursuing). Included in this category would be non-engagement or drop-out due to medico-legal reasons. *Examples*: 'Controlling my temper is not important in my life'; 'I don't want to improve myself'; 'All I want is to do time and not get into trouble'; 'I will be out in six months so there is no point in therapy', 'I have done therapy before and dealt with these problems'; 'His solicitor appears to have advised him not to cooperate in treatment, if he wants to get out of the unit quickly'.

Behavioural factors: This includes evaluations of their problem behaviours (for example, previous offending) as not actually being a problem, help-seeking behaviours and, importantly, the diverse behavioural and cognitive skills required to become engaged in the treatment programme on offer. *Examples*: 'I cannot talk in groups'; 'The homework is too tough'; 'I can't take criticism'.

Identity factors: This includes core values and beliefs that constitute the person's identity. Identity is closely related to how personal goals are prioritised and indicates the kind of life sought and, relatedly, the kind of person he or she would like to be. The important issue for readiness is that an individual's personal identity must allow for the possibility of change and of an offence-free lifestyle and is not based too strongly on being an offender. *Examples*: 'I am a villain, not a patient'; 'I am not someone with mental problems'; 'Men don't talk about feelings'; 'I am not the sort of person who does therapy'.

External readiness factors influencing treatment completion and engagement

Circumstances: Non-engagement or drop-out is attributed to some aspect of external circumstances. *Examples*: 'The facilitator (therapist) left the unit, without a replacement'; 'therapy clashed with urgent medical appointments'.

Location: Non-engagement is attributed to therapy not being available in the setting. *Example*: 'he moved to another ward, which made attending the programme impossible'.

Opportunity: Wishes to engage in treatment but the opportunity is not available. *Example*: 'accepted for violence group, but its not available till next year'.

Resources: Wishes to engage but attendance is impossible for resource reasons. *Example*: 'therapy was cancelled because a room was no longer available'.

Multi-disciplinary team (MDT) exclusion from therapy: This applies where a patient has been excluded from therapy as a result of an external decision. *Example*: 'Patient behaved inappropriately in therapy group', 'Failed to follow group rules'; 'Perceived by clinicians as having too many active treatments'.

Transfer to another facility: Patient is transferred to a prison/other forensic setting, making treatment continuation impossible.

Support: Perceived lack of encouragement and support from family, friends, fellow patients or staff. *Examples*: 'My father kept telling me not to participate'; 'Other people on the ward think this therapy is daft'.

Programme: Low engagement is perceived as caused by some deficit in the programme itself (more than within the patient). *Examples*: 'I am in the substance misuse programme, but I have never drunk alcohol or taken drugs'; 'This patient has brain damage and is unable to cope with DBT' (overlaps with Behavioural factors above).

The reasons for drop-out proved to be straightforward and reliable to rate, though some statements met the criteria for more than one category: for example, cognitive, affective, and volitional. Cognitive factors formed the most endorsed category, comprising negative beliefs as to self-efficacy ('I am terrified of failing again'); negative evaluations, particularly low trust, of therapy staff ('I am misled by the professionals who run the groups'); as well as negative evaluations of fellow therapy participants ('He will not go to Dialectical Behaviour Therapy any more as [another patient] is in that therapy and he does not want to spend time with him'). In this study external, situational factors were recorded, though less frequently than intrapersonal factors. Exclusion of the patient from the therapy by the responsible clinical team was a common external reason, often because of inappropriate or therapy-interfering behaviour in the therapy group by the patient.

An integrated multi-level strategy for improving readiness and engagement in a personality disordered offender service

Little is known, as yet, about what a multi-level and comprehensive approach might look like and how effective it might be, though this is the focus of a long-term project, funded by the National Institute of Health Research (CLAHRC) at the Institute of Mental Health at Nottingham University in the United Kingdom. It is proposed here that a prospective strategy might have the following components, reflecting the MORM model as applied at the individual, programme and organisational levels.

(a) Identify the extent and nature of the problem.

The first step in a strategy in a clinical service is clearly to establish what is the extent of engagement and non-engagement in the therapeutic programmes that are delivered. For this to occur there needs to be in place an auditing system to monitor engagement and non-engagement. It is the experience of the author that formal systems for recording and auditing engagement, including programme completion, are not universally present in services.

(b) Determine in what contexts non-engagement is evident.

Treatment programmes for personality disordered offenders may be multifaceted, including treatments focused on personality traits and disorder and also on associated patterns of offending such as sexual offending, violent offending or substance misuse-related offending (Hogue *et al.* 2007; Tennant and Howells 2010). In addition to these psychological therapies, services often include occupational, educational and other programmes intended to facilitate a 'good life' (Ward and Brown 2004). The question thus arises whether an individual's engagement pattern is consistent across these various therapeutic programmes. A simple correlation coefficient based on the association between rated levels of engagement for a group of patients in different therapy contexts is likely to be useful. Table 9.1 provides illustrative data of this sort for patients in a high-security unit for personality disordered offenders.

At a service level it is also desirable to establish which programme within the system is most problematic in terms of low engagement. A patient may have full engagement in occupational and educational programmes but show minimal participation in formal psychological therapies. Such information illuminates whether non-engagement has trait aspects or is situationally dependent. Evidence that engagement is good in one area but not in others may suggest hypotheses as to what programme features need to be present for engagement to occur and also promotes creative thinking as to how generalisation may be encouraged.

(c) Identify what form non-engagement takes

Non-engagement can take many forms, including refusal to attend sessions, failure to complete the required programme sessions ('drop-

Table 9.1 Engagement in therapy contexts

Ratings were highly positively correlated (rho, $p < 0.001$), suggesting that patients who engage well in one environment/activity tend to engage well in all contexts.

	Named nurse sessions	Day care	Therapy groups	Social learning groups	Individual counselling sessions
Named nurse sessions	–				
Day care/OT	.68	–			
Therapy groups	.73	.71	–		
Social learning groups	.63	.65	.65	–	
Individual sessions	.81	.80	.87	.67	–

Note: We would like to thank Dr Kerry Sheldon and Ms Gita Patel for their help in collecting this data.

out'), treatment-interfering behaviour within sessions, the breaking of therapy rules, failure to complete required therapeutic tasks, such as between-session homework, or failure to form a therapeutic alliance (Drieschner *et al.* 2004; Drieschner and Boomsma 2008).

(d) Work at the individual level

The assessment of the individual patient or offender in terms of intrapersonal factors relevant to readiness and engagement is a necessary part of any strategy. A range of possible assessment methods exist (see Chapter 5). The purpose of such an assessment is to inform a psychological formulation of the readiness and engagement needs of the individual. A theoretical framework or model, derived from previous studies, is necessary for devising a formulation, as is the case in formulating individuals' clinical problems themselves (Sturmey 2009). The MORM model (Ward *et al.* 2004b; Sheldon *et al.*, submitted) is an example of such a model, as discussed in earlier sections of this chapter.

The non-engagement of the person in therapy can be mapped and formulated in terms of such factors, to produce a *dynamic readiness profile*. For example, an individual's drop-out from treatment might be explained in terms of their negative self-efficacy beliefs ('I can't cope with the group treatment setting, I can't get the words out'), his perceived lack of support for engagement by significant others and his difficulties in trusting therapists ('they are out to humiliate me, not help me').

(e) Implement individual level interventions

Such a formulation and profile would directly suggest individualised intervention strategies. Clinical nursing staff, for example, might develop a programme to improve self-efficacy beliefs, either through cognitive therapy to shift what may be an inaccurate self-appraisal or by providing behavioural training to improve group therapy-related skills. Strategies to improve trust in staff are likely to be long term and to require the build-up of trust and a positive relationship through the positive interactions in the course of everyday life and experience of the general milieu, rather than a formal, time-limited 'therapy'. The shifting of unhelpful negative beliefs, in the setting of an institution or residential unit may require an interdisciplinary and consistent strategy, so that such beliefs are undermined through educational, occupational, nursing, social work, psychiatric and psychological staff, working in unison and with a shared understanding of what is to be targeted and achieved. Although an individualised, formulation-driven approach may be desirable, there is clearly also room for group interventions such as motivational interviewing (McMurran 2002) when it is congruent with the formulation made.

An individual-level and multidisciplinary formulation of engagement problems allows for creative, tailored approaches to enhancing engagement. A person who has never achieved any working alliance with a mental health professional, about whom they may be suspicious and hostile, may be enticed into an alliance through working productively on educational or other problems they themselves acknowledge (Jackson *et al*. 2010). Equally, an enthusiasm for music, art, cooking, sport or other occupational activities can form the first step on a path leading to positive relationships with staff and to the beginnings of engagement in formal psychological therapies. Developing readiness and engagement is a milieu task, rather than one addressed only in circumscribed therapy sessions (Burrowes and Needs 2009). The latter authors also draw attention to the importance of the 'catalyst for change'. The individual, the environment and the catalyst are likely to interact rather than be independent influences. A broad strategy would need to incorporate the situational factors identified by MORM and the barriers to change discussed by Burrowes and Needs (2009).

(f) Work at the programme level

Given the argument (above) that non-engagement may reflect the inappropriateness ('unreadiness') of the therapeutic programme for the individual, when the Responsivity principle has been violated, any strategy needs to involve scrutinising the therapeutic programmes being delivered. The critical question is whether the programme has been adequately adapted to meet the particular needs and characteristics of the personality disordered offender. There is a danger that treatment programmes for this population may fall between two stools, in that PDOs may differ from personality disordered people who do not offend but also differ from offenders who do not suffer from a personality disorder. The therapy programmes on offer have typically been derived either from generic treatments for personality disorder or from offence-focused (criminogenic) programmes (Hogue *et al*. 2007). How offence-focused programmes might need to be adapted has only recently begun to be addressed (Jones 2010; Sainsbury 2010). A strategy to improve readiness and engagement in a service would need to give priority to such programme factors. At a research level, there is a need to formally compare adapted and non-adapted interventions in terms of their relative effectiveness.

(g) Work at the institutional or organisational level

The prevailing culture, climate and *modus operandi* of a service would need to be addressed in a comprehensive strategy, or at least assessed to ensure that there are not factors present that might work against readiness and engagement. As suggested above, negative beliefs about treatment on the part of individual patients or offenders could reflect correspondingly negative beliefs on the part of clinicians and service managers, who may subscribe to views that such individuals are not treatable. Staff education is thus a potential strategy for positive change. Explicit and enthusiastic support for, and prioritising of, engagement in therapy at a policy level by senior clinicians and managers of the service is important, as is the clear identification and reinforcement of individuals (staff and patients) who are potential models for good practice. Therapeutic climate (above) needs to be routinely assessed and addressed when found to be deficient. Finally, the structural context of a service may be vitally important (how and why individuals are referred; relationship to funders and external stakeholders). Control over such factors may be limited, but a proper analysis and intervention strategy requires that these broader factors receive consideration.

In conclusion, dealing with problems related to low treatment readiness and engagement are fundamental and as yet largely unaddressed challenges for services for the personality disordered offender. The viability of and public and governmental support for innovative treatment programmes for PDOs within forensic mental health and criminal justice services will depend on our capacity for rigorous analysis and creative solutions for the problems identified in this chapter.

Part Three

Clinical and Therapeutic Approaches to Working with Low Levels of Readiness

Chapter 10

The modification of low readiness

In this book we have understood treatment readiness as the presence of characteristics (states or dispositions) within either the client or the therapeutic situation that are likely to promote engagement in therapy, and thereby are likely to enhance therapeutic change. According to this definition, behaviour change in relation to persistent offending behaviour requires the presence of certain internal and external readiness conditions. It follows from this that when working with those offenders who are assessed as 'not ready' to change (and who may have previously been regarded as 'resistant', 'untreatable' or 'challenging'), a useful starting point will be to identify those internal and external conditions that are required for engagement in a rehabilitation programme to occur, and then modify these as required. Given that our definition of readiness incorporates client, programme and setting factors, increasing readiness can occur by modifying any or all of these factors. In this chapter we discuss each of these in turn, and then review the evidence for one of the most widely used approaches to improving levels of offender motivation: motivational interviewing.

Modifying the setting

Making changes to the setting in which rehabilitation programmes are offered often requires medium- to long-term planning. Setting factors can include the physical and social environment in which programmes are offered, and these are often hard to influence. Such terms are used broadly to refer to the extent to which a particular unit or institution is likely to be conducive to therapeutic change. Investigations into the experiences of those who are held in secure facilities reveal that they typically experience a number of barriers to change in their environments, and express a range of concerns. These include a subjective sense of failure, powerlessness, and the impairment of social identity, concerns about surveillance and the over-regulation of their behaviour, and worries for their personal safety (Quirk and Lelliot 2002; Toch and Adams 2002; Zamble and Porporino 1990). Such experiences are likely to be particularly salient and intense for prisoners, given the additional constraints on their behaviour and actuality of close daily monitoring that is a defining feature of the correctional environment. In addition, the prevalence of aggression and self-harm in prisons suggests that concerns about personal safety may be well founded.

The most relevant body of scientific work for understanding, measuring and modifying negative therapeutic environments and milieux is that on social climate, pioneered and used for over 30 years by Rudolph Moos (Moos 1997) in a range of service settings, including health, mental health and correctional institutions. One of Moos's most important contributions has been the Ward Atmosphere Scale (available in different versions for different settings, including prisons), a 100-item scale that purports to measure ten aspects of the social climate of a unit or institution and is completed by staff and patients. In recent years, the Moos scales have been subject to a number of critiques (for an overview see Schalast *et al.* 2008; see also Chapter 9) identifying problems associated with outdated item content, the time and effort required for completion in disturbed and unmotivated populations, the length of the measures for repeated clinical use, the low internal consistency of some scales, and discrepancies between the scales and the factor structure of the measure. This has prompted new scales to be validated (Schalast *et al.* 2008) that allow for repeated administration such that changes in climate over time can be assessed. It is only then that the effects of any attempt to change the social climate of prison units can be judged. These might include, for example, using the sentence planning process to move offenders to less secure environments to receive programmes, or to promote the active involvement of prison officers in programmes as a means of developing a more therapeutic culture in which pro-social behaviour is both modelled and reinforced outside of the therapeutic session. Developing more treatment supportive settings through training staff in the value of programmes is another obvious way in which readiness might be improved.

There are also a number of organisational and administrative measures that might be used to modify the setting. For example, in relation to the timing of programmes, lower security prisoners or those nearing completion of their sentences might be given the option of attending community-based treatment programmes while on day leave. Systemic issues also appear to exert a great influence on treatment outcomes in community-based programmes. Day and Carson (2009) have observed that court referral and administration by correctional services to intervention programmes for domestically violent men, for example, often takes place after some time (sometimes up to a year or more) after the offence occurred. Such delays can cause offenders to question the relevance of programmes, leading some to claim that they no longer have the need to attend, or that they have a poor recollection of the circumstances of the offence. In addition, the powers to legally enforce an offender's programme attendance can at times be inconsistently applied by both the courts and probation and parole officers, and in many cases non-attendance leads to few (or lenient) statutory consequences. For offenders to be ready to receive community-based programmes they need to be aware that the criminal justice system is seeking particular outcomes from their attendance and participation, and that the consequences for non-attendance will be uniformly applied.

Modify the programme

Another option, and one that is identified most explicitly in the responsivity principle, is to modify the treatment or programme that is offered. This is discussed in Chapter 6 in relation to the treatment of violent offenders, and involves amending treatment methods and programme content such that it is better suited to the needs of the particular client group. This may be in terms of the literacy level required to participate meaningfully in the programme, or the cultural or gender appropriateness of the programme materials. Given that many offenders will arrive in rehabilitation programmes with low levels of readiness, it is particularly important that the content of early sessions is appropriate for these presentations. Of course, this is almost impossible to achieve in programmes that have rolling intakes (where new members join an existing group as they are referred), as is the case in many sexual offender and domestic violence programmes.

Modifying the programme may also involve changing structural components of the programme itself, such as the number of sessions offered. Some offenders may not be willing or indeed able to commit to a programme that lasts over a year (or a very intensive treatment such as that offered in therapeutic communities), but may be willing to engage in programmes that require less commitment.

Although readiness for treatment is likely to be reasonably consistent across most treatment modalities, there may be some occasions where readiness factors differ for different types of treatment. For example, it has been suggested that clients who have low levels of distress may be better suited to more prescriptive interventions (Beutler *et al*. 2000), while those clients who have high levels of distress or specific needs may be better suited to individual methods of delivery rather than group-based approaches. Different types of rehabilitation programme tend to adopt different approaches to the management of therapeutic engagement. The treatment of sexual offenders is relevant here, as it is relatively common for sexual offenders to enter treatment maintaining either that their offending did not happen or that it was not problematic. Low levels of problem recognition and motivation would in some programmes (such as in some substance-use programmes) exclude offenders from participation. In sexual offender treatment, however, denial, unless extreme, is not always grounds for exclusion (see Chapter 7). In our view, the early stages of these programmes should not be considered as treatment, but more as a preparatory stage of treatment where the primary task is to increase readiness. The way in which the programme is delivered and the extent to which programme facilitators are able to respond on a moment-by-moment basis to the changing needs of offenders will also be critical in both the successful formation and the maintenance of a strong therapeutic alliance (see Chapter 12). This is a skilled task, even in programmes that are predominantly psycho-educational in nature.

Theories of behaviour change offer useful frameworks for guiding decisions about the appropriateness of particular approaches for individuals who are at different points in the process of changing their behaviour. Although a number of models of how therapeutic change occurs have been developed, the transtheoretical model of change (TTM) is probably the mostly widely researched and clinically useful models of behaviour change that exists. The TTM suggests that problem resolution typically occurs following a progression through a sequence of change stages, each one characterised by different attitudes, thoughts, beliefs and values. The individual typically experiences a growing awareness of the problem, formulates a decision to do something differently, develops change strategies while in a transitional phase, and finally implements those strategies (see Casey et al. 2005).

The key organising construct of the TMM is the notion of stages (Velicer et al. 1998). Irrespective of whether someone is in or outside formal treatment (and for virtually any type of problem behaviour), behaviour change is thought to occur in a series of six identifiable stages: precontemplation (no wish to change/no recognition of a problem); contemplation (intention to change problem behaviour within the next six months); preparation (intention to take immediate action, usually measured as within the next month); action (characterised by specific, overt modifications within the past six months); maintenance (relapse prevention); and termination (change process is complete/no further need to prevent relapse). Optimal progress through each stage is achieved via different processes of change (which may be either overt or covert).[1] The term 'process' refers to what an individual does to bring about change in affect, behaviour, cognitions or relationships (Prochaska et al. 1988). According to Prochaska and DiClemente (1986), therapeutic interventions should be guided by the processes deemed most appropriate to a particular stage, to ensure progression from one stage to the next.

The Levels of Change dimension of the TTM integrates the various processes and stages of change within the context of five interrelated but distinct levels of psychological problems that can be addressed in treatment: symptom/situational problems; maladaptive cognitions; current interpersonal conflicts; family system conflicts; and intrapersonal conflicts (Prochaska and DiClemente 1984, 1992). Again this is useful in terms of how to modify programmes when offenders present with low levels of readiness as it helps to place the level at which different interventions are offered, and draw attention to areas that may be overlooked (for example, programme content may focus too heavily on maladaptive thinking styles, and underestimate the influence of family systems on behaviour change). Adopting a transtheoretical approach also requires that both therapist and client

[1]Ten processes have received the greatest empirical support in the literature (Prochaska and DiClemente 1983; Prochaska et al. 1988). Of these processes, five are experiential (consciousness raising, dramatic relief, environmental re-evaluation, social liberation, and self re-evaluation), and five are behavioural (stimulus control, helping relationships, counter-conditioning, reinforcement management, and self-liberation).

agree (at least implicitly) about which level an identified problem will be attributed to, and at which level both client and therapist will work to change the problem behaviour. According to Prochaska and DiClemente (1986), the trend in psychological therapies has been to attribute psychological problems to one or two levels, with intervention subsequently focused on these levels (for example, behaviourists focus on the symptom and situational determinants, cognitive therapists on maladaptive cognitions, family therapists at the family/systems level, and psychoanalytic therapists focus on intrapersonal conflicts).

The assimilation model (AM) (Stiles *et al.* 1991; Stiles 2000) is an alternative model of problem resolution, developed primarily on the basis of observations made across a series of intensive psychotherapy case studies. According to this model, 'therapeutic progress consists of the assimilation of problematic experiences into the client's schemata' (Honos-Webb and Stiles 2002: 407). The model describes the likely needs of an individual client at each stage of assimilation. For example, at Stages 0–2 the problematic experience is largely outside of the client's consciousness. Stages 3–4 are characterised by an ability to acknowledge the existence of the problem and to being able to communicate a clear statement of the problem, and stages 5–7 represent stages in which the problem is solved and mastered. In addition, the assimilation model suggests that as individuals pass through the stages of assimilation, they experience a corresponding sequence of emotional reactions, with psychological distress increasing as a function of problem awareness (stages 0–3) and then decreasing with problem clarification, solving and solution (stages 4–7) (Stiles *et al.* 1991).

A particularly important idea in both the transtheoretical and assimilation models is that interventions should be matched to the individual's stage of change. The term 'matching' is commonly used to describe strategies that tailor treatment to clients' baseline characteristics, whereas the term 'adaptive' is commonly used for strategies that continually readjust the interventions during the course of treatment (see Marlowe *et al.* 2007). It follows that the early modules of the rehabilitation programmes should reflect content that aims to increase both self-awareness and problem awareness in ways that may be particularly appropriate for those participants in the earlier stages of change. It is important that facilitators also attend to the needs of those in the later stages, who may benefit from more skills-based approaches. Thus, an individual who is pre-contemplating change might be assisted to develop greater insight into his or her offending and encouraged to think carefully about any decision to (or not to) change. The notion that client needs can change over time suggests that different therapeutic tasks for clients may be required. For example, the therapeutic task for clients at the early stages of assimilation is to increase problem awareness. Low problem awareness is another way of describing what has been referred to as 'denial', although this term can have different meanings, ranging from denial of guilt, denial of responsibility, denial of victim impact, and so on.

It also suggests that both programme content and delivery styles should reflect these needs. For example, problem awareness exercises, such as victim impact work, and more experiential methods of delivery (such as role play and group discussion) may be most valuable in the earlier stages of a programme. As the problem enters awareness, the requirement then moves to facilitating emotional expression. Once the problem has been recognised (from stage 3 onwards), the task is to develop a clearer understanding of the onset, development and maintenance of the problem, before working actively towards solution. Thus, it is suggested that an appropriate therapeutic response is one that meets client requirements at a given stage of assimilation, such that the offender progresses to the next stage of change.

Modifying the offender

For practitioners, attempting to modify the individual client often represents the most realistic and achievable way of changing levels of treatment readiness. Those offender characteristics most closely associated with readiness fall into three domains: the cognitive, the affective, and the behavioural. There are a number of different ways in which these individual low readiness factors can be addressed, and indeed many of the approaches and interventions described below (and elsewhere in this book) are already used informally in rehabilitation programmes. Less commonly, however, are they conceptualised and delivered in relation to the need to improve pre-programme levels of treatment readiness.

Responding to feelings of coercion

Howells and Day (2003) have suggested that for therapeutic goals to be realised, client personal goals need to be constituted by, supportive of, or consistent with, the therapeutic goal. This is a theme of Chapters 3 and 10 of this book. Therapeutic change, therefore, involves the therapist examining the goals that the client is pursuing, how these goals are organised, and how they are being regulated or mis-regulated (Karoly 1999). Karoly (1993) further stresses the need to examine treatment targets in the context of broader client goals and the motivational salience of change. He suggests, also, that 'therapeutic failures of various kinds (premature termination, resistance, relapse etc) can result from the therapist-assessor's failure to appreciate the structural relation between time-limited treatment goals and life goals in general' (1993: 279).

Given that many clients may not, at least in the early stages of intervention, have personal goals that are consistent with programme goals (that is, community safety), or have goals that are incompatible with programme goals (for example, to fulfil the obligations of the order rather than change behaviour), it is perhaps unsurprising that programme facilitators commonly find difficulties in engaging clients in a change process, and often report encountering hostility, resistance and difficulties in engaging men in therapeutic change. Barber (1991) has discussed case work with the 'involuntary client' from a social work perspective, making the following observation:

> Work with involuntary clients must begin with the recognition that the interaction between the worker and client is based on *conflict* rather than co-operation, that social work with involuntary clients is a *political*, not a therapeutic, process involving the socially sanctioned use of power. The political nature of this activity becomes obvious when one calls to mind what it means to be an involuntary client in the first place. (Barber 1991: 45)

He goes on to note that the 'ultimate beneficiary of the work done will be those who in some way suffered from the client's aberrant behaviour in the first place' (1991: 45). Thus for Barber at least the role of the worker is to negotiate a settlement between the client and society at large, and it is important that the client is aware of this from the very outset of any intervention. Barber proposed a six-step model of what he termed 'negotiated casework' (see Table 10.1 below). An advantage of this approach is that it clarifies both the goals of the programme and the responsibilities of the practitioner to other agencies, particularly in regard to reporting or evaluating clients for legal purposes.

Table 10.1 Negotiated casework

Steps	Description
1 Clear the air.	Begin by directing attention to the order that led to the meetings. Read out a copy of the court order, and elicit client perspectives.
2 Identify legitimate client interests.	Attend to any objections to engagement in treatment and the goals of the client.
3 Identify non-negotiable aspects of intervention.	Clarify which aspects cannot be compromised and the reporting requirements (e.g. attendance).
4 Identify negotiable aspects of intervention.	Define the problem and identify possibilities for change.
5 Negotiate the case plan.	The aim here is to make decisions about the way forward, identifying goals and responsibilities.
6 Agree on criteria for progress.	Clarify how judgements will be made about whether the case plan is working or not, and what happens if the client fails to comply with aspects of the case plan.

Source: Adapted from Barber (1991).

We have suggested elsewhere in this book (Chapter 2) that coercing offenders into attending rehabilitation programmes (or placing legal pressure on them to attend) is unlikely in itself to lead to poorer outcomes. Rather, we suggest, it is the perception of coercion that will determine how an offender approaches treatment. Even when offenders perceive they are being coerced, it also seems likely that pre-treatment anti-therapeutic attitudes can change over the course of a programme, such that therapeutic gains (risk reduction) can occur. That is not to say, however, that the needs of those who perceive coercion are the same as those who do not. Engaging coerced clients in treatment is a task that requires great therapeutic skill. Offenders who feel coerced may arrive in treatment with high levels of antipathy towards both programmes and programme providers. The way in which therapists respond to this hostility is likely to be a critical factor in whether perceptions of coercion dissipate over time. In these circumstances, treatment engagement can be enhanced through the provision of accurate information about an individual's legal obligations and consequences of non-participation, as well as by acknowledging explicitly the extent to which the therapist is working for the community as well as for the individual. Offenders in rehabilitation correctly perceive that pressure is exerted to make them engage in programmes but also seem to accept such pressure as 'fair' when it is made clear that it is their decision to accept or refuse treatment (Rigg 2002). Reducing the reality and the perception of excessive and 'unfair' coercion should be an important objective in rehabilitation, for both ethical and practical reasons. Similarly, Cosyns (1999) argues that to maximise treatment efficacy in situations of coercion, an agreement of mutual trust and common goals should exist between the therapist and coercing party. Both parties should hold the client's best interests paramount. It seems that emphasising the negative consequences of non-participation, threatening, and using other forms of coercion such as close monitoring and severe penalties are likely to be less effective than providing accurate and honest information about an offender's circumstances[2] (Maxwell 2000; Young 2002).

There has been much less discussion of the possible role of positive reinforcement for attending treatment, although the introduction of treatment-oriented diversion programmes for mentally disordered and/or substance-using offenders represents a significant development in this area (Murphy 2000). Potentially, there are a number of ways that programme providers in correctional settings can offer incentives for participation. For example, these may include offering salaries to those who attend programmes that are equivalent or greater to those offered at prison workplaces, or additional visits from family and friends.

Those offenders for whom programme participation is highly aversive may need to be treated differently. It would seem untherapeutic at best, and unethical at worst, to enforce a treatment that was likely to traumatise a client, and it seems unlikely that these clients would benefit from the treatment. There is little point in enforcing treatment that is not going to work, and endorsing such an approach would seem to use psychological treatment as a form of punishment. For the majority of offenders who feel coerced into treatment, however, we would argue that interventions to improve treatment readiness are likely to be helpful.

[2]Coercion is distinguished from pressure partly by its exclusive focus on negative consequences or punishment as a means of ensuring compliance.

Problem recognition and motivation to change are important conditions of treatment readiness (see Ward *et al.* 2004b) and interventions such as motivational interviewing (see below) are thought to be useful in improving motivation to attend treatment. Exposure to group treatment in the form of less intensive psycho-educational programmes may also help to allay anxiety in those who are particularly apprehensive about treatment. Similarly, particularly distressed offenders may benefit from learning some life skills in a less coercive 'offence-related' programme prior to participation in 'offence-specific' programmes.

Cognitive factors

We have argued that in the cognitive domain, some degree of problem recognition is likely to be an important readiness factor, along with confidence in the types of programmes and services provided. In Chapter 5 we noted that violent offenders have often been regarded as 'resistant' and unsuitable for treatment, mainly because of their tendency to deny or minimise their abusive behaviour. Instead, they tend to blame others for their problems or justify their use of violence as a reasonable response to provocation. Violent offenders can also be extremely mistrustful, paranoid and suspicious of entering into a therapeutic relationship where they fear they may be perceived as vulnerable. Such negative attitudes and beliefs are likely to impede their readiness to engage in programmes and offenders need to be given feedback that their hostility, while understandable, is inappropriate (see Chambers *et al.* 2008). Negative attitudes about programmes and/or programme providers may be able to be addressed through giving offenders access to information about what programmes actually involve (through videos or even documentary film), or contact with other offenders who have previously participated successfully in the programme.

Affective factors

In the affective domain, some level of general distress (including anxiety and depression, guilt or remorse) is commonly identified as a potentially important readiness factor. One implication of the work described in Chapter 3 is that there is a need for rehabilitation programme providers to pay attention to the assessment and modification of the affective states of their clients if they are to be successfully treated. While this may seem obvious to mental health practitioners where the focus is on the individual well-being of the client, it may be less so for those working in correctional settings who are aware of the empirical evidence that psychological discomfort per se and anxiety are unlikely to be risk factors for reoffending (Bonta 1997), and thus not appropriate targets for intervention. Individualised assessments, such as those proposed by Daffern and Howells (2002) are, in our view, necessary to help determine not only the initial treatment needs of the offender (and the extent to which these differ from identified criminogenic needs) but also guide decisions about the composition of treatment groups.

For some, specific interventions to improve treatment readiness, such as motivational interviewing (see below) may be particularly helpful in reducing anxiety about programme participation. Day, Tucker and Howells (2004) also suggest that exposure to group treatment in the form of less intensive psycho-educational programmes may also help to allay anxiety in those who are particularly apprehensive about treatment. Victim awareness programmes (see Day *et al.*, in press) may serve to increase levels of remorse and guilt, such that offenders are more motivated to seek help to address the causes of their offending behaviour. Other offenders may need to learn how to recognise and respond appropriately to their emotional states. For those who experience too much negative affect, mental health interventions (including pharmacotherapy and counselling) may help an offender contain high levels of arousal to a level that he or she can still engage in treatment. Peer education and mentoring schemes, or access to other services (such as the chaplaincy or culturally-based groups) can also be important here as they have the potential to improve levels of social support and thereby encourage a person to engage in and sustain treatment over time.

Many rehabilitation programmes respond to anxiety about participation by starting with an extensive discussion about the limits of confidentiality and the agreeing of group rules that are likely to facilitate disclosure. It is, however, the skills of the facilitators in developing a safe environment that are likely to be the most influential. While facilitator authenticity (including such things as directness, acceptance, empathy, respect, self-disclosure, non-judgemental attitude) is likely to be important in overcoming client resistance (Milgram and Rubin 1992), it is also apparent that some clients will have greater problems in trusting the facilitator and the group process than others and this will require a higher level of skill from the facilitator.

Low motivation

Low motivation may be addressed using problem recognition and decision-making techniques often used in motivational interviewing (Miller and Rollnick 1991). Motivational interviewing (MI) has also been designed to offer clients a relatively safe and non-threatening introduction to therapy, such that any anxieties about entering treatment are allayed. Hemphill and Hart (2002) have discussed ways of working with psychopathic offenders to increase their motivation. They identify four motivational strengths of psychopaths, associated with a need to feel superior to others, a desire for and tolerance of novelty, good interpersonal skills, and a desire to be in control. They propose, among other things, that interventions that suggest that criminal lifestyles have low status, that help offenders feel in control of their treatment and emphasise self-sufficiency, can all help to motivate the psychopathic offender to engage in treatment.

Brief interventions are often used to increase readiness to change and strengthen self-efficacy (McMurran 2002). There are two characteristics of a brief intervention that exert the greatest influence on readiness to change: the therapeutic style of the programme staff; and the extent to which the client receives personal feedback. Motivational interviewing is one example of a brief treatment approach that is used to increase problem recognition and the probability of treatment entry. MI has been described as 'a client-centered, directive method for enhancing intrinsic motivation to change by exploring and resolving ambivalence' (Miller and Rollnick 2002: 25). This form of intervention is a collaborative method where the therapist finds the potential for change within the client, and facilitates the change process. It thus has the potential to enhance engagement, reduce reactance and increase readiness for treatment.

Motivational interviewing generally involves some discussion regarding the arguments for and against the individual changing their substance-use behaviour (decisional balance), feedback about the risks and benefits of continued substance use, and a description of the available treatment options (see Table 10.2). Brief interventions based on MI typically involve examining the costs and benefits of change, identifying high-risk situations associated with substance use, discussing life goals and how substance use affects these, and learning about the stages of change concept. MI is thought to be particularly useful at the beginning of treatment, providing the foundations of a level of motivation to engage in therapy and change.

Table 10.2 Motivational interviewing

Component	Description
Express empathy	A crucial attitude for therapists to exhibit when working with violent offenders is one of acceptance. This does not mean agreement or approval of their anti-social attitudes or behaviours or labelling the offender as, for example, anti-social or deviant. Instead, skilful, respectful and reflective listening to the offender, with an expressed desire to understand him/her, is crucial. It is important for the therapist to understand that an offender's ambivalence is normal and the therapist should demonstrate an understanding of the client's perspective. Acceptance and respect help to build a working therapeutic alliance, and support the client's self-esteem and self-efficacy, which is an important condition for readiness and motivation to change.
Develop discrepancy	This refers to building a discrepancy between the target behaviour (e.g. violent offending behaviour) and the individual's values, beliefs and goals. With MI the therapist has the opportunity to change the client's perceptions of discrepancy without creating a feeling of being pressured or coerced. It is important for the therapist to clarify important goals for the offender and to explore the consequences of the client's past and potential violent behaviour. When this technique is successful the client rather than the therapist presents the reasons for change.
Avoid argumentation	Any arguments from the therapist in response to the offender's denial or resistance are counter-productive. The therapist should be mindful that an argument can breed defensiveness, and resistance from an offender should be seen as a signal to change strategies. Clearly, if dis-agreements can be resolved, not only will appropriate behaviour be modelled, but also efficacy can be gained through the therapeutic process.

Table 10.2 continues opposite

Table 10.2 continued

Component	Description
Roll with resistance	Therapists need to remain non-defensive and calm when faced with a hostile and resistant offender and avoid confrontation. In managing hostile clients it is important not to oppose the resistance but to understand it, learn its directions and move with its tensions. If resistance does emerge, the therapist should help the offender to shift his/her perceptions by reframing his/her cognitive distortions to create a new momentum towards change. It is important for the therapist to empower the offender to find solutions to his/her own problems and elicit self-motivational statements.
Support self-efficacy	The therapist encourages the offender to believe that she/he has the ability to change. The offender is motivated to take responsibility for choosing and undertaking personal change. The therapist should be affirming of the offender's strengths, which develops the sense of self-efficacy, an important foundation for sustaining change. The therapist should emphasise the value of choice – offenders are more likely to be committed to a freely chosen course of action, such as readiness to engage in therapy, rather than when they feel they have been coerced or pressured to do so.

Source: Adapted from Miller and Rollnick (2002).

This is especially pertinent with offenders, for whom engagement in change is often difficult to achieve.

The efficacy of motivational interviewing has been subjected to two recent meta-analytic reviews (see Burke *et al.* 2003; Hettema *et al.* 2005). Studies reviewed in both meta-analyses were all randomised control studies which, in addition to the random assignment of participants to treatment and control groups, included (a) at least one group or individual intervention with components of MI,[3] (b) at

[3]The research literature indicates that the most widely used MI approach is one where the client is given feedback based on individual assessment

least one control condition or comparison group, and (c) adequate measurement pertaining to pertinent target areas. In the Burke *et al.* (2003) meta-analysis, adaptations of motivational interviewing (AMIs) across a range of problem areas (alcohol problems, drug addiction, smoking cessation, diet and exercise, HIV-risk behaviours) were examined. Twenty of the 30 controlled clinical trials were related to substance misuse (alcohol and drugs). Similarly, of the 72 clinical trials reviewed by Hettema *et al.*, 31 related to alcohol abuse and 14 to drug abuse (62.5 per cent of the total studies).

While the major findings in the Burke *et al.* (2003) meta-analysis were mixed, there were nonetheless positive indicators in support of the use of MI as a brief intervention strategy. For example, AMIs were found to be significantly more effective than either no-treatment or control conditions, with medium effect sizes for drug addiction ($d = .56$) and small to medium for alcohol ($d = .25$ to $.53$), depending on the target measure used. This contrasts with the near zero effect ($d = .02$) for AMIs when compared to other active treatment modalities, although it should be noted that AMIs achieved these same results in substantially fewer treatment sessions (approximately three to four). In this respect, AMIs could be considered a more cost-effective approach than, for example, cognitive behavioural therapy with this client group. In terms of sustained efficacy, those studies with a sufficiently long follow-up period ($N = 9$) showed that the effect size at 20 weeks ($d = .13$) was comparable to the average effect size of 67 weeks ($d = .11$). In other words, irrespective of the comparison group (alternative treatment modality, no treatment, or control), the effects of AMIs did not reduce significantly over time. Clinical impact was also promising, with 51 per cent of clients who received AMI for drug and alcohol problems ($N = 7$ studies) showing either improvements or abstinence on measures taken between four weeks and four years post-treatment. In fact, 54 per cent of clients who receive a single (stand alone) AMI intervention showed noticeable improvement, while 43 per cent of AMIs used as a prelude to further

using standardised measures of drug or alcohol use. This feedback relates to the level of severity on the target symptom as compared to population norms, and is delivered in an MI style, and includes elicitation from the client of possibilities for change, all of which is done in a non-threatening manner. This feedback approach is considered an adaptation of MI (AMI), as the process includes more than just MI. The term AMI can thus be applied to interventions incorporating additional MI techniques, but which maintain the core MI principles (see Burke *et al.* 2003: 844).

treatment also improved. By comparison, significantly fewer clients improved or abstained from drug or alcohol without treatment (38 per cent) or with treatment as usual (35 per cent). This translates to an improvement in client success rates from one-third to one-half following AMI, or the doubling of abstinence rates from one in five to two in five. Finally, AMIs were found to have the same level of effect on social impact measures ($d = .47$) as target symptoms, indicating the positive consequences of treatment for a broad range of important life problems beyond substance-related symptoms.

A particularly important implication of the Burke *et al.* (2003) meta-analysis is the indication that AMIs may in fact be most efficacious as treatment preludes. The researchers point out while 'it is rare that a treatment can be efficacious both as a stand-alone treatment and as a treatment used adjunctively to enhance the efficacy of a variety of other treatments' (2003: 858), their results indicated that this was the case for the AMIs. And while they acknowledge that more detailed research is necessary, it would also seem that the feedback component may be more critical to the success of AMIs than the motivational interviewing *per se*.

In the majority of studies reviewed by Hettema *et al.* (2005), MI was seldom used alone but more often in combination with either feedback or some other form of treatment (such as education, self-help manuals, relapse prevention, cognitive therapy, skills training, Alcoholics Anonymous, stress management). The duration of interventions ranged between 15 minutes and 12 hours (average dose about two sessions; $M = 2.24$ hours, $SD = 2.15$), and in the vast majority of studies (74 per cent), interventions had been standardised by either a manual or specific training. Consistent with other systematic reviews, Hettema *et al.* found considerable variability in effect sizes across studies, even for those within specific problem areas (for example, the observed effects in alcohol studies ranged from $d_c = 0$ to more than 3.0[4]). What this suggests is that despite using the same treatment modality with the same target population, different effects were obtained across both sites and across populations. The implication here is that variation in MI delivery can substantially impact on outcome.

Another observation made by the researchers, and one that is inconsistent with the findings of Burke *et al.* (2003), was the tendency for MI trends to diminish over time. The combined effects across all

[4]An effect size of $d_c = 1$ represents a between-group difference of one standard deviation.

studies showed that whereas d_c = .77 at the 0 to one month point post-treatment, it was reduced to .39 at > 3 to 6 months, .30 at > 6 to 12 months, and .11 at follow-ups longer than 12 months. The exception to this finding was in studies where the additive effect of MI was assessed (where MI is used at the commencement of a standardised or specialised treatment). In these studies, the effect of MI in terms of improved outcome was either maintained or increased over time, generally remaining in the vicinity of d_c = .60. Across all problem domains, the Hettema *et al.* (2005) meta-analysis found the strongest support for MI efficacy was in the area of substance use. The mean effect size across 32 trials which focused on alcohol abuse was .41 at post-treatment and .26 across all follow-up points (range −.08 to 3.07), with the largest effect sizes (all > .70) reported in studies which compared MI with either (a) a no treatment condition, wait-list controls, or education, or (b) adding MI to standard treatment. Where MI was used to treat illicit drug use, the effect sizes ranged from 0 to 1.81, with effects sizes on average being larger at early rather than later follow-up (.51 versus .29).

McMurran (2009a) has recently prepared a review of MI with offenders, identifying a total of 13 outcome studies with offenders and six dissertations. Most of these (N = 10) studies had been conducted with substance-using offenders. Although there were marked variations across studies, the conclusion of the review was that MI can lead to improved retention in treatment, motivation to change and reduced offending, although McMurran notes the importance of maintaining the integrity of treatment. Thus, although MI with offenders probably falls short of fulfilling the criteria for an evidence-based intervention, it is an approach that is likely to be particularly appropriate for use with many offender groups, especially when integrity is increased through the application of practice guidelines.

Conclusion

In this chapter we have discussed some of the ways in which low levels of treatment readiness might be modified. This includes modifying the setting, the programme, and the individual offender. A number of different approaches are described as having potential, although few empirical studies have examined the effectiveness of different approaches. Motivational interviewing is one intervention that has attracted the most attention from researchers, and there is some evidence to support its efficacy with offenders. If attention can also be paid to the environments in which programmes are offered and the match between the needs of individual participants and programme content and structure, then it is likely that low levels of readiness can be successfully modified such that offenders are both willing and able to participate in programmes that seek to address the causes of their offending.

Chapter 11

Goal-focused interventions with offenders

Mary McMurran

Treatment to reduce the likelihood of reoffending operates through requiring offenders to make a range of personal changes, including changing ways of thinking, communicating, behaving and socialising. Motivating offenders to make these relevant personal changes and enabling them to sustain these changes are core aspects of clinical practice. Goal perspectives have proven useful in conceptualising motivation for behaviour in general and change in therapy in particular. This approach also has application in conceptualising motivation for change in offenders. In this chapter, the focus is on goals as a motivational construct and the methods by which offenders may be encouraged to set and pursue pro-social goals.

Goal perspectives

In evolutionary terms, goals are specific representations of what is needed for survival. Maslow (1943) proposed a hierarchy of needs from basic physiological needs (oxygen, food, water), through higher order needs for safety, belonging, esteem and self-actualisation. More recently, researchers have focused on psychological rather than physiological needs, identifying primary needs for autonomy, competence, relatedness, self-transcendence and spirituality (Deci and Ryan 2000; Emmons 2005). Deci and Ryan (2000) define these as 'innate organismic necessities', as opposed to acquired motivations, and say that these needs must be fulfilled for optimal health, well-being and interpersonal functioning.

Innate needs are satisfied through the pursuit of specific goals, which are the 'consciously accessible and personally meaningful objectives that people pursue in their daily lives' (Emmons 2005: 732). As Deci and Ryan (2000) point out, innate needs are what give specific goals their potency and they are important to understanding goal choice, pursuit and attainment. Karoly (1993) defined goals as 'states toward which people intentionally aspire and actively work to bring about (or to avoid)' (1993: 274). Goals are action-oriented and the person strives to attain an identifiable end point. These end points may be of many different types and levels, for instance losing weight, passing an exam, being patient with one's children, and being a kind person. Goals are not stable or static and the effort put into achieving goals is variable, making goals a useful motivational construct (Karoly 1993, 1999).

Emmons (2005) holds goals as central to human functioning. Goals are the concrete expression of a person's life purpose, they represent how people structure their lives, and striving towards worthwhile goals is a key determinant of human health and happiness. In short, a person's goals are synonymous with meaning in life, since they are the route by which the individual fulfils his or her needs for competence, relatedness, self-transcendence and spirituality. Goal strivings or personal concerns have been identified as the middle of three units of personality, where the first is basic tendencies (what one has), the middle is goal strivings (what one does), and the third is personal narratives (who one is) (McAdams 1995).

Goal-based psychological therapies focus upon a person's life goals and goal strivings, attending to the number, range and content of goals a person may be pursuing, the attainability of the goals, the likelihood of satisfaction from goal attainment, and whether goals conflict or cohere (Michalak and Grosse Holtforth 2006). The first step in this therapeutic approach is to define and identify life goals.

Assessing human goals

One theory of motivation in which goal-striving plays a central role is the Theory of Current Concerns, developed originally to understand problem drinking (Klinger and Cox 2004a). In the Theory of Current Concerns, goal pursuit is referred to as a 'current concern', which is a time-limited process initiated when a person becomes committed to a goal and ending when a goal pursuit is terminated.

Cox and Klinger (2004b) identified 11 life areas in which most people aim for satisfaction through goal-setting and striving: (1) home and household matters; (2) employment and finances; (3) partner, family and relatives; (4) friends and acquaintances; (5) love, intimacy and sexual matters; (6) self changes; (7) education and training; (8) health and medical matters; (9) substance use; (10) spiritual matters; and (11) hobbies, pastimes and recreation. These life areas are highly similar to the 'primary human goods' (valued aspects of human functioning and living) identified in Ward and colleagues' Good Lives Model of offender rehabilitation (see Chapter 3; Ward and Brown 2004; Ward and Stewart 2003). The Good Lives Model has as its underlying principle that offenders, like all human beings, seek satisfaction in certain life areas that contain the essential ingredients of human well-being. While we all seek satisfaction in these areas, Ward and colleagues suggest that the offender does so in problematic or distorted ways. The challenge of offender rehabilitation is to encourage offenders to pursue goals that reduce risk and goals that build up a positive, non-criminal identity that helps sustain socially acceptable behaviour (Ward *et al.* 2007).

Focusing on the life areas, Cox and Klinger (Cox and Klinger 2002; Klinger and Cox 2004b) developed the Personal Concerns Inventory, which is an assessment of current concerns along with a number of appraisal dimensions. Respondents are asked to identify their goals in each of the life areas and then rate each goal on a number of scales tapping goal value and likely attainability. We used this assessment procedure with a sample of 129 adult male prisoners to identify their life goals (McMurran *et al.* 2008c). These men identified goals consistent with those treatment targets identified in the risk–needs–responsivity model of offender rehabilitation as likely to reduce reoffending (Andrews and Bonta 2003). They said that they wanted to stop offending, and were aware that to do this they needed to be self-controlled, find and keep jobs, have stable accommodation, quit drink and drugs, change support networks, and find new leisure pursuits. In short, prisoners seem to *want* what professionals think they *need* in rehabilitation. Furthermore, consistent with the Good Lives Model, prisoners expressed life-enhancing goals, such as wanting a better lifestyle, gaining work experience, having good family relationships, gaining skills, and getting fit and healthy. These aspirations translate into approach goals that are likely to provide the rewards that sustain a person in persisting with goals related to risk reduction. So, without being too naive about the possibility that prisoners' responses were coloured by the demands of the situation, it seems that goal-based approaches may be useful in offender rehabilitation.

The question that arises here is, if prisoners have these positive goals, why do they not manage to pursue them successfully? People may have innate tendencies to strive for intrinsically satisfying goals, but these tendencies flourish only where there are supportive conditions (Ryan and Deci 2000). Social exclusion may undermine intrinsic motivation in that some individuals do not have the wherewithal or the opportunities to pursue positive life goals (Bonner 2006). Disadvantage may have been life-long, deriving from family poverty, disadvantaged neighbourhoods, or poor educational opportunities. Alternatively, disadvantage may be a consequence of crime, which often leads to reduced employability, unstable living arrangements and disrupted family and social networks. These problems define poor human and social capital, meaning a lack of resources that people can use to achieve their goals (Farrall 2004). Social changes need to be made to help offenders commit to and realise pro-social goals; however, in this chapter the primary focus is on individual aspects of goal choice and pursuit.

Motivational structure

The Personal Concerns Inventory (PCI) has been used to investigate motivational structure (Cox et al. 2000, 2002). Respondents rate their identified goals on a number of dimensions, including importance, commitment, achievability, likelihood of attainment, control over attainment, imminence of attainment, and happiness resulting from attainment. Analysis of these ratings revealed two factors: (1) an adaptive motivation factor, characterised by high perceived likelihood of goal attainment, expected happiness when goals are attained, and commitment to goal striving; and (2) a maladaptive motivation factor, characterised by rating goals low in importance, expecting no great amount of happiness at goal achievement, and having low commitment to goals. In substance misusing samples, the adaptive factor has been shown as inversely predictive of quantities of alcohol consumption (Cox et al. 2002) and positively predictive of readiness to change (Cox et al. 2000). This suggests that there may be value in developing this assessment for use with offenders.

Scores on the PCI from 129 male prisoners replicated the two original factors: adaptive motivation and maladaptive motivation (Sellen et al. 2009). The replication of these two factors suggests that offenders' motivational structure is similar to that of other populations. An index of adaptive motivation calculated from ratings correlated positively with self-reported internal reasons for entering programmes. An index of maladaptive motivation correlated positively with being in the pre-contemplation stage of change as assessed by the University of Rhode Island Change Assessment (URICA) (McConnaughy *et al.* 1983, 1989) and negatively with staff ratings of motivation for and compliance with treatment. Additionally, some modest changes in motivational structure were observed after the completion of treatment programmes, with improved adaptive motivation scores and reduced maladaptive motivation scores.

In the process of conducting our research on the PCI, we noticed that the process of identifying and rating goals was well received by prisoners. They reported that the interview, which lasted for between one and two hours, helped them identify and clarify their life goals. Additionally, in an offender adaptation of the PCI, we asked prisoners to identify how offending or being in prison helped or hindered goal attainment. This was intended to clarify the impact of offending on their life plan and hopefully motivate them to engage in treatment aimed at reducing their offending. A preliminary investigation into this motivational effect was examined with a small sample of sex offenders who were reluctant to engage in treatment programmes, with some positive indications of a motivational shift, although this needs further investigation (Theodosi and McMurran 2006).

Focusing on goals in treatment

The aim in this section is to outline a goal-focused approach to working with offenders. The overall aim is to assist offenders to identify their personal goals and help them identify ways of working positively and pro-socially towards goal attainment. A goal-focused approach begins by helping the client review, rationalise and prioritise his or her goals. The underlying purpose is to shift the offender's motivational structure in a positive direction by helping him or her aim for valued and achievable goals that form a coherent whole. Then, an action plan for working towards attaining life goals is specified, with engagement in treatment programmes being one option. A second goal-focused approach is problem-solving skills training. The path to attaining life goals is fraught with minor hassles and major life events that can throw us off course, and therefore we need to possess troubleshooting skills. Problem-solving skills training can augment major life goal strivings by helping people avoid maladaptive or anti-social solutions to day-to-day problems.

Goal setting

Based upon the PCI and systematic motivational counselling, which is the intervention that follows from it (Cox and Klinger 2004c), a system for identifying and prioritising life goals, examining obstacles and strengths in relation to goal pursuit, and formulating specific action plans is presented in Tables 11.1 and 11.2. This Goal Positioning System (GPS) is completed with the client over a number of sessions. The information is typed into the system at the end of each therapy session and both the client and the therapist retain a copy after each session to record the progress of therapy. Table 11.1 shows a completed example of a GPS.

Therapy sessions are introduced by explaining the importance of intrinsically rewarding life goals to the client. Life goals may be to do with 'being' – for instance being happy, being loved, or being healthy – but these being goals need to be translated into 'doing' goals: that is, doing the things that will bring happiness, love and good health. Doing goals are often extrinsically motivated in that their attainment is not intrinsically satisfying, but it does assist with the eventual attainment of intrinsically satisfying goals. An example for offenders might be attending treatment programmes: this is not an intrinsically rewarding activity, but it may assist with the attainment of intrinsically rewarding life goals, such as good relationships, a satisfying home life and stable employment. Care must be taken to ensure that extrinsically motivated goals actually do relate to important life goals. The pursuit of money or material goods, for instance, may become disassociated from any basic human need and this pursuit may actually detract from basic need fulfilment, leading to poorer well-being (Ryan and Deci 2000).

The client is then presented with the goal schedule with the explanation that the life areas represent the most important components of human happiness. The first step is to consider each of these areas and identify the principal personal goals. Second, the areas should be ranked in priority order so that the most important, urgent, or manageable areas can be worked through first. Then, focusing on each area in turn, identify the major obstacles to goal attainment. These will include personal (such as substance use), interpersonal (such as conflict in relationships), and social obstacles (unemployment, for example). The focus should then turn to a

Table 11.1 Goal positioning system

Life area	General goals	Rank-ing	Problems	Strengths	Impact of offending	Specific goals
House and home	Get my own flat.	1	No money.	I want to work for my money.	Employers don't want someone with a record.	• Work with my brother.
Employment and finances	Be self-employed.	3	Need to start from scratch.	My brother does painting and decorating – he's said I can do some work with him.	It might be hard to get a job with my record.	• Plan work with my brother.
Education and training	Get a painting and decorating qualification.	2	None.	Can get the training in prison.	Being in prison has helped!	• Complete the course.
Family and relatives	Get back on good terms with my mum.	7	Mum doesn't want to know me.	My step-dad and brother still speak to me.	Mum threw me out of the house because of my drinking and crime.	• Write Mum a letter saying I'm doing courses in here.
Friends and acquaintances	Make new friends who don't get into trouble.	8	Most of my friends go out drinking and get into fights.	My brother and his mates are more settled and don't get into trouble.	If I hadn't been with those people I wouldn't have committed the offence.	• Spend more time with my girl-friend, brother, family and my friends who go out for a quiet drink and don't fight.

Love, intimacy and sexual matters	Stick with my girlfriend.	She doesn't like me getting pissed, fighting and ending up in trouble. She said she'd leave me if I get in trouble again.	4	She hasn't dumped me yet.	She's fed up with me getting sent to prison.	• Get work with my brother. • Cut out the drinking and leave the boys to fight and drink if they want to – I want to make a fresh start.
Health and medical matters	Cut down my drinking.	I spend too much time and money in the pub and I get into fights.	5	I can drink sensibly.	I've got convictions for violence – that's due to drink.	• Drink sensibly with my brother, my girlfriend and mates who don't fight.
Spiritual matters	Be happy.	I've got no flat, no job, my girlfriend is pissed off with me, and my mum has chucked me out.	9	I am young enough to change – my brother will help me.	Drinking, crime, and prison make me unemployed and make my girlfriend and family pissed off with me.	• Cut down drinking. • Get work.
Leisure, hobbies, pastimes	Stop spending my time in the pub.	It's what I do!	6	I have started learning martial arts.	I'll get fit in prison by not drinking and going to the gym.	• Get back into Tai Kwon Do practice.

person's strengths: that is, the assets that may be called upon in the service of goal pursuit. These too will be personal (such as physical fitness), interpersonal (for example, a supportive mother), and social (such as stable accommodation). Attention is drawn to the methods of goal striving by asking offenders about the role of their offending in goal attainment. Does offending help or hinder goal attainment? Offending may help in attaining some life goals but is likely to interfere with others. For instance, burglary may assist with the attainment of material goals, but burglary itself or the criminal justice consequences of it may interfere with harmonious relationships (relatedness), employment prospects (achievement), or feelings of self-satisfaction (self-transcendence). Methods of goal striving that are likely to lead to successful attainment of intrinsically satisfying states should be identified and translated into general goal-directed actions. The next stage is to formulate a single action plan (see Table 11.2). This stage consolidates and further operationalises the goals.

Persistence in goal strivings depends in large part on the value the individual places on the goal outcome. People engage more enthusiastically with goals that are set by the self, compared with those that are externally directed (Deci and Ryan 2000). This has implications for working with offenders, whose goals are often externally directed in the sentence planning process. Even where sentence plan goals are agreed upon by the offender, there is suspicion that they are not genuinely adopted but rather that the offender is simply creating a good impression. The skill is to assist the offender to identify his or her own valued goals and devise non-damaging ways of striving for goal attainment. Entry into offender treatments may be one method of working towards general life goals and if the offender identifies this as a specific goal then this level of self-determination may enhance engagement in the treatment programme. Recidivism outcomes are better for offenders who enter treatment voluntarily compared to those who are mandated or coerced (Parhar *et al.* 2008).

Persistence in goal strivings also depends upon the individual's expectation that an action will result in a specified outcome (Vroom 1964). That is, if a person thinks his or her goal-directed actions are unlikely to lead to positive results, that person is unlikely to put much effort into doing what needs to be done to attain the goal. Expectations of success vary with goal topography (McMurran and Ward 2004). A goal is more likely to be attainable if it is SMART; that is, specific, measurable, achievable, rewarding, and time-limited. Goals that are specifically stated with measurable outcomes allow the individual to set personal performance standards which may be monitored in

Table 11.2 Action plan.

Specific goals	Steps	Contact	Deadline	Life areas this will improve
Start a painting and decorating business.	1 Speak to my brother about setting up a business together.	Brother	Next visit	• Employment and finance • Education and training • House and home • Love, intimacy and sexual matters • Spiritual matters
	2 Complete the painting and decorating course in prison.	Course tutor	End of October	
	3 Get information about setting up a business.	See Education staff about Internet access	Friday	
Cut down drinking.	1 Go on prison alcohol groups.	Personal officer	By end of this week	• Health and medical • Leisure, hobbies, and pastimes • Family and relatives • Friends and acquaintances • Spiritual matters
	2 Book Tai Kwon Do classes to keep me out of the pub.	Tai Kwon Do instructor	Two weeks before release	
	3 Go out with people who don't drink a lot and get into trouble – my brother, my girlfriend, and sensible mates.	Brother, girlfriend	After release	
Get back on good terms with Mum.	1 Decide what I want to say in a letter.		This week	• Family and relatives
	2 Talk it over with my girlfriend.	Girlfriend	Next visit	
	3 Write the letter.	Joe on our wing who helps with letters	End of this month	
	4 Post the letter.	Wing office staff	End of this month	

relation to outcome, thus influencing motivation (Bandura 1986). Goals should be achievable but challenging. As long as the goal is valued, the achievement of a difficult goal is more satisfying (Locke 1996). Goals should be positive and rewarding. Approach goals are usually competency-based, and permit individuals to focus on their successes and mastery of situations, whereas avoidance goals require people to be vigilant for lapses in their good behaviour, and they require individuals to focus on their failures. Approach goals are positively related to well-being, whereas avoidance goals are negatively related (Elliot *et al.* 1997), and approach goals appear to improve offenders' engagement in treatment programmes (Mann *et al.* 2004). The timescale for sub-goals should be fairly short, so that a sense of mastery and achievement is gained rapidly.

Problem-solving

Successful goal-directed behaviour requires that the person has the competencies required for success. The skills necessary include the abilities of emotion control, problem-solving and interpersonal communication, as well as a whole range of practical skills relating to work, finance and the home. Treatment and training programmes to enhance these skills may be available to offenders, and they can be included as appropriate in sentence plans. However, problem-solving skills training is one generic intervention that is goal-based and aims to provide individuals with the skills needed to identify and solve life's problems. Problem-solving approaches may be seen as ways of troubleshooting when the path to one's life goals is thwarted.

Social problem-solving is 'the self-directed cognitive-affective-behavioral process by which an individual attempts to identify or discover solutions to specific problems encountered in everyday living' (D'Zurilla and Nezu 2007: 11). The use of the descriptor 'social' identifies this as problem-solving applied to real-life problems. An effective solution is 'one that achieves the problem-solving goal (i.e., changes the situation for the better and/or reduces the distress that it produces), while at the same time maximizing other positive consequences and minimizing negative consequences ... to others as well as oneself' (D'Zurilla and Nezu 2007: 13). Thus, a solution that disregards the welfare of other people is not an effective solution.

According to social problem-solving theory, problem-solving outcomes are determined by two dimensions: problem orientation, and problem-solving style (D'Zurilla and Nezu 2007). Problem orientation (PO) is the set of cognitive-affective schemas that represent a person's beliefs, attitudes and emotional reactions about problems in living and ability to cope successfully with problems. Problem orientation can be either positive or negative. A positive problem orientation is the tendency to appraise problems as a challenge and be optimistic about problems being solvable if one applies some time and effort to the problem-solving process. A negative problem orientation is the tendency to view problems as a threat, expect problems to be unsolvable, doubt one's own ability to solve problems successfully, and become frustrated and upset when faced with problems. Problem orientation serves a motivational function, with a positive orientation facilitating adaptive problem-solving efforts and a negative orientation serving to inhibit problem-solving attempts. Problem-solving style refers to the cognitive behavioural activities that people engage in when attempting to cope with problems in living. Rational problem-solving is the constructive problem-solving style that involves the systematic application of specific skills, each of which makes a distinct contribution towards the discovery of an adaptive solution or coping response. The specific skills are: defining a problem accurately; setting goals for change; generating a range of alternative solution ideas; considering the costs and benefits of each alternative; developing a solution plan; and evaluating the plan after it is implemented. An impulsivity/carelessness style is characterised by impulsive, hurried and careless attempts at problem resolution, and an avoidance style is characterised by procrastination, passivity and overdependence on others to provide solutions. Both such styles are dysfunctional in nature, usually leading to unsuccessful problem resolution.

Our studies have shown personality disordered offenders and vulnerable prisoners to be poorer at social problem-solving compared with a functioning adult sample (Hayward *et al.* 2008; McMurran *et al.* 2002; McMurran 2009b). Furthermore, poor social problem-solving has been shown to be associated with distress and depression in prisoners (Biggam and Power 1999a, 1999b; McMurran and Christopher 2009). Problem-solving skills training or problem-solving therapy aims to teach people the skills for solving life's problems, and has been used successfully in the treatment a range of problems (Bell and D'Zurilla 2009; Malouff *et al.* 2007).

D'Zurilla and colleagues (D'Zurilla and Goldfried 1971; D'Zurilla and Nezu 1999 2007) describe six separate steps for successful problem-solving: (1) problem orientation, which is acknowledging that problems are a normal part of life, recognising negative emotions as signals that a problem exists, and learning better to manage and use their emotional experiences (for example, viewing bad feelings as a cue that a problem exists); (2) problem definition, which is the ability to define a problem clearly and accurately; (3) goal setting, which is identification of the desired outcome; (4) generation of alternatives, which is the creative generation of a range of possible ways of achieving the goal; (5) decision-making, where after examining the likely positive and negative consequences of each potential solution to both self and others the best options are selected and arranged in logical sequence to form a means–end action plan; and (6) evaluation, which is a review of the success or otherwise of the action plan, either in progress or at its conclusion.

In a problem-solving intervention called Stop and Think!, we have translated these steps into six key questions that guide the problem-solving process in clinical practice: (1) Feeling bad? (2) What's my problem? (3) What do I want? (4) What are my options? (5) What is my plan? (6) How am I doing? These six key questions guide the Stop and Think! sessions, with a focus on each participant's current concerns, aiming not only to solve existing problems but also to teach people the problem-solving strategy. Stop and Think! group sessions have improved problem-solving abilities with mentally disordered male offenders (McMurran *et al.* 1999), personality disordered male offenders (McMurran *et al.* 2001), and vulnerable male prisoners (Hayward *et al.* 2008). Recently, a randomised controlled trial of a combination of 12 group sessions of Stop and Think! preceded by four individual psycho-education sessions improved social functioning in non-offenders diagnosed as having personality disorders (Huband *et al.* 2007).

Problem orientation

A negative problem orientation is strongly associated with anxiety and depression in prisoners (McMurran and Christopher 2009), as well as non-offender populations (Bray *et al.* 2007; Kant *et al.* 1997). A negative problem orientation is where problems engender feelings of nervousness, threat and fear, there are feelings of frustration and upset when problem-solving efforts fail, and there is a lack of confidence in one's ability to solve problems effectively. Clearly, this needs to be a focus in skills training or therapy if people are to be enabled to solve problems effectively.

In two meta-analyses of treatment trials, a major predictor of positive outcome has been the inclusion of components that encourage people to become less negatively oriented and more positively oriented to problem-solving (Bell and D'Zurilla 2009; Malouff *et al.* 2007). In our own research with people diagnosed as having personality disorders, a reduction in negative problem orientation was the most significant predictor of improvements in social functioning (McMurran *et al.* 2008b). When social problem-solving therapy for people diagnosed as having personality disorder works it does so by improving social problem-solving ability, but specifically, by reducing negative problem orientation. Improving problem orientation can be tackled by changing problem appraisal. Instead of viewing problems as insurmountable obstacles that get in the way of happiness, problems are to be seen as a normal part of life and, with a bit of effort, they can be tackled successfully. Problems are normal – we all have them a lot of the time – and they can be solved if you tackle them constructively. Helping a person to experience success in problem-solving is also important, and this often entails giving support in efforts to solve problems. In Stop and Think! participants are offered optional fortnightly individual support sessions, focusing on helping them carry out their problem-solving action plans. Throughout therapy, identifying the client's strengths enhances feelings of competence. Identifying problem-solving successes and praising approximations to success is reinforcing. When problem-solving has not been successful, lack of success should be framed as a learning opportunity. This steers people away from self-criticism and feelings of failure into a more positive approach of enquiry. Why did that not work? How can I do it differently? The ability to be flexible and use alternative strategies when faced with obstacles is associated with good problem-solving skills in prisoners (Christopher and McMurran 2009).

Conclusion

Engagement with a coherent set of valued goals is what gives life meaning, which is associated with happiness and well-being (Emmons and King 1998). The statement of purpose of HM Prison Service for England and Wales refers to its duty to help prisoners to lead law-abiding and useful lives in custody and after release. To lead a law-abiding and useful life captures the quality of transcending self-interest that Emmons (2005) associates with well-being. Helping the offender build a personal narrative or identity in which the self is defined as a law-abiding person who is useful to society is an emerging approach to offender resettlement. Drawing upon principles of restorative justice, Maruna and LeBel (2003) have backed a strengths-based approach to the rehabilitation and resettlement of offenders, focusing on the positive contribution a person can make to society (see also the discussion of the Good Lives Model in Chapter 4). Actively encouraging offenders to contribute to society – and encouraging society to accept offenders as valued members – engenders feelings of belonging. This in turn facilitates the internalisation of what may have begun as externally directed goals, namely becoming a law-abiding and useful member of society.

Chapter 12

Treatment readiness and the therapeutic alliance

Christina Kozar

This chapter discusses how the concept of therapeutic alliance can provide a framework upon which the strength of engagement between the client and the programme provider can be understood, and how programme providers might respond to clients who present with low levels of treatment readiness. Many offenders attend rehabilitation programmes because they are mandated to be there and, as a result, some may be either poorly motivated to attend, or attend unwillingly. It is suggested in this chapter that it is the skill, knowledge and attitude that a programme facilitator or therapist brings to the programme that can determine how well each individual participant engages with programme content, how well group members work together, and, ultimately, exert a profound influence on the extent to which participants benefit from the programme. The argument that is advanced in this chapter, then, is that difficulties in forming an alliance in the early stages of a rehabilitation programme are more likely to occur in offenders who might be considered as having low levels of readiness, but it is the way in which treatment providers respond to this that will ultimately determine how well offenders perform.

What is the therapeutic alliance?

The therapeutic alliance, also known as the working alliance, describes a therapist and client's meaningful and collaborative work towards therapeutic change. Therapists have reflected on the nature of the therapeutic relationship since the days of Freud (1958), but in recent years it has been the work of Bordin (1979, 1994) that has probably been most influential in this area. Bordin suggests that the therapeutic alliance (TA) comprises three distinctive, but interrelated, elements: goals, tasks, and bond. First, the process by which therapist and client mutually agree on *change goals* is regarded as central to the formation of a strong TA. The extent to which therapists can motivate clients into undertaking the *tasks* of therapy (on the basis that this will achieve the agreed goals) is thought to be an important determinant of treatment effectiveness (Bordin 1979). The development of a *bond* is also considered critical, but this is something that should naturally evolve as a part of the process of negotiating goals and completing the tasks required to achieve those goals. This aspect of the alliance is likely to be of particular relevance to forensic practitioners who seek to work with clients on behaviours that may be perceived as shameful. This can only be done within a context where a positive emotional bond has developed between the therapist and the client (Kear-Colwell and Boer 2000). The bond thus describes the quality of the relationship required to work collaboratively on identified change goals (Hatcher and Barends 2006), and for some theorists not only provides a framework from which treatment can be delivered, but rather *is* the treatment (Bordin 1979; Miller, no date). In this respect, the ability of the clinician to make an emotional connection with the client through purposive goal-oriented therapy is regarded as a necessary, if not sufficient, condition for change.

Disagreements on the goals and/or tasks of treatment or strains in the bond are seen as an inevitable consequence of the therapeutic process. Genuine confrontation between the client and the therapist on their specific views, needs and agendas is generally regarded as fundamental to therapeutic change. Bordin (1979), for example, suggests that in successful therapies both parties are required to work through difficulties that emerge in the relationship, given that the client brings things to the therapeutic process that parallel their experiences in other relationships. The resolution of these difficulties is seen by some as the most essential aspect of any therapy. Safran and colleagues (2002), for example, argue that different clients will require different responses from therapists when the alliance ruptures. Ruptures occur when the client confronts the therapist about the therapy, or when the client complies, defers or simply withdraws when confronted with difficulties. Thus effective practice is not simply working collaboratively, but related to the way in which therapists respond to the varying problems that routinely arise within the therapeutic relationship.

The therapeutic alliance in forensic contexts

Any examination of the therapeutic alliance within a forensic context should consider a number of factors over and above those that are thought to be associated with general psychotherapeutic work. Above all, the level of coercion to which clients are subject within prisons or community corrections is likely to have a profound influence of the development of the TA. Forensic clinicians have various obligations relating to the legal context in which they work (including reporting to parole boards, advising correctional case managers/prison staff on the progress of clients). Correctional procedures typically require at least some level of disclosure to other correctional workers around whether clients attend their programme sessions, and the quality of their participation. Often, there is also some expectation that information relating to anti-social activities undertaken by clients while under the purview of correctional services (such as drug-taking, violent behaviour) will be reported if it comes to light during treatment. In a forensic context, then, the alliance will not only comprise those elements traditionally associated with the care of the client (tasks, goals, bond), but must also recognise issues of social control (Skeem *et al.* 2007). It is unavoidable that offenders will be at least wary, if not suspicious, about what clinicians will divulge to correctional staff about them and their participation in treatment. Developing an effective alliance with mandated clients therefore requires a reconciliation of these dual roles.

Another distinctive aspect of forensic or correctional programme delivery is that it invariably occurs in a group format. The alliance in group work is likely to be conceptually different from that in individual treatment (Horvath and Symonds 1991), although, of course, there are fundamental aspects of the therapeutic process that exist across both contexts. The therapist in group programmes must aim to (a) foster group cohesion so that group members are convivial; (b) work through differences between group members; and (c) ensure that group members work together to assist each other during the course of the programme. Serran and colleagues (2003) have argued that the level of group cohesion that develops provides an indication of the level of the TA within offending behaviour programmes. This makes sense. In group interventions clients will benefit from the input of other group members as well as from that of the therapists. Conversely, problems in the relationship with either therapists or other group members are also likely to impinge on the strength of the alliance. Clients are likely to observe closely how therapists respond to ruptures with other group members, and use this to inform their subsequent behaviour in the group. It is, however, a client's individual responses to the therapist's efforts at creating collaborative and purposeful working relationships that is discussed in this chapter.

A myriad issues relating to internal and external treatment readiness factors will affect the course and outcomes of treatment for each individual client in an offending behaviour programme. The complexity of these interactions has been recently highlighted by Ross, Polaschek and Ward (2008), who revised Bordin's (1979) theory of the alliance to incorporate aspects of treatment readiness. They suggest that systemic issues can impinge significantly on the therapeutic alliance: the more difficult the client (complex needs, hostility) and the circumstances (workload, access to training and supervision), the more compromised therapists will be in their attempts to develop an effective alliance. Therapist and client characteristics, including their personality, attachment style and interpersonal schemas, will also influence the interactions that occur within offending behaviour programmes, and the quality of the alliance is more likely to be an outcome of complementary transactions rather than separate actions by either party (Constantino et al. 2002). Indeed, Ross et al. suggest that therapists undertake a wide search to examine which aspects of the model (client, organisational, or other contextual factors, for example) to attend to when ruptures occur.

The therapeutic alliance and treatment outcomes

A number of meta-analytic reviews investigating the impact of the alliance on individual treatment outcomes have consistently shown that the therapeutic alliance has a modest but robust positive impact. Horvath and Symonds (1991), for example, in their analysis of 24 studies relating to the quality of the alliance, found an effect size of 0.26, which they interpreted to mean that at least a quarter of the therapeutic change observed could be directly attributed to the alliance. They observed that the alliance impacts on outcome across different types of therapy, lengths of treatment and sample sizes. Similar observations were made by Martin, Garske and Davis (2000) in their meta-analysis of 79 studies (with a comparable although slightly lower effect size of 0.22).

Various studies have examined the relationship between the alliance and therapeutic outcomes in forensic populations, although few have involved samples solely comprising correctional services clients, and many have focused only on individual treatment. There is, nonetheless, a growing body of evidence supporting the contention that the alliance plays an important role in offender treatment outcomes, although the findings of some studies are inconsistent. In the drug and alcohol field, for example, Meier, Barrowclough and Donmall's (2005) comprehensive review of studies concluded that early alliance seems to be a good predictor of treatment retention, but a less consistent predictor of treatment outcome. Barber *et al.* (2001) also reported that the alliance successfully predicted retention across treatment conditions in a sample of cocaine dependent clients participating in a number of different interventions. In this study, stronger therapeutic alliances were associated with higher rates of retention, although surprisingly this was not the case in the cognitive therapy condition. As in the Meier *et al.* (2005) review, the therapeutic alliance was not correlated with self-reported drug use during the six months of treatment for any treatment condition. These findings conflict, however, with those of an earlier study by Connors and colleagues (1997), who found that a strong alliance in alcoholic community-based clients was significantly associated with treatment participation as well as reduced drinking during 12 weeks of treatment and at 12-month follow-up. Gerstley *et al.* (1989) also found that alliance predicted decreased drug use seven months post-treatment in a sample of anti-social personality disordered methadone-maintained clients. In some ways, of course, whether the alliance impacts on retention or outcome is perhaps two sides of the same coin. Clients who do not experience a collaborative purposeful therapeutic relationship either leave treatment or do not make as many clinical gains compared to other clients.

A critical issue not explored in these studies is the mechanisms at work within therapy that impinge on the development and maintenance of the therapeutic alliance. Issues relating to client motivation, and other aspects of treatment readiness, may have utility in exploring how the alliance is formed and developed. In their review, Meier *et al.* (2005) found a moderate but robust relationship between the alliance, motivation and treatment readiness. A more recent study by Brocato and Wagner (2008) also found that alliance scores (as measured by the Working Alliance Inventory (WAI); Horvath and Greenberg 1989) for clients participating in an alternative-to-prison residential drug treatment programme, were not associated with retention but were associated with motivation to change and treatment readiness. Clients who scored higher on the 'Bond' scale of the WAI (which explores the quality of the relationship within therapy), were also more likely to increase their motivation to change during treatment. This suggests that the alliance both affects and is affected by a client's attitude to being in therapy, and their willingness and capacity to positively change. In line with other chapters in this book, it also suggests that motivation is only one, albeit important, facet of treatment readiness.

A number of studies have examined the impact of the TA in violence intervention programmes, although most of these have focused on treatment for domestic violence or spousal abuse. Brown and O'Leary (2000), for instance, administered the observer-rated WAI in their research and found that while these scores predicted husband abuse at the end of 14 sessions of cognitive behavioural treatment (CBT), they did not predict treatment retention. Similarly, Taft and colleagues (2003) found a relationship between therapist-rated WAI (although not client ratings) and abuse up to six months after 16 CBT group sessions, but no relationship with retention. This latter study also revealed a positive relationship between WAI and readiness to change, psychopathy, borderline personality disorder features (although this was a weaker relationship), and hostile-dominant interpersonal problems, perhaps emphasising the importance of a range of personality and situational factors on the therapeutic alliance. It would seem, therefore, that not only does a client's preparedness and ability to enact change heavily influence the strength of the alliance, but so too do personality characteristics that prohibit the development of close and intimate relationships. Ross (2008), on the other hand, reported less compelling support for the effects of the therapeutic alliance. In a study of a 36-week CBT prison-based treatment programme for violent men, Ross found that the WAI predicted client completion but not outcome (as measured by multiple measures, including the Violence Risk Scale (Wong and Gordon 1999–2003)). WAI scores were also correlated with client motivation, psychopathy and client attitude, but the only factor that remained significant in multiple regression equations was motivation. Structural equation modelling showed that the alliance and motivation mediated both change and programme completion, and that this was bi-directional. Based on these findings, Ross concluded that a strong alliance enhances motivation for treatment (and that motivation for treatment enhances the strength of the alliance), but that personality factors play a less significant role. One possible explanation for the differences in findings between Ross' study and those of Brown and O'Leary and Taft *et al.* concerns the length of treatment. As for drug and alcohol studies, as described above, the greater the time between alliance measure and outcome, the less likely a significant relationship is revealed. This speaks to the possibility of changes over time in the course of the alliance, and it may be that the strength of the alliance plateaus further along in the process of group interventions.

Alliance formation

The development of a therapeutic alliance commences with assessment. A thorough assessment should be conducted to ensure that the learning style and abilities of the client are elucidated prior to treatment so that therapists can be responsive to clients' specific needs (Marshall and Serran 2004). Part of this process should also involve the development of a detailed case formulation to explain the mechanisms underlying offending behaviour and help clients develop greater insight into their own behaviour. The process of developing a case formulation also appears to be associated with therapeutic responses to potential problems in treatment, rather than responses that are simply about offender management (that is the focus is on understanding offending behaviour and opportunities for bringing about change, rather than simply case managing offenders) (Kozar and Day 2009). Throughout this process, clients are oriented to the process of therapy and the nature and expectations of treatment, as this can often be of immense benefit (Constantino *et al.* 2002). Forensic clients in particular may benefit from this strategy, as they may be unfamiliar with therapeutic processes, have suspiciousness about what therapy in a correctional environment will involve, and/ or will demonstrate a number of traits typically associated with poor alliance formation, as outlined below.

Throughout the negotiation of group activities, it is important that interactions between therapists and clients are respectful and work towards positive therapeutic outcomes. Bordin (1994) emphasised that the change goal elicited during treatment must capture something central to the client's concerns. In the forensic context, this will invariably be about the resolution of mechanisms that contribute to previous offending behaviour. Bordin suggested that the identification of these goals should in and of itself have great therapeutic benefit. Marshall and Serran (2004) suggest that strategies that are most effectual include asking open-ended questions, behaving genuinely, offering encouragement, demonstrating care and acceptance, and creating opportunities in group for behaviour to be rewarded. They suggest that directiveness, which involves suggesting possible directions or alternatives to observed behaviours, rather than 'telling' clients what to do, should be used judiciously. Luborsky *et al.* (1997) suggest very similar processes for improving the alliance based on Luborsky's previous work, particularly around providing support and guidance on the client's goals, and offering understanding and acceptance. They also emphasise the importance of conveying realistic hopefulness about the client succeeding, the recognition of progress towards the goals, and finding ways to encourage clients to express themselves on some occasions. The importance of developing a functional means of relating during treatment has also been emphasised by Ross *et al.* (2008), who posit that the therapeutic task for the therapist is to have an awareness of their own schemas and how they interact with the clients' to inform ways of responding in group that are helpful rather than harmful. Where clients have experienced difficulties in relationship formation previously, it stands to reason that difficulties in patterns of relating will continue in the therapeutic context. Therapists must be prepared to work through these issues. The deeper the pathology, the more time needs to be spent on forming the alliance (Bordin 1994).

It is when therapist and client amicably negotiate a means of working together to effect positive change for the client that an adequate TA has been formed. Horvath and Luborsky (1993) contend that this process not only requires the client approving the therapist's style but the therapist communicating the relevance of tasks to goals, and maintaining an awareness of a client's commitment to therapy. They suggest that it is important to negotiate short- and medium-term expectations to foster a strong alliance but that the first phase of therapy is about developing trust and collaboration, and the second concerns challenging dysfunctional patterns. Exploratory strategies are required to undertake this work, but it is recommended that this should only be attempted once a client's distress or other problematic state has been resolved (Constantino *et al.* 2002).

Who will have difficulties in forming an alliance?

Because we know that some client characteristics assist in the formation of positive bonds (for example, quality of object relations stemming from appropriate attachment and bonding with parental figures, expectations of change) while other characteristics do not (avoidance, interpersonal difficulties), it is possible to anticipate when therapists may need to adapt their approach to foster a strong alliance

(Castonguay *et al.* 2006). Many of these internal treatment readiness factors can be easily determined pre-treatment and discussed during the assessment process. For example, clients' poor expectations of improvement is one such factor that has been associated with poor alliance formation (Constantino *et al.* 2002) and in a variety of treatment contexts (Connolly Gibbons *et al.* 2003; Constantino *et al.* 2005). In this situation, clients' goals are not aligned with those of the therapist (who should view therapeutic change as possible for the client).

It makes sense that if clients do not believe that therapeutic interventions will benefit them or are unfamiliar with the process of therapy and what it might offer (even perhaps suspicious), they are unlikely to enthusiastically enter into a therapeutic relationship and create a strong alliance. Hence, openness to being involved in therapy may significantly impact on a client's ability to form a strong alliance (Constantino *et al.* 2002). The most profound way for clients to demonstrate poor alliance formation is to leave treatment. Brown, O'Leary and Feldbau (1997) found that for a group of spousal abusers, a third of non-completers cited treatment-related reasons for ceasing treatment, which included dissatisfaction with the content or structure of the group intervention. So where a client's treatment goals are not aligned or there is disagreement with the tasks required for treatment on offer, a strong alliance is not possible and a decision to leave treatment may be made.

Other treatment readiness factors that potentially impinge on a client's ability to form an alliance concern their mental health. In their review of factors that impede the development of a TA, Constantino *et al.* (2002) stated that severity of psychiatric symptoms equates to greater difficulty in forming the alliance although again there is inconsistency in the research (see Connolly Gibbons *et al.* 2003). Particularly in their more severe forms, however, it makes sense that symptoms of psychosis, depression and/or anxiety would impede clients' ability to relate to therapists and willingness or capacity to disclose issues in treatment due to the range of difficulties these clients would experience in their psychological functioning and ability to relate to others. Brocato and Wagner (2008), for example, found that a high degree of psychological problems and Axis I diagnoses (41 per cent) were found in offenders who prematurely left residential drug and alcohol treatment. It may be, therefore, that if clients are psychologically distressed or have difficulties in controlling their emotions or relating to others, it will be more difficult for them to form an alliance and this will place them at risk of discontinuing treatment.

There are a number of more pervasive client characteristics that seem to impact on the capacity to form a therapeutic alliance. These include clients who have interpersonal difficulties, poor object relations, high levels of defensiveness, or are resistant or hostile (Constantino et al. 2002). It seems likely that these traits would make the development of trusting and intimate relationships more difficult. Hostile-dominant interpersonal problems, which have been correlated in numerous studies with poor alliance formation (see Beauford et al. 1997; Connolly Gibbons et al. 2003; Skeem et al. 2007; Taft et al. 2004) seem particularly relevant to the forensic population. Many offenders have a history of violent behaviour and/or anti-authoritarian attitudes that are likely to create difficulties in their interactions with others. Another relevant factor to the forensic population concerns the difficulty in forming an alliance with clients who experience paranoia. These clients seem to exhibit more difficulty than clients with any of the other personality disorder traits in alliance formation, including those with anti-social personality disorder or borderline personality disorder (Lingiardi et al. 2005). In all, a high prevalence of anti-social or other types of personality disorder exist within the forensic population, and these clients often exhibit other complexities such as substance abuse and other Axis I diagnoses (Blackburn 2000). It should be expected, therefore, that many clients will demonstrate pervasive characteristics that will challenge alliance formation (see Chapter 9). There are, however, various strategies that can be enacted to assist in avoiding difficulties both in the formation of an alliance and in responding to ruptures in these situations (see below). What is critical at the outset, however, is for therapists to identify which clients are likely to have most difficulty in forming alliances during the assessment process, so that when treatment programmes commence therapists possess the requisite skills to assist clients.

Programme setting and therapist characteristics

To date, there has been limited research on the impact of organisational factors on treatment readiness and the therapeutic alliance. Luborsky et al. (1997) suggest that despite the paucity of research in this area, there is some evidence in the substance-abuse field that the qualities of an organisation will strongly influence the alliance. Existing research suggests that providing reward for attendance, such as money or food/refreshments during treatment, is likely to foster the alliance, but further research on this is needed.

It could be hypothesised, however, that if clients perceive that an organisation acts respectfully and looks after their interests with some generosity, they are more likely to come to treatment with a positive attitude and be willing to engage in collaborative working relationships. Organisations that value the provision of support and assistance to encourage programme participation may be more likely to set the scene for therapeutic encounters that foster a strong alliance. Conversely, therefore, organisations whose values are more punitive in nature, and lack sympathy or respect for clients and their circumstances, might discourage trusting and intimate relationships with clients. Some programmes, for example, make offenders pay to attend the sessions (Day *et al.* 2009b), and it may be that this alone leads to lower levels of treatment readiness and greater problems in forming effective alliances. Alternatively it may lead clients to believe that the service is in some way important and valuable. It makes sense that whatever the underlying values an organisation holds towards its clients, these will play out in staff interactions as well as guide the choice of programmes and the manner in which these are delivered.

Serran *et al.* (2003) suggest that clients should be encouraged to work collaboratively not only with therapists but also with each other. They suggest that therapists need to deliver treatment according to standardised manuals flexibly and sensitively, as opposed to strictly adhering to treatment protocols, in order to achieve this end. This highlights a tension that exists in programme delivery. Some correctional service treatment providers suggest that their staff deliver the material in manuals strictly as written, diverging as little as possible if at all, to maintain high levels of programme integrity. Programme integrity refers to attempts to ensure that materials are delivered across a service consistently and with a high level of quality, but this must be balanced against being responsive to the characteristics of clients and the issues they bring to the group. It is likely to be particularly important to diverge from, or at least adapt, programme material and undertake additional activities or group processing when group cohesion is low and ruptures occur.

Few empirical studies have examined therapist skill as a variable that potentially impacts on the alliance with forensic clients, although one study by Barber *et al.* (2008) examined therapist adherence to supportive-expressive (SE) therapy and its association with drug use in cocaine-dependent clients. SE therapy is a manual-based treatment that initially focuses on the development of the alliance in treatment and then examines interpersonal functioning and how this relates to drug abuse. Almost half of this sample met the criteria for anti-social personality disorder, although not all of these clients had a history of conduct disorder. Strong alliance combined with low levels of SE therapy adherence, rather than moderate or high adherence, was associated with better outcomes. The authors concluded that more straightforward drug counselling techniques that target the here-and-now of drug clients' needs may be a better initial choice of therapy for these clients, rather than SE therapy that focuses on understanding maladaptive relationships. So adherence to therapeutic protocols may, at times, reduce the strength of the alliance. Flexibility and responsivity appear to be key in this regard, to ensure that clients continue to be motivated to engage in treatment by having their needs met.

Therapist skill and style are central to alliance development. Constantino et al.'s (2002) review of the development of the alliance in general psychotherapeutic contexts suggests that therapist warmth, support, acceptance, empathy, respect and directiveness are positive therapist attributes that contribute to its development. They also noted that a balance must be struck between challenging clients' problems and being attentive to their needs, and strong or rigid adherence to treatment manuals can be detrimental, particularly when there are relationship problems within the therapy because clients tend to then experience that their individual issues are not being addressed. They pointed out that ruptures may be caused by therapist behaviours, particularly when a technique is used at the wrong time in therapy. Furthermore, accurate interpretation is also likely to be important in the formation of a strong alliance (Castonguay et al. 2006). Other characteristics associated with difficulties in the alliance caused by the therapist's style, such as rigidity, being tense, uncertain, self-focused, aloof, or critical, further suggest that therapists need to make clients feel safe and comfortable. Ackerman and Hilsenroth (2001) also note that the wrong techniques used at the wrong times can create problems in the alliance, such as the inappropriate use of disclosure (therapists discussing their own problems) and transference interpretations (confronting clients about observed interpersonal characteristics too early in therapy). Ackerman and Hilsenroth's review also identified a number of therapist behaviours that are likely to contribute to ruptures in the alliance. These include not being accepting, and rather being unresponsive, closed off, and unwilling to change their view despite client feedback. They suggest that exploratory interventions such as interpretation are best attempted when the alliance is strong, to ensure that a high level of trust and mutual respect has been developed to withstand the potential negative response a client may experience. Supportive interventions are best when the alliance is weak to enhance trust and ensure goals are aligned (Constantino *et al.* 2002). So not only do they reiterate the types of positive characteristics required of therapists, but they further emphasise that therapists need to use their skills flexibly to respond to client needs, which will vary across the treatment experience.

Highly skilled and trained staff are required to undertake the delivery of offending behaviour programmes. Successful programme delivery requires enacting the right action at the right time to respond to both individual and group needs. Not only is knowledge of offenders and offending essential but each therapist has to develop his or her own principles of programme delivery based on training, experience, supervision and organisational practices. This skill and knowledge base in tandem with personal values and attitudes will inform a conceptualisation of how clients can be assisted to change. Primarily this commences with communicating a level of hope that change is possible. Marshall and Serran's (2004) review of their own research with sex offenders suggests that promoting approach goals rather than avoidance goals assists in this end. They suggest that it is more effective to encourage clients to enact a new pro-social behaviour than have them avoid or cease an anti-social behaviour. The four most important therapist characteristics that correlated with clients' positive behaviour change were empathy, warmth, rewardingness and directiveness. This suggests that therapists need to balance humane and amicable approaches with skills largely employed by behaviourists, such as providing specific guidance around client behaviour and using praise when positive changes are observed. Above all, therapists must be perceived as helpful (Serran *et al.* 2003). Respect is also integral to this process as it demonstrates that therapists value and accept clients' strengths and interests. Training in the use of the four positive therapist characteristics also seemed to demonstrate benefits to client outcomes.

In summary, neither confrontational approaches nor unconditional positive regard appear to be effective approaches to working with offenders. A number of other behaviours should also be avoided, including blaming, the therapist behaving as 'expert', or focusing on difficult issues too early. In working with clients who present with low levels of readiness and cautiousness about entering into a therapeutic relationship, the therapist needs to convey support and acceptance in order to foster respect and trust, while also insisting on change and that the client take risks in therapy to explore issues relating to their offending. There are a number of characteristics of clients, therapists, and the setting in which treatment is offered that are likely to impact on the way in which the alliance develops. These include things that the client brings into the treatment environment (such as the personality of the client, his or her relationship history, and experiences of other programmes or psychological treatments) that will influence the motivation and capacity to engage, as well as the ways in which the therapist or programme facilitator delivers the treatment. As the alliance begins to develop, it is then likely that readiness and the alliance will mutually interact and both will change over time. Central to this process, however, is how ruptures to the alliance or problems in therapy are managed by the therapist. It is this area that is explored in the next section.

Working through ruptures in the therapeutic alliance

Identifying ruptures

There is no particular course of rupture and repair patterns that is considered ideal for any particular client group, but there should be an expectation that ruptures will occur during the course of a therapeutic episode when dysfunctional relationship patterns are challenged. Horvath and Luborsky (1993) suggest that if ruptures do not emanate during later therapy, it is perhaps a sign that treatment is 'coasting', and that dysfunctional behaviours are not being challenged or that the client is responding to the therapist in an idealised way. This is a particular issue in some offending behaviour programmes, where there is pressure on both facilitators and clients to avoid confrontation such that participants get through the programme or 'pass the course'. This means that continual reassessment of the therapeutic approach through supervision or peer review processes is required to ensure therapeutic integrity.

A wide variety of client behaviours may indicate when a rupture has occurred. Safran and Muran (2006) distinguish between two different types of ruptures: confrontation ruptures, where the client confronts the therapist about the therapy, and withdrawal ruptures, in which the client complies, defers or withdraws when they are confronted with difficulties. They argue that it is negotiation of needs (rather than collaboration) that most aptly describes the constantly shifting properties of therapeutic interactions, done at both a conscious and an unconscious level. For example, unconscious influences may take the form of projecting onto the therapist unresolved issues stemming from attachment style and replayed without awareness in the therapeutic relationship. Ruptures are defined as a breakdown in or failure to develop collaboration, or periods of poor relatedness between therapist and client. Safran and Muran also add that even the most subtle fluctuation in the quality of therapeutic interactions is worth exploring as it may assist in revealing and resolving client's relational schemas and self-defeating patterns. In addition, failure to explore more dramatic ruptures can lead to treatment failure and drop-out.

Because ruptures may be demonstrated in very subtle ways, it is important to carefully monitor clients' experiences of the therapeutic alliance. Therapists may assume that they are being received very differently from how the client actually perceives them, whether positively or negatively (Constantino et al. 2002). Asking frequently for feedback from clients is essential, and having a structured efficient process to implement this ensures both therapist and client compliance. Duncan et al. (2003) have devised a brief measure of the alliance – the Session Rating Scale (SRS) – for use as a clinical tool. This measure was based largely on Bordin's (1979) concept of the TA as well as Gaston's (1990) notion about the importance of therapist and client having common beliefs around how people change. The SRS requires that the client rate four visual analogue scales: the therapeutic relationship, goals and topics, approach or method, and an overall rating of the session. This measure has demonstrated good test-retest reliability and adequate construct validity, and is moderately, and significantly, correlated with the Outcome Rating Scale (ORS). The ORS (Miller et al. 2003) consists of four analogue scales requiring the client to identify their experience over the previous week. Ratings are made overall, individually, interpersonally and socially. These measures provide immediate feedback to therapists regarding the quality of the experience that clients had during their session, as well as the outcomes they are achieving outside of treatment. They can also become important clinical tools for discussing discrepancies in the therapist's perception of a client's group experience and progress, and how the client rates these experiences. The use of these tools is likely to assist in both the identification of ruptures and ensuring that progress is being made outside of therapy.

Clients are likely to experience difficulties at certain stages within therapy. Marshall and Serran (2004) point out that within forensic settings clients are mistrustful of the professionals running treatment programmes, so it may be that at the outset clients are disgruntled with having to attend treatment. Marshall and Serran suggest that the therapist requires great skill to overcome this mistrust so that they can work effectively with the client, develop group cohesiveness and reduce symptomology. They suggest that the therapist must model how to address others in the group and adjust their style to the needs of clients. Engaging coerced clients requires skills in identifying what client factors might be contributing to an unwillingness to engage in a therapeutic programme, a level of self-awareness to understand their own reactions to a client's behaviour, and an ability to accept and work with the client despite the challenges that arise. Although there is limited research in this area, current research suggests that when faced with anger and hostility, therapists who elicit some self-disclosure from the client in response to the anger, rather than ignore it or avoid responding to it, do better (Castonguay et al. 2006). This suggestion is also consistent with the attributes of being genuine and transparent within treatment programmes. Therapists who attempt to anticipate problems, provide clients with a means of communicating dissatisfaction, and are open to dealing with ruptures as they occur are more likely to foster a strong alliance.

A client's difficulties, of course, may not always be expressed through anger or hostility. Safran et al.'s (2002) review of research suggests that many clients do not express their dissatisfaction with treatment, which emphasises the importance of asking clients for feedback on their experience of the alliance in treatment. Therapists who become aware of clients' negative reactions may stick rigidly to their treatment model rather than respond to the rupture, or they may express their own negative feelings defensively. Conversely, therapists who respond non-defensively and shift their behaviours to respond to the rupture tend to improve the alliance. An alliance is negotiated when there is a willingness and ability to stay in tune with a client, while also accepting and responding to their difficulties.

Responding to ruptures

The manner in which ruptures are dealt with is critical to the course that a programme takes. It is unlikely that taking a punitive approach to difficulties that arise in session will endear therapists to clients. Taking an interest in why clients are unhappy with the treatment process and seeking amicable means of shifting negative behaviour in a group will likely enhance the possibility of resolving a rupture. Serran et al. (2003) note that offenders may minimise their offending in an effort to protect themselves, and this will be demonstrated in a number of ways during the treatment process. They see it as the responsibility of the therapist to create a safe and comfortable environment and build self-esteem to work with these defences. Thus therapist warmth and empathy can assist in reducing resistance when difficulties arise. Treatment providers, therefore, must promote programme practices that seek to resolve difficulties through the use of collaboration and encouragement to ultimately assist in group cohesion and alliance formation. Problems cannot, however, be avoided if ruptures are significant.

Taft and Murphy (2007) caution against the use of confrontational techniques in domestic violence programmes, arguing that they too are not likely to foster a TA and hence may hamper treatment gains. They go on to argue that if a client views relationships as being based on power and control a confrontational approach may affirm this schema, resulting in clients feeling angered if they perceive they are being belittled – clients may respond aggressively in an effort to feel empowered within this type of interaction. They suggest that motivational and other therapeutic strategies to challenge client minimisations and justifications are likely to be more effective at enhancing engagement and making treatment gains. It is encouraging also that the Good Lives Model (see Chapter 4; Ward and Stewart 2003), which promotes the perspective that clients have human needs that can be achieved in pro-social ways using a strength-based approach, is gaining greater acceptance as an approach that can be incorporated into correctional services practices. This approach values clients as humans requiring autonomy and respect, rather than having problems that must be eradicated in therapy.

Enacting appropriate responses to ruptures in the therapeutic relationship is considered key to ensuring a successful therapeutic relationship and maximising clients' positive behaviour change outside of therapy. There is, however, relatively little empirical work examining the impact of ruptures (and attempts to repair ruptures) on treatment outcomes. One study by Strauss et al. (2006) showed that stronger alliances and rupture-repair episodes predicted improvement in both depression and symptoms of personality disorder more than clients who experienced a rupture that was not resolved or those who did not experience a rupture at all. In the context of offending behaviour programmes, it is inevitable that clients will bring to the group those characteristics and behaviours that played a part in their offences, and it is the role of the therapist to identify and intervene at this level during the treatment process. The ability of the therapist to foster the development of the alliance, anticipate ruptures and repair these throughout the therapeutic process should, therefore, also be regarded as a treatment readiness factor in and of itself.

Bennett, Parry and Ryle (2006) examined therapist responses to ruptures in a task analysis of cognitive analytic therapy sessions with borderline personality disordered clients, comparing good and poor client outcomes. Therapists in good outcome cases identified and acknowledged 84 per cent of the ruptures examined in their therapy sessions compared to 34 per cent in poor outcome cases. In addition, therapists in good outcome cases either fully resolved or partially resolved almost all (87 per cent) identified ruptures with their clients, compared to only a third of ruptures identified in poor outcome cases. This study suggests that the process of identifying and having useful ways of responding to ruptures might be a central task relating to therapeutic improvement.

A number of different approaches exist to respond to ruptures, and various commonalities are central to these. Identification and acknowledgement are the first two critical tasks followed by allowing the client to reflect on the nature of the rupture (Bennett *et al.* 2006; Safran *et al.* 2002). Constantino *et al.* (2002) also urge clinicians to 'avoid avoiding', so that if a client is angry it is best to allow a freedom to express that, or the anger is likely to remain present and interfere with treatment. Bennett *et al.* (2006) then suggest invoking processes around negotiating and explaining the threat to the alliance and linking it to the dysfunctional patterns of responding previously identified in the client's case formulation. This should ultimately lead to a revised understanding of the rupture and new ways of relating. This contrasts with Safran *et al.*'s model, which focuses more on the examination of core relational themes derived within the therapeutic process, rather than early formulations of the client's problem overtly discussed within an assessment phase. They also emphasise the importance of having clients express their feelings and identify underlying wishes and needs demonstrated by the ruptures. Within the forensic setting, where previous assessment of the function of offending and the mechanisms underlying this should be elucidated, Bennett *et al.*'s (2006) model has greatest utility. It is commensurate with the notion of exploring offence-paralleling behaviours at appropriate junctures within group treatment (Jones 2004). The relative merits of encouraging self-expression and self-exploration of wants and needs, however, should not be discounted as part of this process.

Consideration of the importance of timing of techniques should again be emphasised within the context of rupture repair processes.

Safran *et al*. (2002) suggest allying with resistance may at times be appropriate in ensuring that clients can use their defences. Similarly, Bennett *et al*. (2006) found that therapists who were involved in good outcome cases were also more likely to collude knowingly with a client at times in order to maintain the relationship when difficulties arose, but they did this with an understanding of what was occurring. This level of insight while concurring with client dysfunction during critical stages of relationship formation contrasted with therapists in poor outcome cases, who colluded without knowing that the therapy may be compromised. Safran *et al*. (2002) also discuss the possibility of dealing with ruptures at times indirectly, such as by shifting tasks or goals, or directly, say by providing an explanation for the use of particular activities, responding to complaints, reframing the meaning of tasks or goals in a manner that the client can relate to, and clarifying misunderstandings.

Conclusion

This chapter has reviewed the construct of the therapeutic alliance and how it might inform how therapists delivering offending behaviour programmes understand and respond to low levels of treatment readiness. It is suggested that the ability to form a therapeutic alliance with offenders and respond appropriately to ruptures when they occur are skills that therapists should possess in working with offenders. They are, however, complex skills that require much organisational support and training. An in-depth knowledge of the client, techniques to assist in alliance formation (particularly with those clients who have demonstrated difficulties in this regard), an ability to present material in a responsive manner, and the flexibility to achieve this while responding to potential ruptures in a group context are all required. There is a plethora of requisite skills and qualities, including openness to feedback when things are not going so well, to ensure this occurs. Those who have limited training and experience seem most likely to struggle with the challenges posed in achieving a strong TA in offending behaviour programmes, and often experience the therapeutic process as something to survive (Kozar and Day 2009). In these situations in particular, correctional providers should ensure adequate resourcing of expert supervision, training and observational feedback so that staff are adequately supported throughout this highly complex process.

Chapter 13

Readiness and risk: a case illustration

The purpose of this chapter is to illustrate some of the concepts presented in this book through a detailed case description. The case is based on material drawn from the authors' clinical experience, combined and altered sufficiently to protect the anonymity of individual offenders. In describing the case, a convicted child sexual offender who is due to appear before a parole board, a number of factors are considered that have the potential to influence the offender's ability to benefit from a treatment programme, such that his level of risk of reoffending is reduced. The chapter starts with a review of the history of the case, current criminal justice and clinical context in which the offender was assessed, before moving on to a consideration of the findings of the initial assessment, case formulation and, finally, treatment recommendations. This is followed by a discussion of treatment readiness, and how this might inform the development of an expanded case formulation and new treatment recommendations.

The case of Mr Jones

Current context and index offending

Mr Jones is a 41-year-old white male prisoner who has been referred to a psychologist by the parole board to ascertain his level of risk of reoffending and current treatment needs. He has been in prison for 12 years. Among the decisions to be made by the board are whether Mr

Jones presents sufficient risk of reoffending to warrant his continued imprisonment; whether additional custodial treatment programmes are needed (and likely to be beneficial); and what treatment, support and supervision conditions will be required if he is to be released back into the community. These are all questions that forensic psychologists are often invited to provide an expert opinion on.

Mr Jones is currently serving a sentence of preventive detention following his conviction for kidnapping, sexual violation and indecent assault of a 15-year-old boy. The offence occurred when Mr Jones was driving in a suburb of the city in which he lives and noticed the victim waiting near a bus stop. He induced the victim to get into the car (rather than wait for a bus), and then drove to a secluded area where he became physically assaultive, striking the boy repeatedly across the face. It is reported in the Police Summary of Facts that Mr Jones kept the victim in the car for approximately 45 minutes, continuing his verbal threats and intimidation, before driving him to another location where he fondled the victim's genitals and, despite the boy's resistance, inserted a foreign object into his anus. Mr Jones then drove the victim back to the bus stop and released him, threatening to have him killed if the incident was reported to the police.

Previous offending

Mr Jones has a history of previous sexual offences of this nature. He was convicted of the indecent assault of a 15-year-old boy some four years prior to the index offence. Before this, Mr Jones's first detected sexual offending was against an eight-year-old boy, for which he was sentenced to 18 months' probation. At age 22 he was again convicted for indecent assault against two boys, aged 10 and 12 years, and sentenced to 19 months' probation and seven months' non-residential periodic detention. This offence also involved a conviction for abducting a child, although no further information on the specifics of this offence is available in the file documentation. At age 25 (four years previous to the current offence), he was convicted on three charges of sexual offending against the 15-year-old male, for which he was sentenced to six months imprisonment.

Mr Jones thus has a pattern of offending sexually against pre-adolescent and adolescent males, with a total of five previous convictions for indecent assaults. There would appear to be a significant increase in the level of violence involved in these offences, although Mr Jones disputes the degree of force and coercion used in

215

some of the earlier offences. All of the convictions were as an adult offender, from the age of 18 until the current (or index) offence which was committed when Mr Jones was aged 29. In previous reports, however, it has been noted that Mr. Jones has also acknowledged an earlier onset of offending and a more extensive number and type of offences than those reflected in his criminal convictions. In addition to his sexual offences, Mr Jones has previous juvenile convictions for vehicle conversion, false statement and theft.

Offender background and offence precipitants

Mr Jones has been assessed on a number of different occasions in the course of his involvement with the criminal justice system, and there are several comprehensive accounts of his social and familial background contained in previous reports. To summarise these, Mr Jones grew up in a suburb of a large industrial city, with his mother, father and younger sister, and reported being doted on and materialistically over-indulged as a child by both his mother and grandmother. His father became ill with some form of progressive dementia when he was eight years of age, and this led to a reduction in parental discipline. There are suggestions that Mr Jones resented the family's focus on his father's illness, and reports indicate that by the age of ten he had begun to behave disrespectfully, or even abusively, towards his father. Indeed, it appears that Mr Jones became exceptionally self-focused and developed a sense of entitlement in relation to his apparently passive, dependent and over-indulgent mother and ineffectual father. As an adolescent he developed the capacity to lie and manipulate his mother in order to get what he wanted: he is described as having poor impulse control, poor ability to delay gratification, and deficits in social skills appropriate for his age, including a lack of empathy for others. These problems indicate difficulties in the pursuit of the goods of relatedness, agency and emotional competency (inner peace), or more specifically, in the internal capabilities required to secure these goods in socially acceptable and personally meaningful ways (Ward and Maruna 2007)

Mr Jones has described himself as a 'slow learner' who preferred to stay at home rather than attend school. He reports being severely teased by his peers regarding his small stature, eczema and chronic asthma. He seems not to have been well accepted by his peers, leading to feelings of social inadequacy and the development of maladaptive strategies to align himself socially, such as telling exaggerated stories and engaging in farcical behaviour, but such attempts ultimately served only to compound his rejection and isolation. These strategies could be viewed as ways of establishing a sense of connectedness to his peers and thus reflect the primary goods of community and relatedness. Mr Jones would socially withdraw and ruminate over others' responses, leading to anger and resentment (problems with emotional competency). These ruminations would escalate his anger to the point that he would sometimes bully more physically and emotionally vulnerable peers.

During this period of adolescence he also appears to have developed a pattern of alleviating his emotional distress through compulsive sexual stimulation and fantasy relating to themes of aggression and dominance. Such sexual stimulation strongly reinforced the fantasies of dominance over others as a way of defending against his feelings of rejection and inadequacy, while simultaneously sexualising his violent impulses. This repeated early pairing of sexual and aggressive retributional drives has been identified as one of the primary risk factors in Mr Jones's sexual offending. In more constructive terms, this issue points to an emerging practical identity revolving around themes of agency and empowerment, albeit translated into destructive ways of relating to others and the broader social world.

At approximately age 15, Mr Jones began teaching martial arts to younger children within an established Judo Dojo. This experience is reported to have contributed to a sense of social efficacy, as he felt admired and respected by the younger students. However, it is also reported that he would fantasise about offending against his pupils and used his position as teacher to gain sexual stimulation from physical contact with both male and female children during classes. It is reported that he would later masturbate to fantasies of abusing children, again further reinforcing these deviant fantasies.

Mr Jones's father died when he was 16 years old and it has been reported that he continues to experience feelings of guilt, shame and anger in relation to his behaviour towards him. Mr Jones left school shortly afterwards to join the workforce, but he demonstrated an unstable work history, losing several jobs in his first year out of school. He has reported that he had difficulty interacting effectively with adults, but that another factor in his employment problems was his sense of entitlement, such that he did not like to be told what to do.

Previous formulations

Previous psychological reports have indicated that Mr Jones has continued to experience difficulties developing and maintaining satisfactory adult relationships, resulting in subjective distress and feelings of isolation. It appears that Mr Jones utilised his previous pattern of sexual preoccupation to mediate stress and regulate his affect, and that fantasies of control and dominance served to soothe his sense of inadequacy while expressing his anger and resentment over the perceived rejections of others. They have noted that Mr Jones's sexual offences against children have become more opportunistic and predatory in nature over time. Specifically, in his most recent offences, Mr Jones drove around in his car to locate a potential victim, an adolescent male that he believed he could intimidate and control. He then physically and sexually abused the victim at different intervals during an extended period of time, and induced a significant level of fear both to gain the victim's compliance and to prevent him from reporting the incident. Such behaviours are thought to manifest Mr Jones's sexualised fantasies of dominance, control and aggression, which then serve to facilitate temporary feelings of power and efficacy that Mr. Jones otherwise lacks.

Previous treatment provided

Mr Jones has now completed a specialised treatment programme for sex offenders on three previous occasions. His response at the completion of his first programme experience was judged to be 'unsatisfactory', and he undertook the programme a second time prior to his release from prison (for his first offence) after he became eligible for parole. At the end of this second attempt at the programme, it was stated that although he was motivated to address treatment issues, 'his inability to be consistent in his application of therapy and an intermittent return to manipulative and dishonest behaviour restricted the progress he made'.

Mr Jones sexually reoffended after a short period of time in the community, and was returned to prison on a sentence of preventive detention. He was again referred to a treatment programme, when it was noted that he had undergone 'a major attitudinal change' and was now 'ready to benefit from treatment'. He subsequently successfully completed the sex offender treatment programme, and although it was noted that while he appeared to have made further progress in the cognitive understanding of the factors contributing to his offences, he was yet to demonstrate a consistent change in his behaviour. Prior reports go on to point out that a particular concern is his pattern of dishonesty, which is described as increasingly more refined and difficult to detect. Although he successfully completed the programme, there were incidents of rule-breaking related to his use of a computer and attempting to communicate inappropriately by letter with another inmate. Following these incidents he was discharged from the programme for short periods, but subsequently allowed to return. An obvious problem in the previous treatment is its tendency to focus on negative treatment goals and failure to engage with Mr Jones's important values and an identity that is focused on a combination of perceived vulnerability and need to dominate or, more accurately, to disempower others. His dishonesty and lack of investment in community norms all point to problems of social consolidation and a view of himself as an outsider: someone who had to fight to survive and be acknowledged by others. In fact, he is eager to be accepted by other people but is unsure of how best to achieve this. It seems obvious that any meaningful treatment plan would need to pick up on these themes and provide constructive ways for him to achieve the needs that underpin them.

Current assessment

Mr Jones had been assessed on a number of occasions for various sentencing and parole board hearings, and has been through a sex offender treatment programme on two separate occasions, with all of the accompanying assessment procedures that are involved in that process. Thus there is an abundance of assessment information available in his file. These are reviewed here relative to the assessment of the current level of risk for sexual reoffending and related barriers to treatment readiness.

Intellectual functioning

One area of previous assessment involved Mr Jones's level of intellectual functioning. This issue is important not as a risk factor *per se*, but rather as a factor that might influence Mr Jones's ability to respond to cognitive behavioural treatment modalities, and as a result limit his ability to successfully implement the relapse prevention strategies that such modalities typically emphasise.

A full scale IQ of 86 was reported following an initial assessment of intellectual functioning using the Revised Wechsler Adult Intelligence Scale over ten years ago. This places Mr Jones in the 'low average' range. His verbal IQ score was recorded as 81, while his performance

IQ was recorded as 98. It was noted that his lower verbal score could be understood in part as related to his poor performance in and early departure from formal education. However, a subsequent administration of the Wechsler Abbreviated Scale of Intelligence three years ago showed a full scale IQ of 106, with a verbal IQ of 104 and a performance IQ of 106, all of which are solidly in the 'average' range of intellectual functioning.

Despite the apparent discrepancy in testing results over time, it seems safe to conclude that Mr Jones is of at least 'low average', and possibly 'average' intelligence, so that formal intellectual deficits do not appear to pose a substantial impediment to his capacity to understand what might be required in participation in a treatment programme.

Assessment of risk to reoffend

In this assessment, Mr Jones's potential to reoffend was evaluated using actuarial risk assessment measures and considering dynamic risk factors. Specifically, he was evaluated using the STATIC-99 (Hanson and Thornton 2000), a risk assessment measure utilising historical offence related variables, as well as the Psychopathy Checklist Revised (PCL-R) (Hare 2003), and the STABLE-2007 (Hanson et al. 2007), a measure of dynamic risk factors for sexual reoffending.

In relation to the STATIC-99, Mr Jones's score placed him in the 'high' range of risk for sexual reoffending, based on his prior sexual offences, his choice of unrelated male strangers as victims, and his lack of long-term intimate adult relationships. Large samples of other sexual offenders scoring in this range on the STATIC-99 have shown sexual recidivism rates of 39 per cent at five years, 45 per cent at ten years, and 52 per cent at 15 years following release to the community (Harris et al. 2003). More recent norms for the STATIC-99 indicate that Mr Jones's score places him in a group that has a five-year sexual recidivism rate of 28.2 per cent for routine correctional samples and 44.0 per cent for high-risk samples, and ten-year sexual recidivism rates of 39.8 per cent for routine samples and 54.3 per cent for high-risk samples (Helmus et al. 2009). Another way of describing risk of reoffence for someone with Mr Jones's STATIC-99 score is that his relative risk of sexual recidivism is four times higher than the average sex offender.

Stable dynamic risk factors are defined by Hanson et al. (2007) as 'personal skill deficits, predilections, and learned behaviors that correlate with sexual recidivism but that can be changed' through intervention (2007: i). The STABLE-2007 assesses 13 dynamic risk factors. Mr Jones scored in the high range on this measure, including high scores on those factors involving lack of positive social influences, capacity for relationship stability, general social rejection, lack of concern for others, impulsivity, poor problem-solving skills, negative emotionality, using sex as coping, and deviant sexual preferences.

It should also be noted that risk assessment with sex offenders also calls for consideration of acute dynamic risk factors, defined as highly transient conditions that only last hours or days. These factors include 'rapidly changing environmental and intrapersonal stresses, conditions, or events that have been shown by previous research to be related to imminent sexual re-offence' (Hanson et al. 2007: i). The ACUTE-2007 (Hanson et al. 2007) is designed to assess these factors, including items such as victim access, rejection of supervision, collapse of social supports, and substance abuse, among others. However, because these factors exert an influence in the immediate environment in close temporal proximity to potential sexual offending, it is not possible to assess these factors meaningfully while an offender remains incarcerated (unless the concern is over sexual reoffending in the custodial environment). One may attempt to anticipate the likely factors that may be present in the post-release environment and extrapolate from current functioning, but any attempt to do this is ultimately speculative and does not reflect the application for which the ACUTE-2007 was designed: to provide an ongoing assessment measure for monitoring the risk of sex offenders under supervision in the community.

Psychopathy, which represents a severe form of personality disorder with a strong empirical association with a variety of clinical and criminal justice outcomes, including recidivism, was also reassessed using the revised Psychopathy Checklist (PCL-R). Mr Jones was scored in the 'moderately high' range of the PCL-R. Thus while he demonstrates moderately high levels of psychopathic traits, he does not meet the criteria to be classified as a psychopath and does not reach the level of psychopathy considered to be in the same class of offenders as those who have consistently demonstrated the worst outcomes for treatment failure and serious reoffending.

The combination of deviant arousal and psychopathy have been associated with some of the highest observed rates of sexual reoffending. The strongest predictor of sexual reoffending is the combination of high levels of psychopathy and the presence of deviant sexual interest or arousal, defined as arousal to sexual activities with children or coercive sex with non-consenting adults. In a recent example of such findings, Hildebrand, de Ruiter and de Vodel (2004) examined the sexual recidivism rates among a sample of treated rapists. They reported a sexual reconviction rate of 82 per cent over an average follow-up of 11.8 years for offenders who were both psychopathic and sexually deviant, compared to 18 per cent for offenders who were both non-psychopathic and non-deviant. Similar outcomes have been observed with other samples including child molesters (Rice and Harris 1997). The assessment of sexual deviance thus warrants close consideration. It appears that risk assessment experts sometimes conclude that deviant sexual arousal must be present based solely on the presence of convictions for sexual offences. Yet sexual offending alone is not sufficient evidence for the presence of sexual deviance. International experts such as Hart and Kropp (2009) have stated:

> Mental health professionals should attempt a direct and comprehensive evaluation of sexual deviance, gathering information about normal and abnormal sexual thoughts, urges, images, fantasies, behavior, and physiological arousal. An important corollary of this standard is that assessments of sexual deviance should avoid over-focusing on convictions for sexual offenses. Sexual offenses are neither necessary nor sufficient for a diagnosis of sexual deviance. Many people with sexual deviance never act on their thoughts, images, urges, or fantasies; and many of those who act in a manner consistent with their sexual deviance do so in a way that may be perfectly legal. Also, many – perhaps the majority – of people who commit sexual offenses do not suffer from sexual deviance. Sexual offenses may be the result of other causal factors, including such things as anger, generalized negative attitudes toward women, poor impulse control, poor heterosexual skills, and inappropriate sexualization of nonsexual needs. Assuming that all sexual offenders have sexual deviance is as illogical as assuming that all thieves have kleptomania or that all arsonists have pyromania. (2009: 560).

In the case of Mr Jones, there is sufficient evidence that he experiences deviant sexual arousal. The assessments conducted as part of his treatment programme participation included the Penile Plethysmograph, which indicated significant levels of arousal to coercive sexual stimuli with pre- and post-pubescent males and females. He also has self-reported sexual arousal to fantasies of dominance and physically coercive sex with adolescent boys.

In light of the results of the current assessment of static and dynamic factors, Mr Jones is still considered to present a 'high risk' for sexual reoffending.

Assessment of needs

Considering personality features more broadly as they relate to treatment considerations, the results of a Millon Clinical Multiaxial Inventory, third edition (MCMI-III) provide a profile of Mr Jones's personality features. As far as can be assessed from scores on this measure, he appears to display prominent avoidant, dependent and self-defeating personality features, marked by a significant level of reported anxiety. Despite remarks regarding a sense of entitlement presented in various earlier reports, Mr Jones had a particularly low score on the scale measuring narcissistic traits, which are often associated with a sense of entitlement.

Case formulation

Identification of the factors contributing to and maintaining Mr Jones's offending behaviour have been presented in previous reports, and will be briefly integrated into an explanatory formulation here. This could be summarised as follows.

Mr Jones's early life experiences included rejection and ridicule by his peers, combined with over-indulgence by his mother and ineffectual discipline related to his progressively disabled father. These conditions led to the development of a profound sense of inadequacy and anxiety, social incompetence and isolation, along with a sense of entitlement and the use of manipulation and lying to get his way within the family. Although he had a strong desire to connect interpersonally with others, he did not develop the social skills or interpersonal sensitivity to achieve lasting relationships.

When his dependency needs were not met and he experienced, instead, the teasing and ridicule of his peers, he appears to have begun to comfort himself through sexual stimulation, with fantasies of control, aggression and retribution. His offending thus results from a highly sexualised ideation of others, particularly physically and emotionally less mature males with whom he can act out the deviant sexual fantasies that boost his sense of efficacy and power.

It also appears that Mr Jones displays entitlement stemming from his over-indulgence as a child and his limited capacity to recognise the impact of his behaviour on others or the consequences to himself. Unlike the overtly grandiose sense of self-worth associated with narcissism, Mr Jones in fact struggles with a profound sense of inadequacy and social incompetence, contributing to his anxiety and occasional depression. The potentially positive side of those with essentially avoidant personality patterns is that they can be extremely sensitive to the needs and perspective of others. They can potentially show substantial compassion and understanding and be emotionally responsive, if they can set aside their mistrust and expectation of rejection or ridicule to develop more direct and less reactive interactions with others.

Such a formulation is consistent with the results of the Minnesota Multiphasic Personality Inventory (MMPI) personality assessment. Individuals with the personality profile of Mr Jones desperately want to be accepted and involved with other people, but this desire is blocked by intense fear of being rejected or ridiculed. They scan their environment for threats to their self-esteem and try to present themselves in a favourable manner, but are seldom successful, as they feel a continual sense of uneasiness and anxiety, tending to overreact to minor events. They typically perceive themselves as socially inept, inferior and inadequate. Because of a fear of social situations and close relationships, such individuals may rely heavily on fantasy to gratify their needs for affection and to cope with their anger. This has the potential to restrict them to a solitary life where they are more likely to reactivate memories of past social rejections, rather than risk forming new, more satisfactory relationships. However, passive aggressive elements may also be present, as indicated by moodiness and resentment, with significant difficulty trusting others. This is consistent with previous descriptions of Mr Jones's vacillating between being friendly and cooperative and then being hostile, followed by apologies.

Conceptualising Mr Jones from a Good Lives Model (see Chapter 4) perspective, it would appear that his 'practical identity' was based on the primary goods of agency and relatedness and he sees himself as a person who needs to fight back and gain respect from others through dominating and sexually abusive behaviour. His perceived vulnerability and trouble articulating his needs to others also highlights difficulties with emotional competency. Taking all this into account, a good lives plan needs to emphasise the importance of establishing meaningful relationships and to find a way of enhancing his sense of agency and personal control. This should be done by carefully considering his social ecology and the level of resources available within the community he is likely to be released into.

Typical treatment recommendations

Treatment goals for someone with Mr Jones's history and presentation typically involve the continuation of the treatment that has already been started. There are some indications of progress: Mr Jones appears, for example, to have a solid cognitive understanding of his offence cycle, including the precursors and high-risk situations associated with his sexual offences. Furthermore, he states that he continues to practise the masturbatory reconditioning techniques that he has been taught in order to strengthen his arousal to appropriate adult partners and decrease his interest in young males like those he has victimised. The areas where he needs to demonstrate continuing progress involve applying the skills and insights that he has learned in his current everyday interpersonal relationships. He also accurately identifies that he needs to work on being consistently open and honest in his dealing with others and eliminate his use of deceit, manipulation and secrecy, as these behaviours have contributed to the development of situations in which he has offended, as well as interfered with his capacity to benefit from interventions.

Specific treatment goals for Mr Jones have been consistently identified in previous psychological reports. These have often been listed as follows:

- Develop an understanding of how he came to offend.
- Learn how to maintain healthy adult relationships.
- Replace sexual thoughts of children with appropriate adult fantasies.
- Replace coercive sexual thoughts with appropriate intimate fantasies.
- Learn appropriate interpersonal boundaries.
- Develop alternative coping strategies during time of negative emotions.
- Learn not to see children as sex objects.
- Understand the effects of offending on victims and develop empathy.
- Challenge thinking errors.

- Learn warning signs and high-risk situations and how to manage these.
- Take full responsibility for his offending (this is an ethical issue as well).
- Integrate all the above within a good lives plan and his practical identities and associated values.

Assessment of treatment readiness

This is where traditional assessment and treatment recommendation reports often end. However, to be of maximum utility, assessment and treatment planning reports should also, in our view, include an explicit consideration of treatment readiness.

There is quite a lot of information already available from this assessment that is directly relevant to understanding Mr Jones's readiness for further treatment, and his likely prognosis. It may also be helpful, however, to administer some measures of treatment readiness (described in Chapter 5). For example, the Corrections Victoria Treatment Readiness Questionnaire (CVTRQ) (Casey et al. 2007), although not validated specifically for use with sexual offenders, purports to assess readiness to engage in a treatment programme through four subscales: attitudes and motivation, emotional reactions, offending beliefs, and efficacy. This measure does not provide cut-off scores, but had it been administered, Mr Jones would have an overall score that would place him in the moderate range of treatment readiness (a total score of around 70) when compared with other offenders.[1] However, closer examination of his subscale scores may be more informative. They would reveal, for example, that he scored in the high range of the attitudes and motivation subscale and the emotional reactions subscale (higher scores indicate higher levels of treatment readiness), but in the low range of the Offending Beliefs and Efficacy subscales.

This would suggest that Mr Jones has a relatively positive attitude towards treatment programmes, but is not happy being identified as an offender. He regrets his past offences and wants to stop offending. These are all positive indicators of his readiness for treatment. On the other hand, his responses indicate that he blames others rather

[1] A CVTRQ score of over 72 suggests that an individual displays a capacity to engage in a treatment programme, but this measure was only validated for prisoners attending cognitive skills programmes.

than himself for his offending, feels that he doesn't deserve his current sentence, and is angry with others regarding his sentence (offending beliefs). He also does not see himself as well organised, hates being told what to do, and generally does not trust other people (efficacy). These factors present barriers to his current treatment readiness.

An assessment of this type can then be linked back to the formulation of his offending. It identifies core beliefs about himself and other people (for example, his sense of entitlement and injustice) as representing significant barriers to any positive and genuine engagement in a programme. Perhaps even more important from a readiness perspective is the detection of his core values and associated identity. It is likely that Mr Jones has a number of potentially maladaptive schemas that will influence both his treatment readiness and his treatment needs. These include schemas related to disconnection and rejection, such as abandonment/instability, which lead him to believe that others will not be able to provide emotional support and practical protection. Related schemas of mistrust/abuse and emotional deprivation may also be present, with the expectation that one's desire for normal degrees of emotional support will not be met. A defectiveness/shame schema may also be present in some form, with the feeling that he is defective, inferior and unwanted, or that he would be found to be unlovable by significant others if his true self is exposed. Related to all of these may be a schema involving social isolation/alienation, in which Mr Jones feels isolated from the rest of the world, and different from other people.

Other potential schemas for Mr Jones include those related to impaired autonomy, such as dependency/incompetence schemas (the belief that one is unable to handle one's everyday responsibilities and take care of oneself); failure (the belief that one has failed and will inevitably fail, one is fundamentally inadequate relative to others in achievement, that one is stupid, inept and untalented); and an insufficient self-control/self-discipline schema (a pervasive difficulty in exercising self-control and frustration tolerance, or to restrain one's impulses).

Given this, it might be possible to predict that Mr Jones would willingly attend treatment sessions, and present himself as someone who is genuinely interested in changing his behaviour, and willing to learn from others in the treatment group. However, he is likely to experience significant difficulties in full and frank self-disclosure (of the type required in offender treatment), and this may be understood in terms of a pervasive lack of confidence that others will be willing to support him emotionally, or perhaps will judge him negatively. It may be expected, therefore, that while he may be able to form an apparently strong therapeutic alliance with programme staff in the early stages of treatment, significant ruptures will occur as soon as he is challenged about those aspects of his offending that he finds uncomfortable or shameful. At this time he might experience programme staff as punitive and uncaring, and become angry about the requirement for him to attend.

Mr Jones is also a person who is likely to vacillate between being friendly and cooperative and then being hostile, followed by apologies to become accepted again. As he is often uncomfortable with others' anger, he may also resort to covert expressions of hostility, such as passive obstructionism. It is not difficult to predict that as a direct consequence of this interpersonal style he will experience problems in his relationships with other group members, although he may also seek to intimidate members of the group whom he considers to be less powerful.

In addition, while his PCL-R scores were not sufficiently elevated to warrant his categorisation as highly psychopathic, Mr Jones did score highly on items that will affect his treatment readiness. The personality and interpersonal characteristics that Mr. Jones has been assessed as demonstrating, such as lying, manipulation, lack of remorse and empathy, impulsivity and irresponsibility, may make it more difficult for Mr Jones to internalise and consistently utilise the gains he has made in treatment. He may also believe that ultimately, treatment is likely to be ineffective, given that he experiences so little control over his behaviour. These considerations make it imperative that things that matter to him are identified and made a focus of any intervention plan. It is much easier to motivate people to engage in the process of behaviour change if they believe their needs and values have been sufficiently addressed and are built into an intervention plan (Ward and Maruna 2007). Traditional risk reduction treatment plans are unlikely to appeal to someone like Mr Jones.

External readiness factors

There are a number of external factors that might also influence Mr Jones's readiness to effectively engage in treatment at this stage. One set of factors relates to the circumstances in which treatment will occur. Although treatment is not legally mandated for Mr Jones, it is apparent that the parole board will not seriously consider his release until he has more satisfactorily completed a specialised sex offender treatment programme. Thus there is considerable pressure, if not outright coercion, to engage in treatment. To the degree that treatment goals are congruent with Mr Jones's personal goals, and the recognition that successful completion of a treatment programme will be beneficial in personally meaningful ways, his perception of coercion and the attendant impediments to treatment readiness may be minimised. This means that clinicians need to take the time to sit down with Mr Jones and enquire about his interests and aspirations, and how the personal concerns evident in his past offending can be translated into treatment goals and form the basis of a good lives plan.

Another external readiness factor relates to the availability of adequate treatment resources. Engaging offenders such as Mr Jones in treatment is a task that requires great therapeutic skill. Therefore, one of the resource factors that will influence Mr Jones's treatment readiness will be the availability of well-trained and highly experienced treatment staff with the skills to work with offenders who present with his particular challenging risk factors, personality features and prior treatment experiences. The ability to engage with Mr Jones in a warm, empathic, respectful and rewarding manner, especially when he becomes aggressively defensive, evasive or manipulative, will have a substantial impact on his initial levels of treatment readiness; as will his ability to remain engaged in treatment when it becomes more directly focused on the personal factors that contribute to his risk of reoffending. These therapeutic skills will, of course, also interact with other, internal readiness factors, such as Mr Jones's enduring mistrust of others.

There are also programme factors that will influence Mr Jones's treatment readiness. Particularly in light of his previous treatment experiences with limited success, there will be a need for flexibility in the identification of treatment goals and the application of suitable treatment approaches for Mr Jones. If the programme attempts to impose a rigidly defined set of avoidance goals broadly associated with reducing risk, and implements treatment with a strict adherence to treatment manuals, it is less likely that Mr Jones will become engaged in the treatment process. Conversely, to the degree that the programme staff can collaborate with Mr Jones to define treatment goals that are individually relevant and valued, and tailor the pace, content and modality of treatment delivery to match his individual needs, treatment readiness is likely to be maximised.

A final set of external readiness factors relate to opportunity, location and support for treatment. Opportunities for Mr Jones to demonstrate and practise the treatment gains he desires to make in an ecologically valid manner will be severely limited while he remains incarcerated. This is one of the dilemmas facing those responsible for the treatment and supervision of sex offenders: the effectiveness of treatment in custodial settings may be lower than treatment in community settings (perhaps partly because of the more coercive nature of the custodial environment and the lack of ecological validity to practising treatment gains in that setting), but offenders are often not considered safe to release to the community until they have demonstrated sufficient treatment gains. It would probably be beneficial if Mr Jones is provided with the opportunity to move into a supervised community setting at the earliest stage of the treatment process, ideally through a series of progressive temporary community visits resulting in some form of conditional release to a supported community treatment setting.

Finally, Mr Jones, like many offenders, is largely estranged from family, most of whom now live some distance from the prison where he resides, and he has few pro-social friends. Support for his treatment must, therefore, come primarily from treatment and custodial staff. To the extent that there is a unified and consistently supportive approach taken by those in his prison environment, treatment readiness is likely to be enhanced. Conversely, if he gets mixed messages from different staff, some of whom express doubt or even overt denigration of the treatment programme, treatment readiness is likely to be diminished.

Implications for treatment readiness

So, how might this consideration of treatment readiness inform answers to the questions raised by the parole board? In light of Mr Jones's extensive treatment history, it is anticipated that little more is to be gained from additional intensive residential treatment for his sexual offending. He would appear to have acquired, at a cognitive level, an adequate understanding of the precursors to his offending and the factors associated with increased risk of reoffending. He has also been taught a variety of cognitive and behavioural techniques for managing this risk. What remains is the need for Mr Jones to further internalise these treatment gains and demonstrate a consistent adherence to candid, honest, pro-social behaviour in his daily interactions.

To assist with this, treatment providers will need to attend much more closely to the way in which Mr Jones relates to others, and provide clear, consistent and supportive feedback about how this might reflect beliefs about himself and the world that also contribute to the causes of his offending. They will need to expect significant ruptures in the therapeutic alliance to occur, and respond to these in ways that are both therapeutic and informed by the case formulation. It may, of course, be that this style of working is beyond the skills or resources of some programmes (which may, for example, be psycho-educational in nature, involving large groups of offenders), and if this is the case there would be little reason to expect that further participation would be particularly beneficial. It may also, of course, compromise the treatment of other participants.

There are other ways in which risk can be managed outside of a formal treatment programme. A key factor in minimising risk in this case, for example, will be the adequacy of his close relationships with appropriate adult partners. The distress, isolation and frustration that have resulted from previous situations in which Mr Jones has failed to establish adequate relationships with other adults have directly contributed to his sexual offences. Therefore, it is important for Mr Jones to establish and maintain a strong social network of individuals familiar with his offence cycle who can be actively involved in his transition to an offence-free lifestyle in the community. Setting such a goal is, of course, much more compatible with Mr Jones's professed desire to form age-appropriate and fulfilling relationships than goals that relate to him *not* behaving in particular ways.

An adequate release or good lives plan for Mr Jones could also include consideration of his living situation, with particular attention to the nature of his close interpersonal relationships. The lack of stable, healthy relationships with appropriate adult friends or partners has been a significant factor to the isolation and distressing emotions that contribute to his sexual offending. Mr Jones also recognises that placing himself in situations where he is alone, especially if he is driving around in a car with access to potential victims, will put him at particularly high risk of reoffending. Having a supportive social network available, and suitable activities accessed through reliable modes of public transportation, will correspondingly reduce his immediate level of risk, especially if these are areas that can be adequately monitored in the community on an ongoing basis.

Conclusion

In this chapter we have attempted to discuss some of the ways in which a consideration of treatment readiness can not only inform decisions about whether or not to refer an offender to a particular rehabilitation programme, but also how an understanding of readiness can also assist in the process of determining treatment needs and manage risk. This is not to suggest that this chapter provides a template for how to work with offenders, as any assessment will be determined by the particular context in which it occurs and the questions that it seeks to address.

The case we developed for use in this chapter was of someone with a long history of treatment experiences, and for whom significant concerns remained about his future risk, despite participation in programmes that was at times adequate. He was referred for assessment because of an upcoming parole board hearing, the results of which would have significant implications for his future. While there are a number of complicating factors in relation to assessing offenders such as Mr Jones, we chose this example because it is not an uncommon presentation. Offenders typically arrive for assessment with histories of attendance at a range of different programmes, beliefs about what is reasonable and to be expected from them in treatment, and often a desire to negotiate the easiest pathway out of the criminal justice system. Our conclusion here is that any assessment of readiness of treatment should be closely and inextricably linked to the assessment of risk of reoffending and treatment needs, and undertaken with the goal of developing comprehensive case formulations that allow programme content to be individualised to meet the needs of each and every participant. Had treatment readiness been considered in the original assessment and treatment planning process, it is possible that these previous attempts at rehabilitation may have proven more successful. In our view this entails taking Mr Jones's personal concerns and values seriously and attempting to understand his offending and his associated lifestyle from the viewpoint of what matters to him. Strength-based approaches aim first to identify an individual's core values and then to ascertain just what internal and external resources he requires to secure them in ways that also reduce risk. The prospect of a future life that revolves primarily around risk reduction and avoidance is arguably empty, and unlikely to motivate an offender to desist from further sexually abusive actions. Focusing instead on the pursuit of personally valued goals, and on constructive, collaborative approaches to their achievement, may offer a more promising transition to a better life.

Chapter 14

Ways forward and conclusions

Wormwith *et al.* (2007) have suggested that much of the future understanding about correctional intervention 'is likely to come from moving beyond the simple, but important, treatment-recidivism study, to the examination of in-program issues' (2007: 882). They identify non-engagement, non-completion and drop-out as some of the most critical factors that influence rehabilitative outcomes. In this book we have described and discussed how treatment readiness is likely to be an important determinant of programme engagement and completion, and offered a framework from which to understand and assess readiness, as well as to inform interventions that might be used to modify or address low levels of readiness.

It is evident to us, in writing this book, that while managing offenders who are not ready for rehabilitation is clearly a difficult and challenging task for those involved in programme delivery, there is a very limited evidence base from which to inform their practice. Although much has been written about managing resistance, and responding to low levels of motivation, few empirical studies have been conducted with offenders who are referred to offence-specific rehabilitation programmes. This includes research on both the level of readiness (and how this might inform referral to programmes), and on the impact of attempts to improve readiness on programme outcomes. A prerequisite for such research, however, is the development of measures that can reliably measure treatment readiness, that have established norms and cut-off points, and that can be used to assess changes in readiness over time. Some promising approaches to assessing readiness have been developed, but much more work is needed to validate these measures.

The challenge for practitioners is to work in ways that most closely match the needs and aspirations of offenders to those of the criminal justice system, and by extension the broader community. It is reasonable to expect those who have committed serious offences to consider seriously the ways in which they might be able to change their behaviour. It is also to be expected that many will not see the need to do this, or have confidence that the programmes and services that are offered to them will be able to meet these needs. In our view finding new ways to understand the barriers that stand in the way of effective rehabilitation, and allow offenders to become more meaningfully engaged in a process of behaviour change, can only lead to better programme outcomes and improved community safety.

Appendix

Measures of Treatment Readiness

University of Rhode Island Change Assessment

Citation: McConnaughy, E. A., Prochaska, J. O. and Velicer, W. F. (1983) 'Stages of change in psychotherapy: Measurement and sample profiles', *Psychotherapy: Theory, Research and Practice*, 20: 368–75.

Instructions: Please read each statement below carefully and then decide whether you agree or disagree with each statement. Circle the number that best represents how you feel. Please circle one and only one number for every statement.

	Strongly disagree	Disagree	Undecided	Agree	Strongly agree
1. As far as I'm concerned, I don't have any problems that need changing.	1	2	3	4	5
2. I think I might be ready for some self-improvement.	1	2	3	4	5
3. I am doing something about the problems that had been bothering me.	1	2	3	4	5
4. It might be worthwhile to work on my problem.	1	2	3	4	5
5. I'm not the problem one. It doesn't make much sense for me to be here.	1	2	3	4	5

6. It worries me that I might slip back on a problem I have already changed, so I am here to seek help. ① ② ③ ④ ⑤

7. I am finally doing some work on my problem. ① ② ③ ④ ⑤

8. I've been thinking that I might want to change something about myself. ① ② ③ ④ ⑤

9. I have been successful in working on my problem but I'm not sure I can keep up the effort on my own. ① ② ③ ④ ⑤

10. At times my problem is difficult, but I'm working on it. ① ② ③ ④ ⑤

11. Being here is pretty much a waste of time for me because the problem doesn't have to do with me. ① ② ③ ④ ⑤

12. I'm hoping this place will help me to better understand myself. ① ② ③ ④ ⑤

13. I guess I have faults, but there's nothing that I really need to change. ① ② ③ ④ ⑤

14. I am really working hard to change. ① ② ③ ④ ⑤

15. I have a problem and I really think I should work at it. ① ② ③ ④ ⑤

16. I'm not following through with what I had already changed as well as I had hoped, and I'm here to prevent a relapse of the problem. ① ② ③ ④ ⑤

17. Even though I'm not always successful in changing, I am at least working on my problem. ① ② ③ ④ ⑤

18. I thought once I had resolved my problem I would be free of it, but sometimes I still find myself struggling with it. ① ② ③ ④ ⑤

19. I wish I had more ideas on how to solve the problem. ① ② ③ ④ ⑤

20. I have started working on my problems but I would like help. ① ② ③ ④ ⑤

21. Maybe this place will be able to help me. ① ② ③ ④ ⑤

22. I may need a boost right now to help me maintain the changes I've already made.   ①   ②   ③   ④   ⑤

23. I may be part of the problem, but I don't really think I am.   ①   ②   ③   ④   ⑤

24. I hope that someone here will have some good advice for me.   ①   ②   ③   ④   ⑤

25. Anyone can talk about changing; I'm actually doing something about it.   ①   ②   ③   ④   ⑤

26. All this talk about psychology is boring. Why can't people just forget about their problems?   ①   ②   ③   ④   ⑤

27. I'm here to prevent myself from having a relapse of my problem.   ①   ②   ③   ④   ⑤

28. It is frustrating, but I feel I might be having a recurrence of a problem I thought I had resolved.   ①   ②   ③   ④   ⑤

29. I have worries but so does the next guy. Why spend time thinking about them?   ①   ②   ③   ④   ⑤

30. I am actively working on my problem.   ①   ②   ③   ④   ⑤

31. I would rather cope with my faults than try to change them.   ①   ②   ③   ④   ⑤

32. After all I had done to try to change my problem, every now and again it comes back to haunt me.   ①   ②   ③   ④   ⑤

Scoring protocol

Precontemplation items: 1, 5, 11, 13, 23, 26, 29, 31

Contemplation items: 2, 4, 8, 12, 15, 19, 21, 24

Action items: 3, 7, 10, 14, 17, 20, 25, 30

Maintenance items: 6, 9, 16, 18, 22, 27, 28, 32

To obtain a Readiness to Change score, first sum items from each subscale and divide by 7 to obtain the mean for each subscale. Then sum the means from the Contemplation, Action, and Maintenance subscales and subtract the Precontemplation mean (C + A + M − PC = Readiness). Scores of 8 and less are classified as Precontemplators, 8→11 are Contemplators, and 11→14 are Preparation to Action Takers.

(For further details see www.uri.edu/research/cprc/measures.htm)

Readiness to Change Questionnaire

Citation: Rollnick, S., Heather, N., Gold, R. and Hall, W. (1992) 'Development of a short readiness to change questionnaire for use in brief opportunistic interventions among excessive drinkers', *British Journal of Addiction*, 87: 743–54.

Instructions: Please read each question below carefully and then decide whether you agree or disagree with the statements. Please circle the answer of your choice to each question. If you have any problems please ask the questionnaire administrator.

Key: **SD = Strongly disagree D = Disagree U = Unsure A = Agree SA = Strongly agree**

1. I don't think that I drink too much.	SD	D	U	A	SA
2. I am trying to drink less than I used to.	SD	D	U	A	SA
3. I enjoy my drinking, but sometimes I drink too much.	SD	D	U	A	SA
4. Sometimes I think I should cut down on my drinking.	SD	D	U	A	SA
5. It's a waste of time thinking about my drinking.	SD	D	U	A	SA
6. I have just recently changed my drinking habits.	SD	D	U	A	SA
7. Anyone can talk about wanting to do something about drinking, but I am actually doing something about it.	SD	D	U	A	SA
8. I am at the stage where I should think about drinking less alcohol.	SD	D	U	A	SA
9. My drinking is a problem sometimes.	SD	D	U	A	SA
10. There is no need for me to think about changing my drinking.	SD	D	U	A	SA
11. I am actually changing my drinking habits right now.	SD	D	U	A	SA
12. Drinking less alcohol would be pointless for me.	SD	D	U	A	SA

Scoring protocol

Precontemplation items: 1, 5, 10, 12

Contemplation items: 3, 4, 8, 9

Action items: 2, 6, 7, 11

To calculate the score for each scale, simply add the items score for the scale in question. The range on each scale is –8 through 0 to +8. A negative scale score reflects an overall disagreement with items measuring the stage of change, whereas a positive score represents overall agreement. The highest score represents the Stage of Change Designation.

Note: If two or more scale scores are equal, then the scale farthest along the continuum of change (Precontemplation–Contemplation–Action) represents the Stage of Change Designation. For example, if a someone scores 6 on the Precontemplation scale, 6 on the Contemplation scale, and –2 on the Action scale, then that person is assigned to the Contemplation stage.

If one of the four items on a scale is missing, the individual's score for that scale should be pro-rated (i.e. multiplied by 4/3 or 1.33). If two or more items are missing, the scale score cannot be calculated. In this case, the Stage of Change Designation will be invalid.

Revised Readiness to Change Questionnaire

[Treatment Version]

Citation: Heather, N. and Honekopp, J. (2008) 'A revised edition of the Readiness to Change Questionnaire [Treatment Version]', *Addiction Research and Theory*, 16: 421–33.

Instructions: The following questions are designed to identify how you personally feel about your drinking right now. Please think about your current situation and drinking habits, even if you given up drinking completely. Read each question below carefully and then decide whether you agree or disagree with the statements. Please circle the answer of your choice to each question. If you have any problems please ask the questionnaire administrator.

Key: SD = Strongly disagree D = Disagree U = Unsure A = Agree SA = Strongly agree

1. It's a waste of time thinking about my drinking because I do not have a problem.	SD	D	U	A	SA
2. I enjoy my drinking but sometimes I drink too much.	SD	D	U	A	SA
3. There is nothing seriously wrong with my drinking.	SD	D	U	A	SA
4. Sometimes I think I should quit or cut down on my drinking.	SD	D	U	A	SA
5. Anyone can talk about wanting to do something about their drinking, but I'm actually doing something about.	SD	D	U	A	SA
6. I am a fairly normal drinker.	SD	D	U	A	SA
7. My drinking is a problem sometimes.	SD	D	U	A	SA
8. I am actually changing my drinking habits right now (either cutting down or quitting).	SD	D	U	A	SA
9. I have started to carry out a plan to cut down or quit drinking.	SD	D	U	A	SA
10. There is nothing I really need to change about my drinking.	SD	D	U	A	SA
11. Sometimes I wonder if my drinking is out of control.	SD	D	U	A	SA
12. I am actively working on my drinking problems.	SD	D	U	A	SA

Scoring protocol

Precontemplation items: 1, 3, 6, 10

Contemplation items: 2, 4, 7, 11

Action items: 5, 8, 9, 12

Follow the scoring protocol for the Readiness to Change Questionnaire.

Personal Drinking Questionnaire

(SOCRATES 8A)

Citation: Miller, W. R. and Tonigan, J. S. (1996) 'Assessing drinkers' motivation for change: The Stages of Change Readiness and Treatment Eagerness Scale (SOCRATES)', *Psychology of Addictive Behaviors*, 10: 81–9.

Instructions: Please read the following statements carefully. Each one describes a way that you might (or might not) feel about your drinking. For each statement, circle one number from 1 to 5, to indicate how much you agree or disagree with it right now. Please circle one and only one number for every statement.

	Strongly disagree	Disagree	Undecided	Agree	Strongly agree
1. I really want to make changes in my drinking.	1	2	3	4	5
2. Sometimes I wonder if I am an alcoholic.	1	2	3	4	5
3. If I don't change my drinking soon, my problems are going to get worse.	1	2	3	4	5
4. I have already started making some changes in my drinking.	1	2	3	4	5
5. I was drinking too much at one time, but I've managed to change my drinking.	1	2	3	4	5
6. Sometimes I wonder if my drinking is hurting other people.	1	2	3	4	5
7. I am a problem drinker.	1	2	3	4	5
8. I'm not just thinking about changing my drinking, I'm already doing something about it.	1	2	3	4	5
9. I have already changed my drinking, and I am looking for ways to keep from slipping back to my old pattern.	1	2	3	4	5
10. I have serious problems with drinking.	1	2	3	4	5
11. Sometimes I wonder if I am in control of my drinking.	1	2	3	4	5

12. My drinking is causing a lot of harm. ① ② ③ ④ ⑤

13. I am actively doing things now to cut down or stop drinking. ① ② ③ ④ ⑤

14. I want help to keep from going back to the drinking problems that I had before. ① ② ③ ④ ⑤

15. I know that I have a drinking problem. ① ② ③ ④ ⑤

16. There are times when I wonder if I drink too much. ① ② ③ ④ ⑤

17. I am an alcoholic. ① ② ③ ④ ⑤

18. I am working hard to change my drinking. ① ② ③ ④ ⑤

19. I have made some changes in my drinking, and I want some help to keep from going back to the way I used to drink. ① ② ③ ④ ⑤

Scoring protocol

Recognition (Re):   1, 3, 7, 10, 12, 15, 17

Ambivalence (Am):   2, 6, 8, 11, 16

Take steps (Ts):   4, 5, 8, 9, 13, 14, 18, 19

Sum each of the items to yield a score for each subscale. Then transfer the total scale scores into the empty boxes at the bottom of the profile sheet. For each scale, CIRCLE the same value above it to determine the decile range.

Profile sheet

DECILE SCORES	Recognition	Ambivalence	Taking steps
90 Very high		19–20	39–40
80		18	37–38
70 High	35	17	36
60	34	16	34–35
50 Medium	32–33	15	34
40	31	14	32–33
30	29–30	12–13	31
20	27–28	9–11	29–30
10	7–26	4–8	8–25
RAW SCORES	Re =	Am =	Ts = 111

The following are provided as general guidelines for interpretation of scores, but it is wise in an individual case also to examine individual item responses for additional information.

Recognition

HIGH scorers directly acknowledge that they are having problems related to their drinking, tending to express a desire for change and to perceive that harm will continue if they do not change.

LOW scorers deny that alcohol is causing them serious problems, reject diagnostic labels such as 'problem drinker' and 'alcoholic', and do not express a desire for change.

Ambivalence

HIGH scorers say that they sometimes wonder if they are in control of their drinking, are drinking too much, are hurting other people, and/or are alcoholic. Thus a high score reflects ambivalence or uncertainty. A high score here reflects some openness to reflection, as might be particularly expected in the contemplation stage of change.

LOW scorers say that they do not wonder whether they drink too much, are in control, are hurting others, or are alcoholic. Note that a person may score low on ambivalence either because they 'know' their drinking is causing problems (high recognition), or because they 'know' that they do not have drinking problems (low recognition). Thus a low ambivalence score should be interpreted in relation to the recognition score.

Taking steps

HIGH scorers report that they are already doing things to make a positive change in their drinking, and may have experienced some success in this regard. Change is under way, and they may want help to persist or to prevent backsliding. A high score on this scale has been found to be predictive of successful change.

LOW scorers report that they are not currently doing things to change their drinking, and have not made such changes recently.

Personal Drug Use Questionnaire

(SOCRATES 8D)

	Strongly disagree	Disagree	Undecided	Agree	Strongly agree
1. I really want to make changes in my use of drugs.	1	2	3	4	5
2. Sometimes I wonder if I am a drug addict.	1	2	3	4	5
3. If I don't change my use of drugs soon, my problems are going to get worse.	1	2	3	4	5
4. I have already started making some changes in my use of drugs.	1	2	3	4	5
5. I was using drugs too much at one time, but I've managed to change that.	1	2	3	4	5
6. Sometimes I wonder if my drug use is hurting other people.	1	2	3	4	5
7. I have a drug problem.	1	2	3	4	5
8. I'm not just thinking about changing my drug use, I'm already doing something about it.	1	2	3	4	5
9. I have already changed my drug use, and I am looking for ways to keep from slipping back to my old pattern.	1	2	3	4	5
10. I have serious problems with drugs.	1	2	3	4	5
11. Sometimes I wonder if I am in control of my drug use.	1	2	3	4	5
12. My drug use is causing a lot of harm.	1	2	3	4	5
13. I am actively doing things now to cut down on my use of drugs.	1	2	3	4	5
14. I want help to keep from going back to the drug problems that I had before.	1	2	3	4	5
15. I know that I have a drug problem.	1	2	3	4	5
16. There are times when I wonder if I use drugs too much.	1	2	3	4	5
17. I am a drug addict.	1	2	3	4	5

18. I am working hard to change my
    drug use.   ① ② ③ ④ ⑤
19. I have made some changes in my
    drug use, and I want some help
    to keep from going back to the way
    I used before.   ① ② ③ ④ ⑤

Scoring protocol

Use the same protocol as that provided above for the Personal Drinking Questionnaire.

Corrections Victoria Treatment Readiness Questionnaire

Citation: Casey, S., Day, A., Howells, K. and Ward, T. (2007) 'Assessing suitability for offender rehabilitation: Development and validation of the Treatment Readiness Questionnaire', *Criminal Justice and Behaviour*, 34: 1427–40.

Instructions: Please read each statement below carefully and then decide whether you agree or disagree with each statement. Circle the number that best represents how you feel. Please circle one and only one number for every statement.

	Strongly disagree	Disagree	Undecided	Agree	Strongly agree
1. Treatment programs are rubbish.	1	2	3	4	5
2. I want to change.	1	2	3	4	5
3. Generally I can trust other people.	1	2	3	4	5
4. I am not able to do treatment programs.	1	2	3	4	5
5. I am to blame for my offending.	1	2	3	4	5
6. Treatment programs don't work.	1	2	3	4	5
7. When I think about my last offence I feel angry with myself.	1	2	3	4	5
8. Others are to blame for my offending.	1	2	3	4	5
9. I am upset about being a corrections client.	1	2	3	4	5
10. Stopping offending is really important to me.	1	2	3	4	5
11. I am well organised.	1	2	3	4	5
12. I feel guilty about my offending.	1	2	3	4	5
13. I have not offended for some time now.	1	2	3	4	5
14. I don't deserve to be doing a sentence.	1	2	3	4	5
15. Being seen as an offender upsets me.	1	2	3	4	5
16. When I think about my sentence I feel angry with other people.	1	2	3	4	5
17. I regret the offence that led to my last sentence.	1	2	3	4	5

18. I feel ashamed about my offending.	①	②	③	④	⑤
19. I hate being told what to do.	①	②	③	④	⑤
20. Treatment programs are for wimps.	①	②	③	④	⑤

Scoring protocol

Attitudes and motivation items: 1, 2, 4, 6, 10, 20

Emotional reactions items: 7, 9, 12, 15, 17, 18

Offending beliefs items: 5, 8, 14, 16

Efficacy items: 3, 11, 13, 19

To obtain a Treatment Readiness reverse code items numbered 1, 4, 6, 8, 14, 16, 19 and 20 and then sum all items to obtain a total readiness score. Subscale scores can be obtained by summing the relevant items. These scores can be used as an indicator for areas for intervention when readiness scores are low. While Casey *et al.* recommend a cut-off score of 72 as indicative of readiness for treatment, any decision about cut-offs needs to be made in conjunction with other treatment considerations (including decisions about the percentage of false positives and false negatives considered acceptable).

Violence Treatment Readiness Questionnaire

Citation: Day, A., Howells, K., Casey, S., Ward, T., Chambers, J. and Birgden, A. (2009) 'Assessing treatment readiness in violent offenders', *Journal of Interpersonal Violence*, 24: 618–35.

Instructions: Please read each statement below carefully and then decide whether you agree or disagree with each statement. Circle the number that best represents how you feel. Please circle one and only one number for every statement.

	Strongly disagree	Disagree	Undecided	Agree	Strongly agree
1. Treatment programs are rubbish.	①	②	③	④	⑤
2. I want to change.	①	②	③	④	⑤
3. Generally I can trust other people.	①	②	③	④	⑤
4. I am not able to do treatment programs.	①	②	③	④	⑤
5. I am to blame for my violence.	①	②	③	④	⑤
6. Treatment programs don't work.	①	②	③	④	⑤
7. When I think about my last offence I feel angry with myself.	①	②	③	④	⑤
8. Others are to blame for my violence.	①	②	③	④	⑤
9. I am upset about being a corrections client.	①	②	③	④	⑤
10. Stopping offending is really important to me.	①	②	③	④	⑤
11. I am well organised.	①	②	③	④	⑤
12. I feel guilty about my offending.	①	②	③	④	⑤
13. I have not acted violently for some time now.	①	②	③	④	⑤
14. I don't deserve to be doing a sentence.	①	②	③	④	⑤
15. Being seen as an offender upsets me.	①	②	③	④	⑤
16. When I think about my sentence I feel angry with other people.	①	②	③	④	⑤
17. I regret the offence that led to my last sentence.	①	②	③	④	⑤

18. I feel ashamed about my
    violence. ① ② ③ ④ ⑤
19. I hate being told what to
    do. ① ② ③ ④ ⑤
20. Treatment programs are for
    wimps. ① ② ③ ④ ⑤

Scoring protocol

Use the same protocol as that provided above for the Corrections Victoria Treatment Readiness Questionnaire.

Selected journal articles

Casey, S., Day, A. and Howells, K. (2005) 'The application of the transtheoretical model to offender populations: Some critical issues', *Legal and Criminological Psychology*, 10: 1–15.

Casey, S., Day, A., Howells, K. and Ward, T. (2007) 'Assessing suitability for offender rehabilitation: Development and validation of the treatment readiness questionnaire', *Criminal Justice and Behavior*, 34: 1427–40.

Chambers, J. C., Eccleston, L., Day, A., Ward, T. and Howells, K. (2008) 'Treatment readiness in violent offenders: The influence of cognitive factors on engagement in violence programs', *Aggression and Violent Behavior*, 13: 276–84.

Day, A. and Carson, E. (2009) 'Intervention programs for male perpetrators of domestic violence: Program goals and the role of the practitioner in legally coerced services', *Psychology Journal*, 6(4).

Day, A., Bryan, J., Davey, L. and Casey, S. (2006) 'Processes of change in offender rehabilitation', *Psychology, Crime and Law*, 12(5): 473–89.

Day, A., Howells, K., Casey, S., Ward, T. and Birgden, A. (2007) 'Treatment readiness: An overview of Australasian work', *Issues in Forensic Psychology*, Special Issue on readiness for treatment in offenders, 7: 19–23. British Psychological Society, Leicester.

Day, A., Howells, K., Casey, S., Ward, T., Chambers, J. C. and Birgden, A. (2009) 'Assessing treatment readiness in violent offenders', *Journal of Interpersonal Violence*, 24(4): 618–35.

Day, A., Tucker, K. and Howells, K. (2004) 'Coercing offenders into treatment', invited paper for special issue of *Psychology, Crime and Law*, 10: 259–69.

Howells, K. and Day, A. (2003) 'Readiness for anger management: Clinical and theoretical issues', *Clinical Psychology Review*, 23: 319–37.

Howells, K. and Day, A. (2006) 'Affective determinants of treatment engagement in violent offenders', *International Journal of Offender Rehabilitation and Comparative Criminology*, 50: 174–86.
Howells, K. and Day, A. (2007) 'Readiness for treatment in high risk offenders with personality disorders', *Psychology, Crime and Law*, 13(1): 47–57: Special Issue: High risk Offenders with Personality Disorders: Conceptual and scientific bases.

Ward, T., Day, A., Howells, K. and Birgden, A. (2004) 'The multifactor offender readiness model', *Aggression and Violent Behavior*, 9: 645–73.
Williamson, P., Day, A., Howells, K., Bubner, S. and Jauncey, S. (2003) 'Assessing offender motivation to address problems with anger', *Psychology, Crime and Law*, 9(4): 295–307.

References

Abel, G. G., Becker, J. V. and Cunningham-Rathner, J. (1984) 'Complications, consent and cognitions in sex between children and adults', *International Journal of Law and Psychiatry*, 7: 89–103.

Abel, G. G., Mittleman, M., Becker, J., Rathner, J. and Rouleau, J. (1988) 'Predicting child molesters' response to treatment', *Annals of the New York Academy of Science*, 528: 223–35.

Abram, K. M., Teplin, L. A. and McClelland, G. M. (2003) 'Comorbidity of severe psychiatric disorders and substance use disorders among women in jail', *American Journal of Psychiatry*, 160: 1007–10.

Ackerman, S. J. and Hilsenroth, M. J. (2001) 'A review of therapist characteristics and techniques negatively impacting the therapeutic alliance', *Psychotherapy*, 38(2): 171–85.

Aharonovich, E., Brooks, A. C., Nunes, E. V. and Hasin, D. S. (2008) 'Cognitive deficits in marijuana users: Effects on motivational enhancement therapy plus cognitive behavioral therapy treatment outcome', *Drug and Alcohol Dependence*, 95: 279–83.

Aharonovich, E., Hasin, D. S., Brooks, A. C., Liu, X., Bisaga, A. and Nunes, E. V. (2006) 'Cognitive deficits predict low treatment retention in cocaine dependent patients', *Drug and Alcohol Dependence*, 81: 313–22.

Allen, L. C., MacKenzie, D. L. and Hickman, L. J. (2001) 'The effectiveness of cognitive behavioral treatment for adult offenders: A methodological, quality-based review', *International Journal of Offender Therapy and Comparative Criminology*, 45: 498–514.

Alterman, A. I. and Cacciola, J. S. (1991) 'The antisocial personality disorder diagnosis in substance abusers', *Journal of Nervous and Mental Disease*, 179: 401–9.

Alterman, A. I. and Hall, J. G. (1989) 'Effects of social drinking and familial alcoholism risk on cognitive functioning: Null findings', *Alcoholism: Clinical and Experimental Research*, 13: 799–803.

American Psychiatric Association (1994) *Diagnostic and Statistical Manual of Mental Disorders*, 4th edn. Washington, DC: APA.

Andrews, D. A. (2006) 'Enhancing adherence to risk–need–responsivity: Making equality a matter of policy', *Criminology and Public Policy*, 5: 595–602.

Andrews, D. A. and Bonta, J. (1998) *The Psychology of Criminal Conduct*, 2nd edn. Cincinnati, OH: Anderson.

Andrews, D. A. and Bonta, J. (2003) *The Psychology of Criminal Conduct*, 3rd edn. Cincinnati, OH: Anderson.

Andrews, D. A. and Bonta, J. (2006) *The Psychology of Criminal Conduct*, 4th edn. Cincinnati, OH: Anderson.

Andrews, D. A. and Dowden, C. (2007) 'The risk–need–responsivity model of assessment and human service in prevention and corrections: Crime-prevention jurisprudence', *Canadian Journal of Criminology and Criminal Justice*, 49: 439–64.

Andrews, D. A. and Kiessling, J. J. (1980) 'Program structure and effective correctional practices: A summary of the CaVIC research', in R. R. Ross and P. Gendreau (eds) *Effective Correctional Treatment*. Toronto: Butterworth.

Andrews, D. A., Zinger, I., Hoge, R. D., Bonta, J., Gendreau, P. and Cullen, F. T. (1990) 'Does correctional treatment work? A clinically relevant and psychologically informed meta analysis', *Criminology*, 28: 369–404.

Anglin, M. D. and Perrochet, B. (1998) 'Drug use and crime: A historical review of research conducted by the UCLA Drug Abuse Research Center', *Substance Use and Misuse*, 33: 1871–914.

Anglin, M. D., Longshore, D. and Turner, S. (1999) 'Treatment alternatives to street crime', *Criminal Justice and Behavior*, 26: 168–95.

Anstiss, B., Polaschek, D. L. L. and Wilson, M. J. (in press) 'A brief motivational interviewing intervention with prisoners: When you lead a horse to water, can it drink for itself?', *Psychology, Crime and Law*.

Archer, J. (2000) 'Sex differences in aggression between heterosexual partners: A meta-analytic review', *Psychological Bulletin*, 126: 651–80.

Archer, J. (2004) 'Sex differences in aggression in real-world settings: A meta-analytic review', *Review of General Psychology*, 8: 291–322.

Archer, M. S. (2000) *Being Human: The Problem of Agency*. Cambridge: Cambridge University Press.

Arnkoff, D. B., Glass, C. R. and Shapiro, S. J. (2002) 'Expectations and preferences', in J. C. Norcross (ed.) *Psychotherapy Relationships that Work: Therapist Contributions and Responsiveness to Patients*. New York: Oxford University Press.

Aspinwall, L. G. and Staudinger, U. M. (eds) (2003) *A Psychology of Human Strengths: Fundamental Questions and Future Directions for a Positive Psychology*. Washington, DC: American Psychological Association.

ATSA (Association for the Treatment of Sexual Abusers) (2005) *Practice Standards and Guidelines for the Evaluation, Treatment and Management of Adult Male Sexual Abusers*. Beaverton, OR: ATSA.

Austin, J. T. and Vancouver, J. B. (1996) 'Goal constructs in psychology: Structure process and content', *Psychological Bulletin*, 120: 338–75.

Averill, J. R. (1983) 'Studies on anger and aggression: Implications for theories of emotion', *American Psychologist*, 38: 1145–60.

Babcock, J. C., Green, C. E. and Robie, C. (2004) 'Does batterers' treatment work? A meta-analytic review of domestic violence treatment', *Clinical Psychology Review*, 23: 1023–53.

Baker, E. and Beech, A. R. (2004) 'Dissociation and variability of adult attachment dimensions and early maladaptive schemas in sexual and violent offenders', *Journal of Interpersonal Violence*, 19(10): 1119–36.

Bandura, A. (1986) *Social Foundations of Thought and Action.* Englewood Cliffs, NJ: Prentice Hall.

Bandura, A. (1997) *Self-efficacy: The Exercise of Control.* New York: Freeman.

Bandura, A. and Locke, E. A. (2003) 'Negative self-efficacy and goal effects revisited', *Journal of Applied Psychology*, 88: 87–99.

Barbaree, H. E. (1991) 'Denial and minimization among sex offenders: Assessment and treatment outcome', *Forum on Corrections Research*, 3: 30–3.

Barber, J. G. (1991) *Beyond Casework.* Basingstoke: Macmillan.

Barber, J. P., Gallop, R., Crits-Christoph, P., Barrett, M. S., Klosterman, S., McCarthy, K. S. and Sharpless, B. A. (2008) 'The role of the alliance and techniques in predicting outcome of supportive-expressive dynamic therapy for cocaine dependence', *Psychoanalytic Psychology*, 25(3): 461–82.

Barber, J. P., Luborsky, L., Gallop, R., Frank, A., Weiss, R. D., Thase, M., Connolly, M. B., Gladis, M., Foltz, C. and Siqueland, L. (2001) 'Therapeutic alliance as a predictor of outcome and retention in the National Institute on Drug Abuse Collaborative Cocaine Treatment Study', *Journal of Consulting and Clinical Psychology*, 69(1): 119–24.

Barlow, D. H. (2004) 'Psychological treatments', *American Psychologist*, 59: 869–78.

Barratt, E. S. and Slaughter, L. (1998) 'Defining, measuring and predicting impulsive aggression: A heuristic model', *Behavioral Sciences and the Law*, 16: 285–302.

Barrett, K. C. (1995) 'A functionalist approach to shame and guilt', in J. P. Tangney and K. W. Fischer (eds) *Self-conscious Emotions: The Psychology of Shame, Guilt, Embarrassment and Pride.* New York: Guilford Press.

Barrett, M., Wilson, R. J. and Long, C. (2003) 'Measuring motivation to change in sexual offenders from institutional intake to community treatment', *Sexual Abuse: A Journal of Research and Treatment*, 15(4): 269–83.

Bau, C. H. D., Spode, A., Ponso, A. C., Elias, E. P., Garcia, C. E. D., Costa, F. T. and Hutz, M. H. (2001) 'Heterogeneity in early onset alcoholism suggests a third group of alcoholics', *Alcohol*, 23: 9–13.

Baxter, D. J., Marion, A. and Goguen, B. (1995) 'Predicting treatment response in correctional settings', *Forum on Corrections Research*, 7.

Beauford, J. E., McNiel, D. E. and Binder, R. L. (1997) 'Utility of the initial therapeutic alliance in evaluating psychiatric patients risk of violence', *American Journal of Psychiatry*, 154(9): 1272–6.

Bechara, A. and Damasio, H. (2002) 'Decision making and addiction, Part 1: Impaired activation of somatic states in substance-dependent individuals when pondering decision with negative future consequences', *Neuropsychologia*, 40: 1675–89.

Bechara, A., Tranel, D. and Damasio, A. R. (2002) 'The somatic marker hypothesis and decision-making', in F. Boller, J. Grafman and G. Rizzolatti (eds) *Handbook of Neuropsychology*, 2nd edn. Amsterdam: Elsevier.

Beck, A. T. (1964) 'Thinking and depression: 2. Theory and therapy', *Archives of General Psychiatry*, 9: 324–33.

Beck, A. T. (1967) *Depression: Causes and Treatment*. Philadelphia: University of Pennsylvania Press.

Beck, A. T., Freeman, A. and Davis, D. D. (2004) *Cognitive Therapy of Personality Disorders*. New York: Guilford Press.

Beech, A. R. and Hamilton-Giachritsis, C. E. (2005) 'Relationship between therapeutic climate and treatment outcome in group-based sexual offender treatment programs', *Sexual Abuse: A Journal of Research and Treatment*, 17(2): 127–40.

Begun, A. L., Shelley, G., Strodthoff, T. and Short, L. (2001) 'Adopting a stages of change approach for individuals who are violent with their intimate partners', *Journal of Aggression, Maltreatment and Trauma*, 5(2): 105–27.

Bell, A. C. and D'Zurilla, T. J. (2009) 'Problem-solving therapy for depression: A meta-analysis', *Clinical Psychology Review*, 29: 348–53.

Bennett, D., Parry, G. and Ryle, A. (2006) 'Resolving threats to the therapeutic alliance in cognitive analytic therapy of borderline personality disorder: A task analysis', *Psychology and Psychotherapy: Theory, Research and Practice*, 79: 395–418.

Berger, P., Berner, W., Bolterauer, J., Gutierrez, K. and Berger, K. (1999) 'Sadistic personality disorder in sex offenders: Relationship to antisocial personality disorder and sexual sadism', *Journal of Personality Disorder*, 13: 175–86.

Berkowitz, L. (1999) 'Anger', in T. Dalgleish and M. Power (eds) *Handbook of Cognition and Emotion*. Chichester: John Wiley.

Beutler, L. E., Clarkin, J. F. and Bongar, B. (2000) *Guidelines for the Systematic Treatment of the Depressed Patient*. London: Oxford University Press.

Beyko, M. J. and Wong, S. C. P. (2005) 'Predictors of treatment attrition as indicators for program improvement not offender shortcomings: A study of sex offender treatment attrition', *Sexual Abuse: A Journal of Research and Treatment*, 17(4): 375–89.

Biggam, F. H. and Power, K. G. (1999a) 'A comparison of the problem solving abilities and psychological distress of suicidal, bullied and protected prisoners', *Criminal Justice and Behavior*, 26: 196–216.

Biggam, F. H. and Power, K. G. (1999b) 'Social problem-solving skills and psychological distress among incarcerated young offenders: The issue of bullying and victimization', *Cognitive Therapy and Research*, 23: 307–26.

Birgden, A. and Vincent, F. (2000) 'Maximizing therapeutic effects in treating sexual offenders in an Australian correctional system', *Behavioral Sciences and the Law*, 18(4): 479–88.

Blackburn, R. (2000) 'Treatment or incapacitation? Implications of research on personality disorders for the management of dangerous offenders', *Legal and Criminological Psychology*, 5: 1–21.

Blair, R. J. R. (2004) 'The roles of orbital frontal cortex in the modulation of antisocial behaviour', *Brain and Cognition*, 55: 198–208.

Blair, R. J. R. (2008) 'The amygdala and ventomedial prefrontal cortex: functional contributions and dysfunction in psychopathy', in S. Hodgins, E. Viding and A. Plodowski (eds) *The Neurobiology of Violence: Implications for Prevention and Treatment*, Philosophical Transactions of the Royal Society, 363: 2557–66.

Blanchette, K. and Moser, A. (2006) *The Integrated Correctional Intervention Strategies (ICIS) Pilot Project: Preliminary Results*. Correctional Service Canada.

Boldero, J. and Fallon, B. (1995) 'Adolescent help-seeking: What do they get help for and from whom?', *Journal of Adolescence*, 18: 193–209.

Bonner, A. (2006) *Social Exclusion and the Way Out: An Individual and Community Response to Human Social Dysfunction*. Chichester: John Wiley.

Bonta, J. (1997) *Offender Rehabilitation: From Research to Practice*, Report No. 1997–01. Ottawa, Canada: Solicitor General Canada.

Bonta, J., Hanson, K. and Law, M. (1998) 'The prediction of criminal and violent recidivism among mentally disordered offenders: A meta-analysis', *Psychological Bulletin*, 123: 123–42.

Bonta, J., Rugge, T., Scott, T., Bourgon, G. and Yessine, A. K. (2008) 'Exploring the black box of community supervision', *Journal of Offender Rehabilitation*, 47: 248–70.

Bordin, E. (1979) 'The generalizability of the psychoanalytic concept of the working alliance', *Psychotherapy: Theory, Research and Practice*, 16(3): 252–60.

Bordin, E. (1994) 'Theory and research on the therapeutic working alliance: New Directions', in A. Horvath and L. Greenberg (eds) *The Working Alliance: Theory, Research and Practice*. New York: John Wiley.

Brady, T. M. and Ashley, O. S. (eds) (2005) *Women in Substance Abuse Treatment: Results from the Alcohol and Drug Services Study (ADSS)*, DHHS Publication No. SMA 04–3968, Analytic Series A–26. Rockville, MD: Substance Abuse and Mental Health Services Administration, Office of Applied Studies.

Bray, S., Barrowclough, C. and Lobban, F. (2007) 'The social problem-solving abilities of people with borderline personality disorder', *Behaviour Research and Therapy*, 45: 1409–17.

Brecht, M. L., Anglin, M. D. and Wang, J. C. (1993) 'Treatment effectiveness of legally coerced vs voluntary methadone maintenance clients', *American Journal of Drug and Alcohol Abuse*, 19: 89–106.

Brocato, J and Wagner, E. F. (2008) 'Predictors of retention in an alternative-to-prison substance abuse treatment program', *Criminal Justice and Behavior*, 35(1): 99–119.

Brown, P. D. and O'Leary, K. D. (2000) 'Therapeutic alliance: Predicting continuance and success in group treatment for spouse abuse', *Journal of Consulting and Clinical Psychology*, 68(2): 340–5.

Brown, P. D., O'Leary, K. D. and Feldbau, S. R. (1997) 'Dropout in a treatment program for self-referring wife abusing men', *Journal of Family Violence*, 12(4): 365–87.

Brown, V. B., Melchior, L. A., Panter, A. T., Slaughter, R. and Huba, G. J. (2000) 'Women's steps of change and entry into drug abuse treatment: A multidimensional stages of change model', *Journal of Substance Abuse Treatment*, 18, 231–40.

Bumby, K. M., Marshall, W. L. and Langton, C. (1999) 'A theoretical model of the influences of shame and guilt on sexual offending', in B. K. Schwartz (ed.) *The Sex Offender: Theoretical Advances, Treating Special Populations*. Civic Research Institute.

Burdon, W. M. and Gallagher, C. A. (2002) 'Coercion and sex offenders: Controlling sex-offending behavior through incapacitation and treatment', *Criminal Justice and Behavior*, 29(1): 87–109.

Burke, P. and Tonry, M. (2006) *Successful Transition and Reentry for Safer Communities: A Call to Action for Parole*. Silver Spring, MD: Center for Effective Public Policy.

Burke, B. L., Arkowitz, H. and Menchola, M. (2003) 'The efficacy of motivational interviewing: A meta-analysis of controlled clinical trials', *Journal of Consulting and Clinical Psychology*, 71(5): 843–61.

Burnett, R. (2002) *The Dynamics of Recidivism*. Oxford: University of Oxford Centre for Criminological Research.

Burrowes, N. and Needs, A. (2009) 'Time to contemplate change? A framework for assessing readiness to change with offenders', *Aggression and Violent Behavior*, 14: 39–49.

Bushman, B. J. and Anderson, C. A. (2001) 'Is it time to pull the plug on the hostile versus instrumental aggression dichotomy?', *Psychological Review*, 108: 273–9.

Buttell, F. P. and Carney, M. M. (2008) 'A large sample investigation of batterer intervention program attrition: Evaluating the impact of state program standards', *Research on Social Work Practice*, 18: 177–88.

Campbell, A. (2006) 'Sex differences in direct aggression: What are the psychological mediators?', *Aggression and Violent Behavior*, 11: 237–64.

Casey, S., Day, A. and Howells, K. (2005) 'The application of the transtheoretical model to offender populations: Some critical issues', *Legal and Criminology Psychology*, 10: 157–71.

Casey, S., Day, A., Howells, K. and Ward, T. (2007) 'Assessing suitability for offender rehabilitation: Development and validation of the Treatment Readiness Questionnaire', *Criminal Justice and Behavior*, 34(11): 1427–44.

Castonguay, L. G., Constantino, M. J. and Grosse Holtforth, M. (2006) 'The working alliance: Where are we and where should we go?', *Psychotherapy: Theory, Research, Practice, Training*, 43(3): 271–9.

Cavell, T. A. and Malcolm, K. T. (eds) (2007) *Anger, Aggression and Interventions for Interpersonal Violence*. Mahwah, NJ: Lawrence Erlbaum.

Chaiken, J. and Chaiken, M. (1990) 'Drugs and predatory crime', in M. Tonry and J. Wilson (eds) *Drugs and Crime*. Chicago: University of Chicago Press.

Chambers, J. (2006) 'The Violence Situation: A Descriptive Model of the Offence Process of Assault for Male and Female Offenders', PhD thesis, Department of Criminology, University of Melbourne.

Chambers, J. C., Eccleston, L., Day, A., Ward, T. and Howells, K. (2008) 'Treatment readiness in violent offenders: The influence of cognitive factors on engagement in violence programs', *Aggression and Violent Behavior*, 13: 276–84.

Chambless, D. L. and Hollon, S. D. (1998) 'Defining empirically supported therapies', *Journal of Consulting and Clinical Psychology*, 66: 7–18.

Chew, F., Palmer, S., Slonska, Z. and Subbiah, K. (2002) 'Enhancing health knowledge, health beliefs and health behaviour in Poland through a health promoting television program series', *Journal of Health Communication*, 7: 179–96.

Childress, A. R., McElgin, W., Mozley, D., Fitzgerald, J., Reivich, M. and O'Brien, C. P. (1999) 'Limbic activation during cue-induced cocaine craving', *American Journal of Psychiatry*, 156: 11–18.

Christopher, G. and McMurran, M. (2009) 'Alexithymia, empathic concern, goal management and social problem solving in adult male prisoners', *Psychology, Crime and Law*, 15: 697–709.

Clark, A. (2007) 'Soft selves and ecological control', in D. Spurrett, D. Ross, H. Kincaid and L. Stephens (eds) *Distributed Cognition and the Will*. Cambridge, MA: MIT Press.

Clark, A. (2008) *Supersizing the Mind: Embodiment, Action and Cognitive Extension*. New York: Oxford University Press.

Clark, L. and Robbins, T. W. (2002) 'Decision-making deficits in drug addiction', *Trends in Cognitive Sciences*, 6: 361–3.

Cohen, S. and Parkman, H. P. (1998) 'Esophageal manometry in clinical practice: The need for evidence-based assessment of clinical efficacy', *American Journal of Gastroenterology*, 93: 2319–20.

Collins, J. J. (1993) 'Drinking and violence: An individual offender focus', in S. E. Martin (ed.) *Alcohol and Interpersonal Violence: Fostering Multidisciplinary Perspectives*. Rockville, MD: National Institute of Health.

Collins, J. J. and Messerschmidt, P. M. (1993) 'Epidemiology of alcohol-related violence', *Alcohol Health and Research World*, 17: 93–100.

Connolly Gibbons, M. B., Crits-Christoph, P., de la Cruz, C., Barber, J. P., Siqueland, L. and Gladis, M. (2003) 'Pretreatment expectations, interpersonal functioning and symptoms in the prediction of the therapeutic alliance across supportive-expressive psychotherapy and cognitive therapy', *Psychotherapy*, 13(1): 59–76.

Connors, G. J., Carroll, K. M., DiClemente, C. C., Longabaugh, R. and Donovan, D. M. (1997) 'The therapeutic alliance and its relationship to alcoholism treatment participation and outcome', *Journal of Consulting and Clinical Psychology*, 65(4): 588–98.

Constantino, M. J., Arnow, B. A., Blasey, C. and Agras, W. S. (2005) 'The association between patient characteristics and the therapeutic alliance in cognitive-behavioural and interpersonal therapy for bulimia nervosa', *Journal of Consulting and Clinical Psychology*, 73(2): 203–11.

Constantino, M. J., Castonguay, L. G. and Schut, A. J. (2002) 'The Working Alliance: A flagship for the "scientist-practitioner" model in psychotherapy', in G. S. Tryon (ed.) *Counseling Based on Process Research: Applying What We Know*. Boston, MA: Allyn and Bacon.

Cooper, S. (2005) 'Understanding, treating and managing sex offenders who deny their offence', *Journal of Sexual Aggression*, 11(1): 85–94.

Corcoran, M. and Corcoran, J. (2001) 'Retrospective reasons for the initiation of substance use: Gender and ethnic effects', *Journal of Ethnic and Cultural Diversity in Social Work*, 10: 69–83.

Correctional Service of Canada (2009) http://www.csc–scc.gc.ca/text/prgrms-eng.shtml. Retrieved 27 October 2009.

Cosyns, P. (1999) 'Treatment of sexual offenders in Belgium', *Journal of Interpersonal Violence*, 14: 396–410.

Cox, W. M. and Klinger, E. (2002) 'Motivational structure: Relationships with substance abuse and processes of change', *Addictive Behaviors*, 27: 925–40.

Cox, W. M. and Klinger, E. (2004a) 'Measuring motivation: The Motivational Structure Questionnaire and Personal Concerns Inventory', in W. M. Cox and E. Klinger (eds) *Handbook of Motivational Counselling: Concepts, Approaches and Assessment*. Chichester: John Wiley.

Cox, W. M. and Klinger, E. (2004b) 'A motivational model of alcohol use: Determinants of use and change', in W. M. Cox and E. Klinger (eds) *Handbook of Motivational Counselling: Concepts, Approaches and Assessment*. Chichester: John Wiley.

Cox, W. M. and Klinger, E. (2004c) 'Systematic motivational counselling: The Motivational Structure Questionnaire in action', in W. M. Cox and E. Klinger (eds) *Handbook of Motivational Counselling: Concepts, Approaches and Assessment*. Chichester: John Wiley.

Cox, W. M., Blount, J. P., Bair, J. and Hosier, S. G. (2000) 'Motivational predictors of readiness to change chronic substance abuse', *Addiction Research*, 8: 121–8.

Cox, W. M., Schippers, G. M., Klinger, E., Skutle, A., Stuchlikova, I., Man, F., King, A. L. and Inderhaug, R. (2002) 'Motivational structure and alcohol use of university students across four nations', *Journal of Studies on Alcohol*, 63: 280–5.

Craissati, J. and Beech, A. (2001) 'Attrition in a community treatment program for child sexual abusers', *Journal of Interpersonal Violence*, 16: 205–21.

Craissati, J., Webb, L. and Keen, S. (2008) 'The relationship between developmental variables, personality disorder and risk in sex offenders', *Sexual Abuse: A Journal of Research and Treatment*, 20(2): 119–38.

Cunha, P. J., Nicastri, S., Gomes, L. P., Moino, R. M. and Peluso, M. A. (2004) 'Neuropsychological impairments in crack cocaine-dependent inpatients: Preliminary findings', *Brazilian Journal of Psychiatry*, 26: 103–06.

Daffern, M. and Howells, K. (2002) 'Psychiatric inpatient aggression: A review of structural and functional assessment approaches', *Aggression and Violent Behavior*, 3: 1–21.

Daffern, M., Howells, K. and Ogloff, J. R. P. (2006) 'What's the point? Towards a methodology for assessing the function of psychiatric inpatient aggression', *Behaviour Research and Therapy*, 45(1): 101–11.

Davidson, R., Rollnick, S. and MacEwan, I. (1991) *Counselling Problem Drinkers*. London: Routledge.

Davies, S. (2004) 'Secure psychiatric services', in P. Campling, S. Davies and G. Farquharson (eds) *From Toxic Institutions to Therapeutic Environments: Residential Settings in Mental Health Services*. London: Gaskell Press.

Day, A. (2009) 'Offender emotion and self-regulation: Implications for offender rehabilitation programming', *Psychology, Crime and Law*, 15: 119–30.

Day, A. and Carson, E. (2009) 'Intervention programs for male perpetrators of domestic violence: Program goals and the role of the practitioner in legally coerced services', in A. Day, D. Justo, P. O'Leary and D. Chung (eds) *Integrated Responses to Domestic Violence: Research and Practice Experiences in Working with Men*. Annandale, NSW: Federation Press.

Day, A. and Howells, K. (2008) *Theory Manual for the Violent Offender Treatment Program*. Department of Correctional Services, WA.

Day, A., Bryan, J., Davey, L. and Casey, S. (2006) 'The process of change in offender rehabilitation programmes', *Psychology, Crime and Law*, 12(5): 473–87.

Day, A., Casey, S. and Gerace, A. (in press) 'Interventions to improve empathy awareness in sexual and violent offenders: Conceptual, empirical and clinical issues', *Aggression and Violent Behavior*.

Day, A., Howells, K., Casey, S., Ward, T. and Birgden, A. (2007) 'Treatment readiness: An overview of Australasian work', *Issues in Forensic Psychology*, 7: 21–25.

Day, A., Howells, K., Casey, S., Ward, T., Chambers, J. C. and Birgden, A. (2009a) 'Assessing treatment readiness in violent offenders', *Journal of Interpersonal Violence*, 24: 618–35.

Day, A., O'Leary, P., Chung, D. and Justo, D. (2009b) *Integrated Responses to Domestic Violence: Research and Practice Experiences in Working with Men*. Annandale, NSW, Federation Press.

Day, A., Tucker, K. and Howells, K. (2004) 'Coerced offender rehabilitation – A defensible practice?', *Psychology, Crime and Law*, 10(3): 259–69.

Day, K. (2000) 'Offenders with mental retardation', in C. R. Hollin (ed.) *Handbook of Offender Assessment and Treatment*. Chichester: John Wiley.

Dear, G., Beers, K. A., Dastyar, G., Hall, F., Kordanovski, B. and Pritchard, E. C. (2002) 'Prisoners' willingness to approach prison officers for support: The officers' views', *Journal of Offender Rehabilitation*, 34: 33–46.

Deci, E. L. and Ryan, R. M. (2000) 'The "what" and "why" of goal pursuits: Human needs and the self-determination of behavior', *Psychological Inquiry*, 11, 227–68.

Deci, E. L., Koestner, R. and Ryan, R. M. (1999) 'A meta-analytic review of experiments examining the effects of extrinsic rewards on intrinsic motivation', *Psychological Bulletin*, 125: 627–68.

Delva, J., Wallace, J. M., O'Malley, P. M., Bodman, J. G., Johnston, L. D. and Schulberg, J. E. (2005) 'The epidemiology of alcohol, marijuana and cocaine use among Mexican, Puerto Rican, Cuban American and other Latin American eighth grade students in the United States: 1991–2002', *American Journal of Public Health*, 95: 696–702.

Denny, D. (2005) *Risk and Society*. London: Sage.

Department of Justice (2002) *Victorian Prison Drug Strategy 2002*. Melbourne, Victoria.

DiClemente, C. C. (2005) 'Conceptual models and applied research: The ongoing contribution of the Transtheoretical Model', *Journal of Addictions Nursing*, 16: 5–12.

DiClemente, C. C. and Hughes, S. (1990) 'Stages of change profiles in outpatient alcoholism treatment', *Journal of Substance Abuse*, 2: 217–35.

DiClemente, C. C., Nidecker, M. and Bellack, A. S. (2008) 'Motivation and the stages of change among individuals with severe mental illness and substance abuse disorders', *Journal of Substance Abuse Treatment*, 34: 25–35.

DiClemente, C. C., Schlundt, D. and Gemmell, L. (2004) 'Readiness and stages of change in addiction treatment', *American Journal on Addictions*, 13: 103–19.

Doss, A. J. (2005) 'Evidence-based diagnosis: Incorporating diagnostic instruments into clinical practice', *Journal of the American Academy of Child and Adolescent Psychiatry*, 44: 947–52.

Dowden, C. and Blanchette, K. (2002) 'An evaluation of the effectiveness of substance abuse programming for female offenders', *International Journal of Offender Therapy and Comparative Criminology*, 46: 220–30.

Dowden, C., Blanchette, K. and Serin, R. (1999) *Anger Management Programming for Federal Inmates: An Affective Intervention*. Ottawa: Correctional Services Canada, Research Branch.

Drake, R. E., Mueser, K. T., Clark, R. E. and Wallach, M. A. (1996) 'The course, treatment and outcome of substance disorder in persons with severe mental illness', in L. Davidson, C. Harding and L. Spaniol (eds) *Recovery from Severe Mental Illnesses: Research Evidence and Implications for Practice*, Vol. 1. Boston, MA: Center for Psychiatric Rehabilitation.

Drapeau, M. (2005) 'Research on the processes involved in treating sexual offenders', *Sexual Abuse: A Journal of Research and Treatment*, 17(2): 117–25.

Draycott, S. (2007) 'Hunting the snark: The concept of motivation', *Issues in Forensic Psychology*, 7: 24–32.

Drieschner, K. H. and Boomsma, A. (2008) 'Validation of the Treatment Motivation Scales for forensic outpatient treatment', *Assessment*, 15: 242–55.

Drieschner, K. H., Lammers, S. M. M. and van der Staak, C. P. F. (2004) 'Treatment motivation: An attempt for clarification of an ambiguous concept', *Clinical Psychology Review*, 23: 1115–37.

Duggan, C. (2009) 'A treatment guideline for people with antisocial personality disorder: Overcoming attitudinal barriers and evidential limitations', *Criminal Behaviour and Mental Health*, 19: 219–23.

Duggan, C. and Howard, R. C. (2009) 'The functional link between personality disorder and violence: A critical appraisal', in M. McMurran and R. C.

Howard (eds) *Personality, Personality Disorder and Violence*. Chichester: John Wiley.

Duggan, C., Huband, N., Smailagic, N., Ferriter, M. and Adams, C. (2007) 'The use of psychological treatments for people with personality disorder: A systematic review of randomized controlled trials', *Personality and Mental Health*, 1: 95–125.

Duncan, B. L., Miller, S. D., Sparks, J. A., Claud, D. A., Reynolds, L. R., Brown, J. and Johnson, L. D. (2003) 'The Session Rating Scale: Preliminary psychometric properties of a "working" alliance measure', *Journal of Brief Therapy*, 3(1): 3–12.

D'Zurilla, T. J. and Goldfried, M. R. (1971) 'Problem solving and behavior modification', *Journal of Abnormal Psychology*, 78: 107–26.

D'Zurilla, T. J. and Nezu, A. M. (1999) *Problem-solving Therapy: A Social Competence Approach to Clinical Intervention*, 2nd edn. New York: Springer.

D'Zurilla, T. J. and Nezu, A. M. (2007) *Problem-solving Therapy: A Social Competence Approach to Clinical Intervention*, 3rd edn. New York: Springer.

El-Bassel, N., Schilling, R. F., Ivanoff, A., Chen, D., Hanson, M. and Bidassie, B. (1998) 'Stages of change profiles among incarcerated drug-using women', *Addictive Behaviors*, 23: 389–94.

Elliot, A. J., Sheldon, K. M. and Church, M. A. (1997) 'Avoidance personal goals and subjective well-being', *Personality and Social Psychology Bulletin*, 23: 915–27.

Emmons, R. A. (1999) *The Psychology of Ultimate Concerns*. New York: Guilford Press.

Emmons, R. A. (2003) 'Personal goals, life meaning and virtue: Wellsprings of a positive life', in C. L. M. Keyes and J. Haidt (eds) *Flourishing: Positive Psychology and the Life Well-lived*. Washington, DC: American Psychological Association.

Emmons, R. A. (2005) 'Striving for the sacred: Personal goals, life meaning and religion', *Journal of Social Issues*, 61: 731–45.

Emmons, R. A. and King, L. A. (1988) 'Conflict among personal strivings: Immediate and long-term implications for psychological and physical well-being', *Journal of Personality and Social Psychology*, 54: 1040–8.

Fallon, M. (2005) *The Road to Dharamsala: My Unexpected Life*. Milton, QLD: Wiley Australia.

Fals-Stewart, W. (1993) 'Neurocognitive defects and their impact on substance abuse treatment', *Journal of Addictions and Offender Counseling*, 13: 46–57.

Farabee, D., Prendergast, M. and Anglin, D. (1998) 'The effectiveness of coerced treatment for drug-abusing offenders', *Federal Probation*, 62: 3–10.

Farrall, S. (2004) 'Social capital and offender reintegration: Making probation desistance focused', in S. Maruna and R. Immarigeon (eds) *After Crime and Punishment: Pathways to Offender Reintegration.* Cullompton: Willan Publishing.

Fiorentine, R., Anglin, M. D., Gil-Rivas, V. and Taylor, E. (1997) 'Drug treatment: Explaining the gender paradox', *Substance Use and Misuse,* 32: 653–78.

Fishbein, D., Sheppard, M., Hyde, C., Hubal, R., Newlin, D., Serin, R. C., Chrousos, G. and Alesci, S. (2009) 'Deficits in behavioural inhibition predict treatment engagement in prison inmates', *Law and Human Behavior,* 33: 419–35.

Ford, M. E. (1992) *Motivating Humans: Goals, Emotions and Personal Agency Beliefs.* Newbury Park, CA: Sage.

Forth, A. and Kroner, D. (1995) 'The Factor Structure of the Revised Psychopathy Checklist with Incarcerated Rapists and Incest Offenders', unpublished manuscript.

Frank, J. D. (1974) 'Therapeutic components of psychotherapy: A 25 year progress report of research', *Journal of Nervous and Mental Disease,* 159: 325–42.

Freud, S. (1958) 'The dynamics of transference', in J. Strachey (ed.) *The Complete Standard Edition of the Complete Psychological Works of Sigmund Freud.* London: Hogarth Press.

Frijda, N. H. (1986) *The Emotions.* Cambridge: Cambridge University Press.

Garfield, S. L. (1994) 'Research on client variables in psychotherapy', in A. E. Bergin and S. L. Garfield (eds) *Handbook of Psychotherapy and Behavior Change,* 4th edn. New York: John Wiley.

Gaston, L. (1990) 'The concept of the alliance and its role in psychotherapy: Theoretical and empirical considerations', *Psychotherapy,* 27: 143–53.

Gentilello, L. M., Rivara, F. P., Donovan, D. M., Villaveces, A., Daranciang, E., Dunn, C. W. and Ries, R. R. (2000) 'Alcohol problems in women admitted to a level I trauma center: A gender-based comparison', *Journal of Trauma,* 48(1): 108–14.

German, D. and Sterk, C. (2002) 'Looking beyond stereotypes: Exploring life structure and access to crack', *Journal of Psychoactive Drugs,* 34: 383–392.

Gerstley, L., McLellan, A. T., Woody, G., Luborsky, L. and Prout, M. (1989) 'Ability to form an alliance with the therapist: A possible maker of prognosis for patients with antisocial personality disorder', *American Journal of Psychiatry,* 146(4): 508–12.

Gibbs, J. C., Potter, G. B. and Goldstein, A. P. (1995) *The EQUIP Program: Teaching Youth to Think and Act Responsibly Through a Peer-helping Approach.* Champaign, IL: Research Press.

Gilchrist, E. (2009) 'Implicit thinking about implicit theories in intimate partner violence', *Psychology, Crime and Law,* 15: 131–45.

Ginsberg, J. I. D., Mann, R. E., Rotgers, F. and Weekes, J. R. (2001) 'Motivational interviewing with criminal justice populations', in W. R. Miller and S. Rollnick (eds) *Motivational Interviewing: Preparing People for Change.* London: Guilford.

Goldstein, P. J. (1985) 'The drugs/violence nexus: A tripartite conceptual framework', *Journal of Drug Issues,* 39: 143–74.

Gondolf, E. W. (2008) 'Program completion in a specialized batterer counseling for African-American men', *Journal of Interpersonal Violence*, 23: 94–116.

Gorman, D. and White, H. R. (1995) 'You can choose your friends, but do they choose your crime? Implications of differential association theories for crime prevention policy', in H. Barlow (ed.) *Criminology and Public Policy: Putting Theory to Work*. Boulder, CO: Westview Press.

Gowing, L., Proudfoot, H., Henry-Edwards, S. and Teeson, M. (2001) *The Effectiveness of Interventions for Illicit Drug Use*, ANCD Research Paper. Woden, ACT: Australian National Council on Drugs.

Graves, K. N. (2006) 'Not always sugar and spice: Expanding theoretical and functional explanations of why females aggress', *Aggression and Violent Behavior*, 12(2).

Graycar, A. (2001) 'Crime in twentieth century Australia', in *Australian Bureau of Statistics, Year Book Australia 2001* (ABS Cat. No. 1302. 0). Canberra: Australian Bureau of Statistics.

Green, C. A., Polen, M. R., Dickinson, D. M., Lynch, F. L. and Bennett, M. D. (2002) 'Gender differences in predictors of initiation, retention and completion in an HMO-based substance abuse treatment program', *Journal of Substance Abuse Treatment*, 23: 285–95.

Gregoire , T. K. and Burke, A. C. (2004) 'The relationship of legal coercion to readiness to change among adults with alcohol and other drug problems', *Journal of Substance Abuse Treatment*, 26: 35–41.

Grossman, L. S., Haywood, T. W., Cavanaugh, J. L., Davis, J. M. and Lewis, D. A. (1995) 'State hospital patients with past arrests for violent crime', *Psychiatric Services*, 46: 790–5.

Grubin, D. and Thornton, D. (1994) 'A national program for the assessment and treatment of sex offenders in the England prison system', *Criminal Justice and Behavior*, 21: 55–71.

Hanby, L. J., Serin, R. C. and Vuong, B. (2009) 'Offender Competencies and their Relationship to Correctional Program Performance', manuscript in preparation.

Hanson, R. K. and Bussiere, M. T. (1998) 'Predicting relapse: A meta-analysis of sexual offender recidivism studies', *Journal of Consulting and Clinical Psychology*, 66: 348–62.

Hanson, R. K. and Harris, A. J. R. (2000) 'Where should we intervene? Dynamic predictors of sexual offense recidivism', *Criminal Justice and Behavior*, 27: 6–35.

Hanson, R. K. and Morton-Bourgon, K. (2004) *Predictors of Sexual Recidivism: An Updated Meta-analysis*. Ottawa: Department of the Solicitor General of Canada.

Hanson, R. K. and Morton-Bourgon, K. (2005) 'The characteristics of persistent sexual offenders: A meta-analysis of recidivism studies', *Journal of Consulting and Clinical Psychology*, 73: 1154–63.

Hanson, R. K. and Thornton, D. (2000) 'Improving risk assessment for sex offenders: A comparison of three actuarial scales', *Law and Human Behaviour*, 24: 119–36.

Hanson, R. K., Gordon, A., Harris, A. J. R., Marques, J. K., Murphy, W., Quinsey, V. and Seto, M. (2002) 'First report of the collaborative outcome data project on the effectiveness of psychological treatment for sex offenders', *Sexual Abuse: A Journal of Research and Treatment*, 14(2): 169–95.

Hanson, R. K., Harris, A. J. R., Scott, T. L. and Helmus, L. (2007) *Assessing the Risk of Sexual Offenders on Community Supervision: The Dynamic Supervision Project*. Public Safety Canada. Available at www.publicsafety.gc.ca/res/cor/rep/_fl/crp2007-05-en.pdf (retrieved 25 January 2008).

Hanson, K. L., Luciana, M. and Sullwold, K. (2008) 'Reward-related decision-making deficits and elevated impulsivity among MDMA and other drug users', *Drug and Alcohol Dependence*, 96: 99–110.

Hare, R. D. (2003) *Hare Psychopathy Checklist*, 2nd edn. Toronto: Multi-Health Systems.

Harkins, L. and Beech, A. R. (2007) 'A review of the factors that can influence the effectiveness of sexual offender treatment: Risk, need, responsivity and process issues', *Aggression and Violent Behavior*, 12: 615–27.

Harris, A., Phenix, A., Hanson, R. K. and Thornton, D. (2003) *Static-99 Coding Rules: Revised 2003*. Ottawa: Department of the Solicitor General of Canada.

Hart, S. D. and Kropp, P. R. (2008) 'Sexual deviance and the law', in D. R. Laws and W. T. O'Donohue (eds) *Sexual Deviance: Theory, Assessment and Treatment*. New York: Guilford Press.

Hasin, D. S. (1994) 'Treatment/self-help for alcohol-related problems: Relationship to social pressure and alcohol dependence', *Journal of Studies on Alcohol*, 55: 660–6.

Hatcher, R. L. and Barends, A. W. (2006) 'How a return to theory could help alliance research', *Psychotherapy: Theory, Research, Practice, Training*, 43(3): 292–9.

Hayward, J., McMurran, M. and Sellen, J. (2008) 'Social problem solving in vulnerable adult prisoners: Profile and intervention', *Journal of Forensic Psychiatry and Psychology*, 19: 243–8.

Heather, N. and Honekopp, J. (2008) 'A revised edition of the Readiness to Change Questionnaire [Treatment Version]', *Addiction Research and Theory*, 16: 421–33.

Heather, N., Luce, A., Peck, D., Dunbar, B. and James, I. (1999) 'Development of a treatment version of the Readiness to Change Questionnaire', *Addiction Research*, 7: 63–83.

Heilbrun, K. S., Bennett, W. S., Evans, J. H., Offult, R. A., Reiff, H. J. and White, A. J. (1992) 'Assessing treatability in mentally disordered offenders: Strategies for improving reliability', *Forensic Reports*, 5: 85–96.

Helmus, L., Hanson, R. K. and Thornton, D. (2009) 'Reporting Static-99 in light of new research on recidivism norms', *The Forum*, 21(1): 38–45.

Hemphill, J. F. and Hart, S. D. (2002) 'Motivating the unmotivated: Psychopathy, treatment and change', in M. McMurran (ed.) *Motivating Offenders to Change: A Guide to Enhancing Engagement in Therapy*. Chichester: John Wiley.

Henderson, D. J., Boyd, C. and Mieczkowski, T. (1994) 'Gender, relationships and crack cocaine: A content analysis', *Research in Nursing and Health*, 17: 265–72.

Heseltine, K., Howells, K. and Day, A. (2009) 'Brief anger interventions with offenders may be ineffective: A replication and extension', *Behaviour Research and Therapy*, DOI.

Hettema, J., Steele, J. and Miller, W. R. (2005) 'Motivational interviewing', *Annual Review of Clinical Psychology*, 1: 91–111.

Hildebrand, M., de Ruiter, C. and de Vogel, V. (2004) 'Psychopathy and sexual deviance in treated rapists: Association with sexual and nonsexual recidivism', *Sexual Abuse: A Journal of Research and Treatment*, 16: 1–24.

Hiller, M. L., Knight, K. and Simpson, D. D. (1999) 'Prison-based substance abuse treatment, residential aftercare and recidivism', *Addiction*, 94: 833–43.

Hiller, M. L., Knight, K., Broome, K. M. and Simpson, D. D. (1998) 'Legal pressure and treatment retention in a national sample of long-term residential programs', *Criminal Justice Behavior*, 25: 463–81.

Hobbs, G. and Dear, G. E. (2000) 'Prisoners' perceptions of prison officers as sources of support', *Journal of Offender Rehabilitation*, 31: 127–42.

Hodge, J. E. and Renwick, S. J. (2002) 'Motivating mentally disordered offenders', in M. McMurran (ed.) *Motivating Offenders to Change: A Guide to Enhancing Engagement in Therapy*. Chichester: John Wiley.

Hodgins, S. and Muller-Isberner, R. (2000) *Violence, Crime and Mentally Disordered Offenders*. Chichester: John Wiley.

Hodgins, S., Viding, E. and Plodowski, A. (eds) (2008) *The Neurobiology of Violence: Implications for Prevention and Treatment*, Philosophical Transactions of the Royal Society, 363.

Hogue, T. E., Jones, L., Talkes, K. and Tennant, A. (2007) 'The Peaks: A clinical service for those with dangerous and severe personality disorder', *Psychology, Crime and Law*, 13: 57–68.

Hollin, C. R. (2000) *Handbook of Offender Assessment and Treatment*. Chichester: John Wiley.

Hollin, C. R. and Palmer, E. J. (2006) *Offending Behaviour Programmes: Controversies and Resolutions*. Chichester: John Wiley.

Honos-Webb, L. and Stiles, W. B. (2002) 'Assimilative integration and responsive use of the Assimilation Model', *Journal of Psychotherapy Integration*, 12: 406–20.

Horowitz, M. J. (1998) *Cognitive Psychodynamics*. New York: John Wiley.

Horvath, A. O. and Greenberg, L. S. (1989) 'Development and validation of the Working Alliance Inventory', *Journal of Counseling Psychology*, 36: 223–33.

Horvath, A. O. and Luborsky, L. (1993) 'The role of the therapeutic alliance in psychotherapy', *Journal of Consulting and Clinical Psychology*, 61(4): 561–73.

Horvath, A. O. and Symonds, B. D. (1991) 'Relation between working alliance and outcome in psychotherapy: A meta-analysis', *Journal of Consulting and Clinical Psychology*, 38(2): 139–49.

Howells, K. (2008) 'The treatment of anger in offenders', in A. Day, M. Nakata and K. Howells (eds) *Anger in Indigenous Men*. Federation Press.

Howells, K. (2009) 'Angry affect, aggression and personality disorder', in M. McMurran and R. Howard (eds) *Personality, Personality Disorder and Risk of Violence*. Chichester: John Wiley.

Howells, K. (in press) 'Distinctions within distinctions: The challenges of heterogeneity and causality in the formulation and treatment of violence', in M. Daffern, L. Jones and J. Shine (eds) *Offence-paralleling Behaviour*. Chichester: John Wiley.

Howells, K. and Day, A. (2003) 'Readiness for anger management: Clinical and theoretical issues', *Clinical Psychology Review*, 23: 319–37.

Howells, K. and Day, A. (2006) 'Affective determinants of treatment engagement in violent offenders', *International Journal of Offender Therapy and Comparative Criminology*, 50(2): 174–86.

Howells, K. and Day, A. (2007) 'Readiness for treatment in high risk offenders with personality disorders', *Psychology, Crime and Law*, 13: 47–56.

Howells, K. and Tennant, A. (2007) 'Ready or not they are coming: Dangerous and severe personality disorder and treatment engagement', in E. Sullivan and R. Shuker (eds) *Issues in Forensic Psychology No. 7: Readiness for Treatment*. Leicester: British Psychological Society.

Howells, K., Day, A. and Thomas-Peter, B. (2004a) 'Changing violent behaviour: criminological models compared', *Journal of Forensic Psychiatry and Psychology*, 15: 391–406.

Howells, K., Day, A. and Wright, S. (2004b) 'Affect, emotions and sex offending', *Psychology, Crime and Law*, 10(2): 179–95.

Howells, K., Day, A., Williamson, P., Bubner, S., Jauncey, S., Parker, A. and Heseltine, K. (2005) 'Brief anger management programs with offenders: Outcomes and predictors of change', *Journal of Forensic Psychiatry and Psychology*, 16: 296–311.

Howells, K., Krishnan, G. and Daffern, M. (2007) 'Challenges in the treatment of dangerous and severe personality disorder', *Advances in Psychiatric Treatment*, 13: 325–32.

Howells, K., Tonkin, M., Milburn, C., Lewis, K., Draycot, S., Cordwell, J., Price, M., Davies, S. and Schalast, N. (2009) 'The EssenCES measure of social climate: A preliminary validation and normative data in UK high secure hospital settings', *Criminal Behaviour and Mental Health*, 19(5): 308–20.

Hsu, L. M. (2002) 'Diagnostic validity statistics and the MCMI–III', *Psychological Assessment*, 14: 410–22.

Huband, N., McMurran, M., Evans, C. and Duggan, C. (2007) 'Social problem solving plus psychoeducation for adults with personality disorder: A pragmatic randomised controlled trial', *British Journal of Psychiatry*, 190: 307–13.

Hunsley, J. (2003) 'Introduction to the special section on incremental validity and utility in clinical assessment', *Psychological Assessment*, 15: 443–45.

Hunsley, J. and Mash, E. J. (2005) 'Introduction to the special section on developing guidelines for the evidence-based assessment (EBA) of adult disorders', *Psychological Assessment*, 17: 251–5.

Hunsley, J. and Mash, E. J. (2007) 'Evidence-based assessment', *Annual Review of Clinical Psychology*, 3: 57–79.

Hunsley, J. and Mash, E. J. (2008) 'Developing criteria for evidence-based assessment: An introduction to assessments that work', in J. Hunsley and

E. J. Mash (eds) *A Guide to Assessments that Work*. New York: Oxford University Press.

Hunsley, J., Crabb, R. and Mash, E. J. (2004) 'Evidence-based clinical assessment', *Clinical Psychologist*, 57: 25–32.

Hutchins, W. (2003) 'Impact of sex offender programs on parole applications: Rehabilitate or perish', paper presented to a symposium, *Rehabilitate or Perish*, Institute of Criminology, University of Sydney, June.

Jackson, P., Thurlow, C. and Underwood, D. (2010) 'Adult learning and personality disorders', in A. Tennant and K. Howells (eds) *Using Time, Not Doing Time: Practitioner Perspectives on Personality Disorder and Risk*. Chichester: Wiley-Blackwell.

Joe, G. W., Simpson, D. D. and Broome, K. M. (1998) 'Effects of readiness for drug treatment on client retention and assessment of process', *Addiction*, 93: 1177–91.

Johnson, H. (2004) *Drugs and Crime: A Study of Incarcerated Female Offenders*, Research and Public Policy Series No. 63. Canberra: Australian Institute of Criminology.

Johnson, M. (2007) *The Meaning of the Body: Aesthetics of Human Understanding*. Chicago: University of Chicago Press.

Jones, L. (2004) 'Offence paralleling behaviour (OPB) as a framework for assessment and intervention with offenders', in A. Needs and G. Towl (eds) *Applying Psychology to Forensic Practice*. Oxford: Blackwell.

Jones, L. (2010) 'Working with people who have committed sexual offences with personality disorders', in A. Tennant and K. Howells (eds) *Using Time, Not Doing Time: Practitioner Perspectives on Personality Disorder and Risk*. Chichester: Wiley-Blackwell.

Kant, G. L., D'Zurilla, T. J. and Maydeu-Olivares, A. (1997) 'Social problem solving as a mediator of stress-related depression and anxiety in middle-aged and elderly community residents', *Cognitive Therapy and Research*, 21: 73–96.

Karoly, P. (1993) 'Goal systems: An organising framework for clinical assessment and treatment planning', *Psychological Assessment*, 5: 273–80.

Karoly, P. (1999) 'A goal systems self-regulatory perspective on personality, psychopathology and change', *Review of General Psychology*, 3: 264–91.

Kazdin, A. E. (2005) 'Evidence-based assessment of child and adolescent disorders: Issues in measurement development and clinical application', *Journal of Child Clinical and Adolescent Psychology*, 34: 253–76.

Kazdin, A. E., Kratochwill, T. R. and VandenBos, G. R. (1986) 'Beyond clinical trials: Generalizing from research to practice', *Professional Psychology: Research and Practice*, 17: 391–8.

Kear-Colwell, J. and Boer, D. P. (2000) 'The treatment of pedophiles: Clinical experience and the implications of recent research', *International Journal of Offender Therapy and Comparative Criminology*, 44: 593–605.

Kear-Colwell, J. and Pollock, P. (1997) 'Motivation or confrontation: Which approach to the child sex offender?', *Criminal Justice and Behavior*, 24(1): 20–33.

Kekes, J. (1989) *Moral Tradition and Individuality*. Princeton, NJ: Princeton University Press.

Kendler, K. S. and Prescott, C. A. (1998) 'Cannabis use, abuse and dependence in a population-based sample of female twins', *American Journal of Psychiatry*, 155: 1016–22.

Kendler, K. S., Bulik, C. M., Silberg, J., Hettema, J. M., Myers, J. and Prescott, C. A. (2000) 'Childhood sexual abuse and adult psychiatric and substance use disorders in women: An epidemiological and co-twin control analysis', *Archives of General Psychiatry*, 57: 953–9.

Kennedy, S. M. and Serin, R. C. (1997) 'Treatment responsivity: Contributing to effective correctional programming', *International Community Corrections Association Journal*, 7: 46–52.

Kessler, R. C. (2004) 'Impact of substance abuse on the diagnosis, course and treatment of mood disorders: The epidemiology of dual diagnosis', *Biological Psychiatry*, 56: 730–7.

Kessler, R. C., Crum, R. M., Warner, L. A., Nelson, C. B., Shulenberg, J. and Anthony, J. C. (1997) 'Lifetime occurrence of DEM-III-R alcohol abuse and dependence with other psychiatric disorders in the National Comorbidity Survey', *Archives of General Psychiatry*, 54: 313–21.

Khantzian, E. J. (1985) 'The self-medication hypothesis of addictive disorders: Focus on heroin and cocaine dependence', *American Journal of Psychiatry*, 142: 1259–64.

Kirsch, I. (1990) *Changing Expectations: A Key to Effective Psychotherapy*. Pacific Grove, CA: Brooks/Cole.

Klag, S., O'Callaghan, F. and Creed, P. (2005) 'The use of legal coercion in the treatment of substance abusers: An overview and critical analysis of thirty years of research', *Substance Use and Misuse*, 40: 1777–95.

Kleinig, J. (2004) 'Ethical issues in substance abuse intervention', *Substance Use and Misuse*, 39: 369–98.

Klinger, E. and Cox, W. M. (2004a) 'Motivation and the theory of current concerns', in W. M. Cox and E. Klinger (eds) *Handbook of Motivational Counselling: Concepts, Approaches and Assessment*. Chichester: John Wiley.

Klinger, E. and Cox, W. M. (2004b) 'The Motivational Structure Questionnaire and Personal Concerns Inventory: Psychometric properties', in W. M. Cox and E. Klinger (eds) *Handbook of Motivational Counselling: Concepts, Approaches and Assessment*. Chichester: John Wiley.

Koob, G. F. and Bloom, F. E. (1998) 'Cellular and molecular mechanisms of drug dependence', *Science*, 242: 715–23.

Korsgaard, C. M. (1996) *The Sources of Normativity*. Cambridge: Cambridge University Press.

Korsgaard, C. M. (2009) *Self-constitution: Agency, Identity and Integrity*. New York: Oxford University Press.

Kouri, E. M., Pope, H. G., Powell, K. F., Oliva, P. S. and Campbell, C. (1997) 'Drug use history and criminal behavior among 133 incarcerated men', *American Journal of Drug and Alcohol Abuse*, 23: 413–20.

Kozar, C and Day, A. (2009) 'Developing the therapeutic alliance in offending behaviour programs: A qualitative study of its perceived impact on treatment outcomes', presentation to Australian Psychological Society's Forensic College conference, Melbourne.

Kreek M. J. and Koob, G. F. (1998) 'Drug dependence: Stress and dysregulation of brain reward pathways', *Drug and Alcohol Dependence*, 51: 23–47

Krishnamurthy, R., VandeCreek, L., Kaslow, N. J., Tazeau, Y. N., Milville, M. L. and Kerns, R. (2004) 'Achieving competency in psychological assessment: Directions for education and training', *Journal of Clinical Psychology*, 80: 725–40.

Kyvik, K. O., Green, A. and Beck-Nielsen, H. (1995) 'Concordance rates of insulin dependent diabetes mellitus', *British Medical Journal*, 311: 913–17.

Lamers, C. T., Bechara, A., Rizzo, M. and Ramaekers, J. G. (2006) 'Cognitive function and mood in MDMA/THC users, THC users and non-drug using controls', *Journal of Psychopharmacology*, 20: 302–11.

Langan, N. and Pelissier, B. M. M. (2001) 'Gender differences among prisoners in drug treatment', *Journal of Substance Abuse*, 13: 291–301.

Langlands, R., Ward, T. and Gilchrist, E. (2009) 'Applying the Good Lives Model to male perpetrators of domestic violence', in P. Lehmann and C. Simmons (eds) *Strengths Based Batterer Intervention: A New Paradigm in Ending Domestic Violence*. New York: Springer.

Langton, C. M., Barbaree, H. E., Harkins, L., Arenovich, T., McNamee, J., Peacock, E. J., Dalton, A., Hansen, K. T., Luong, D. and Marcon, H. (2008) 'Denial and minimization among sex offenders: Posttreatment presentation and association with sexual recidivism', *Criminal Justice and Behavior*, 35(1): 69–98.

Latendresse, M. (2006) 'Predicting Sex Offender Program Attrition: The Role of Denial, Motivation and Treatment Readiness', unpublished master's thesis. Carleton University, Ottawa, Canada.

Lawental, E., McLellan, A. T., Grissom, G. R., Brill, P. and O'Brien, C. (1996) 'Coerced treatment for substance abuse problems detected through workplace urine surveillance: Is it effective?', *Journal of Substance Abuse*, 8: 115–28.

Laws, D. R. and Ward, T. (in press) *People Like Us: Desistance from Crime and Paths to the Good Life*. New York: Guilford Press.

Leahy, R. L. (2001) *Overcoming Resistance in Cognitive Therapy*. New York: Guilford Press.

LeBel, T. P., Burnett, R., Maruna, S. and Bushway, S. (2008) 'The 'chicken and egg' of subjective and social factors in desistance from crime', *European Journal of Criminology*, 5: 131–59.

Lee, Y. (2005) Personal communication, 30 September 2005.

Levenson, J. S. and Macgowan, M. J. (2004) 'Engagement, denial and treatment progress among sex offenders in group therapy', *Sexual Abuse: A Journal of Research and Treatment*, 16(1): 49–63.

Levesque, D. A., Gelles, R. J. and Velicer, W. F. (2000) 'Development and validation of a Stages of Change measure for men in batterer treatment', *Cognitive Therapy and Research*, 24: 175–99.

Lewis, M. (1995) 'Self-conscious emotions', *American Scientist*, 83: 68–78.

Li, F., Barrera, M., Hops, H. and Fisher, K. (2002) 'The longitudinal influence of peers on the development of alcohol use in late adolescence: A growth mixture analysis', *Journal of Behavioral Medicine*, 25: 293–315.

Lingiardi, V., Filippucci, L. and Baiocco, R. (2005) 'Therapeutic alliance evaluation in personality disorders psychotherapy', *Psychotherapy Research*, 15(1–2): 45–53.

Link, M. and Stueve, A. (1994) 'Psychotic symptoms and the violent/illegal behaviour of mental patients compared to community controls', in J. Monahan and H. Steadman (eds) *Violence and Mental Disorder: Developments in Risk Assessment*. Chicago, IL: University of Chicago Press.

Linley, P. A. and Joseph, S. (2004) 'Applied positive psychology: A new perspective for professional practice', in P. A. Linley and S. Joseph (eds) *Positive Psychology in Practice*. New Jersey: John Wiley.

Littell, J. H. and Girvin, H. (2002) 'Stages of change: A critique', *Behavior Modification*, 26: 223–72.

Little, B. R. (1983) 'Personal projects: A rationale and method for investigation', *Environment and Behavior*, 16: 273–309.

Livesley, W. J. (2003) *Practical Management of Personality Disorders*. New York: Guilford Press.

Livesley, W. J. (2007) 'The relevance of an integrated approach to the treatment of personality disordered offenders', *Psychology, Crime and Law*, 13: 27–46.

Lloyd, C. D. and Serin, R. C. (2009) 'Agency and Outcome Expectancies for Crime Desistance: Measuring Internal Mechanisms of Offender Change', manuscript submitted for publication.

Locke, E. A. (1996) 'Motivation through conscious goal setting', *Applied and Preventive Psychology*, 5: 117–24.

Luborsky, L., Barber, J. P., Siqueland, L., McLellan, A. T. and Woody, G (1997) 'Establishing a therapeutic alliance with substance abusers', in L. S. Onken, J. D. Blaine and J. J. Boren (eds) *Beyond the Therapeutic Alliance: Keeping the Drug-Dependent Individual in Treatment*. Rockville: National Institute on Drug Abuse Research Monograph.

Lund, C. A. (2000) 'Predictors of sexual recidivism: Did meta-analysis clarify the role and relevance of denial?', *Sexual Abuse: A Journal of Research and Treatment*, 12(4): 275–87.

Lyon, J., Dennison, C. and Wilson, A. (2000) *Messages from Young People in Custody: Focus Group Research*, Home Office Research Findings 127. London: HMSO.

Maher, B., Marazita, M., Zubenko, W., Kaplan, B. and Zubenko, G. (2002) 'Genetic segregation analysis of alcohol and other substance use disorders in families with recurrent, early onset major depression', *American Journal of Drug and Alcohol Abuse*, 28: 711–31.

Makkai, T. (2000) *Drug Use Monitoring in Australia: 1999 Annual Report*, Research and Public Policy Series No. 26. Canberra: Australian Institute of Criminology.

Makkai, T. and Payne, J. (2003) *Key Findings from the Drug Use Careers of Offenders (DUCO) Study*, Trends and Issues in Crime and Criminal Justice No. 267. Canberra: Australian Institute of Criminology.

Malcolm, P. B. (2002) *Child Molester Denial: Utilizing A Multi-Method Assessment Approach.* Dissertation Abstracts International, 63 (4–B), 2064.

Maletzky, B. M. (1991). *Treating the Sexual Offender.* Newbury Park, CA: Sage.

Malouff, J. M., Thorsteinsson, E. B. and Schutte, N. S. (2007) 'The efficacy of problem solving therapy in reducing mental and physical health problems: A meta-analysis', *Clinical Psychology Review*, 27: 46–57.

Mann, R. E. and Beech, A. R. (2003) 'Cognitive distortions, schemas and implicit theories', in T. Ward, D. R. Laws and S. M. Hudson (eds) *Sexual Deviance: Issues and Controversies.* Thousand Oaks, CA: Sage.

Mann, R. E. and Marshall, W. L. (2009) 'Advances in the treatment of adult incarcerated sex offenders', in A. R. Beech, L. A. Craig and K. D. Browne (eds) *Assessment and Treatment of Sex Offenders: A Handbook.* Chichester: John Wiley.

Mann, R. E. and Shingler, J. (2006) 'Schema-driven cognition in sexual offenders: Theory, assessment and treatment', in W. L. Marshall, Y. M. Fernandez, L. E. Marshall and G. A. Serran (eds) *Sexual Offender Treatment: Controversial Issues.* Chichester: John Wiley.

Mann, R. E., Webster, S. D., Schofield, C. and Marshall, W. L. (2004) 'Approach versus avoidance goals in relapse prevention with sex offenders', *Sexual Abuse: A Journal of Research and Treatment*, 16(1): 65–75.

Marlowe, D. B. (2001) 'Coercive treatment of substance abusing criminal offenders', *Journal of Forensic Science*, 1: 65–73.

Marlowe, D. B., Festinger, D. S., Dugosh, K. L., Lee, P. A. and Nenasutti, K. M. (2007) *Drug and Alcohol Dependence*, 88S, S4–S13.

Marques, J. K., Wiederanders, M., Day, D. M., Nelson, C. and van Ommeren, A. (2005) 'Effects of a relapse prevention program on sexual recidivism: Final results from California's Sex Offender Treatment and Evaluation Project (SOTEP)', *Sexual Abuse: A Journal of Research and Treatment*, 17: 79–107.

Marshall, W. L. (1994) 'Treatment effects on denial and minimization in incarcerated sex offenders', *Behavior Research and Therapy*, 32(5): 559–64.

Marshall, W. L. (2005) 'Therapist style in sexual offender treatment: Influence on indices of change', *Sexual Abuse: A Journal of Research and Treatment*, 17(2): 109–16.

Marshall, W. L. and Serran, G. A. (2004) 'The role of the therapist in offender treatment', *Psychology, Crime and Law*, 10(3): 309–20.

Marshall, W. L., Anderson, D. and Fernandez, Y. M. (1999) *Cognitive Behavioral Treatment of Sexual Offenders.* Chichester: John Wiley.

Marshall, W. L., Champagne, F., Sturgeon, C. and Bryce, P. (1997) 'Increasing the self-esteem of child molesters', *Sexual Abuse: A Journal of Research and Treatment*, 9: 321–33.

Marshall, W. L., Marshall, G. A., Serran, G. A. and O'Brien, M. D. (2009) 'Self-esteem, shame, cognitive distortions and empathy in sexual offenders: Their integration and treatment implications', *Psychology, Crime and Law*, 15: 217–34.

Marshall, W. L., Marshall, L. E., Serran, G. A. and Fernandez, Y. M. (2006) *Treating Sexual Offenders: An Integrated Approach*. New York: Routledge, Taylor and Francis.

Marshall, W. L., Ward, T., Mann, R. E., Moulden, H., Fernandez, Y. M., Serran, G. and Marshall, L. E. (2005) 'Working positively with sexual offenders: Maximizing the effectiveness of treatment', *Journal of Interpersonal Violence*, 20(9): 1096–114.

Martin, D. J., Garske, J. P. and Davis, M. K. (2000) 'Relation of the therapeutic alliance with outcome and other variables: A meta-analytic review', *Journal of Consulting and Clinical Psychology*, 68(3): 438–50.

Martinson, R. (1974) 'What Works: Questions and answers about prison reform', *Public Interest*, 35: 22–54.

Maruna, S. (2001) *Making Good: How Ex-convicts Reform and Rebuild their Lives*. Washington, DC: American Psychological Association.

Maruna, S. and LeBel, T. P. (2003) 'Welcome home? Examining the "re-entry court" concept from a strengths-based perspective', *Western Criminology Review*, 4: 91–107.

Maruna, S. and Mann, R. E. (2006) 'A fundamental attribution error? Rethinking cognitive distortions', *Legal and Criminological Psychology*, 11: 155–77.

Mash, E. J. and Hunsley, J. (2005) 'Evidence-based assessment of child and adolescent disorders: Issues and challenges', *Journal of Clinical Child and Adolescent Psychology*, 34: 362–79.

Maslow, A. H. (1943) 'A theory of human motivation', *Psychological Review*, 50: 370–96.

Massoglia, M. and Uggen, C. (2007) 'Subjective desistance and the transition to adulthood', *Journal of Contemporary Criminal Justice*, 23: 90–103.

Maxwell, S. (2000) 'Sanction threats in court ordered programs: Examining their effects on offenders mandated into drug treatment', *Crime and Delinquency*, 46: 542–63.

McAdams, D. P. (1995) 'What do we know when we know a person?', *Journal of Personality*, 63: 365–96.

McConnaughy, E. A., DiClemente, C. C., Prochaska, J. O. and Velicer, W. F. (1989) 'Stages of change in psychotherapy: A follow-up report', *Psychotherapy*, 26: 494–503.

McConnaughy, E. A., Prochaska, J. O. and Velicer, W. F. (1983) 'Stages of change in psychotherapy: Measurement and sample profiles', *Psychotherapy: Theory, Research and Practice*, 20: 368–75.

McCrady, B. S. and Smith, D. E. (1986) 'Implications of cognitive impairment for the treatment of alcoholism', *Alcoholism: Clinical and Experimental Research*, 10: 145–9.

McEllistrem, J. E. (2004) 'Affective and predatory violence: A bimodal classification system of human aggression and violence', *Aggression and Violent Behavior*, 10: 1–30.

McFall, R. M. (2005) 'Theory and utility – key themes in evidence-based assessment: Comment on the special section', *Psychological Assessment*, 17: 312–23.

McGovern, M. P., Xie, H., Segal, S. R., Siembab, L. and Drake, R. E. (2006) 'Addiction treatment services and co-occurring disorders: Prevalence estimates, treatment practices and barriers', *Journal of Substance Abuse Treatment*, 31: 267–75.

McGuire, J. (2001) 'Defining correctional programs', in L. L. Motiuk and R. C. Serin (eds) *Compendium 2000 on Effective Correctional Programming*. Ottawa: Correctional Service Canada.

McGuire, J. (2004) 'Commentary: Promising answers and the next generation of questions', *Psychology, Crime and Law*, 10: 335–45.

McGuire, J. (2008) 'A review of effective interventions for reducing aggression and violence', *Philosophical Transactions of the Royal Society B*: 1–21.

McLellan, A. T., Lewis, D. C., O'Brien, C. P. and Kleber, H. D. (2000) 'Drug dependence, a chronic medical illness: Implications for treatment, insurance and outcome evaluation', *Journal of the American Medical Association*, 284: 1689–95.

McMurran, M. (2002) *Motivating Offenders to Change: A Guide to Enhancing Engagement in Therapy*. Chichester: John Wiley.

McMurran, M. (2009a) 'Motivational interviewing with offenders: A systematic review', *Legal and Criminological Psychology*, 14: 83–100.

McMurran, M. (2009b) 'Social problem solving, personality and violence', in M. McMurran and R. C. Howard (eds) *Personality, Personality Disorder and Violence*. Chichester: John Wiley.

McMurran, M. and Christopher, G. (2009) 'Social problem solving, anxiety and depression in adult male prisoners', *Legal and Criminological Psychology*, 14: 101–7.

McMurran, M. and Howard, R. (eds) (2009) *Personality, Personality Disorder and Risk of Violence*. Chichester: John Wiley.

McMurran, M. and Theodosi, E. (2007) 'Is treatment non-completion associated with increased reconviction over no treatment?', *Psychology, Crime and Law*, 13: 333–43.

McMurran, M. and Ward, T. (2004) 'Motivating offenders to change in therapy: An organizing framework', *Legal and Criminological Psychology*, 9: 295–311.

McMurran, M., Blair, M. and Egan, V. (2002) 'An investigation of the correlations between aggressiveness, impulsiveness, social problem-solving and alcohol use', *Aggressive Behavior*, 28: 439–45.

McMurran, M., Egan, V., Richardson, C. and Ahmadi, S. (1999) 'Social problem-solving in mentally disordered offenders: A brief report', *Criminal Behaviour and Mental Health*, 9: 315–22.

McMurran, M., Fyffe, S., McCarthy, L., Duggan, C. and Latham, A. (2001) 'Stop and Think!: Social problem solving therapy with personality disordered offenders', *Criminal Behaviour and Mental Health*, 11: 273–85.

McMurran, M., Huband, N. and Duggan, C. (2008a) 'A comparison of treatment completers and non-completers of an inpatient treatment programme for male personality-disordered offenders', *Psychology and Psychotherapy: Theory, Research and Practice*, 81: 193–8.

McMurran, M., Huband, N. and Duggan, C. (2008b) 'The role of social problem solving in improving social functioning in therapy for adults with personality disorder', *Personality and Mental Health*, 2: 1–6.

McMurran, M., Huband, N. and Overton, E. (2009) 'Non-completion of personality disorder treatments: A systematic review of correlates, consequences and interventions', *Clinical Psychology Review*, doi:10.1016/j.cpr.2009.12.002.

McMurran, M., Theodosi, E. and Sellen, J. (2006) 'Measuring engagement in therapy and motivation to change in adult prisoners: A brief report', *Criminal Behaviour and Mental Health*, 16: 124–9.

McMurran, M., Theodosi, E., Sweeney, A. and Sellen, J. (2008c) 'What do prisoners want? Current concerns of adult male prisoners', *Psychology, Crime and Law*, 14: 267–74.

McMurran, M., Tyler, P., Hogue, T., Cooper, K., Dunseath, W. and McDaid, D. (1998) 'Measuring motivation to change in offenders', *Psychology, Crime and Law*, 4: 43–50.

Meir, P. S., Barrowclough, C. and Donmall, M. C. (2005) 'The role of the therapeutic alliance in the treatment of substance misuse: A critical review of the literature', *Addiction, 100*, 304–316.

Messina, N., Burdon, W. M. and Prendergast, M. L. (2003) 'Assessing the needs of women in institutional therapeutic communities', *Journal of Offender Rehabilitation*, 37: 89–106.

Messina, N., Burdon, W., Hagopian, G. and Prendergast, M. (2006) 'Predictors of prison TC treatment outcomes: A comparison of men and women participants', *The American Journal of Drug and Alcohol Abuse*, 32: 7–28.

Michalak, J. and Grosse Holtforth, M. (2006) 'Where do we go from here? The goal perspective in psychotherapy', *Clinical Psychology: Science and Practice*, 13: 346–65.

Michenbaum, D. and Turk, D. C. (1987) *Facilitating Treatment Adherence: A Practitioner's Guidebook*. New York: Plenum.

Milgram, D. and Rubin, J. S. (2000) 'Resisting resistance: Involuntary substance abuse group therapy', *Social Work with Groups*, 15: 95–110.

Miller, S. D. (no date) *Therapeutic alliance: What works in therapy?* [CD–ROM] Chicago: Institute for the Study of Therapeutic Change.

Miller, S. D., Duncan, B. L., Brown, J., Sparks, J. A. and Claud, D. A. (2003) 'The Outcome Rating Scale: A preliminary study of the reliability, validity and feasibility of a brief visual analog measure', *Journal of Brief Therapy*, 2(2): 91–100.

Miller, W. R. and Rollnick, S. (1991) *Motivational Interviewing: Preparing People to Change Addictive Behavior*. New York: Guilford Press.

Miller, W. R. and Rollnick, S. (2002) *Motivational Interviewing: Preparing People for Change*, 2nd edn. New York: Guilford Press.

Miller, W. R. and Tonigan, J. S. (1996) 'Assessing drinkers' motivation for change: The Stages of Change Readiness and Treatment Eagerness Scale (SOCRATES)', *Psychology of Addictive Behaviors*, 10: 81–9.

Milner, L., Mouzos, J. and Makkai, T. (2004) *Drug Use Monitoring in Australia: 2003: Annual Report on Drug Use among Police Detainees*, Research and Public Policy Series No. 58. Canberra: Australian Institute of Criminology.

Mitchell, D., Francis, J. P. and Tafrate, R. C. (2005) 'The psychometric properties of the Stages of Change and Treatment Eagerness Scale (SOCRATES) in a clinical sample of active duty military service members', *Military Medicine*, 170: 960–3.

Moos, R. H. (1997) *Evaluating Treatment Environments: The Quality of Psychiatric and Substance Abuse Programs*. New Brunswick, NJ: Transaction Publishers.

Moulden, H. M. and Marshall, W. L. (2005) 'Hope in the treatment of sexual offenders: The potential application of hope theory', *Psychology, Crime and Law*, 11: 329–42.

Murdoch, S., Vess, J. and Ward, T. (in press) 'A descriptive model of the offence process of women violent offenders: Distal background variables', *Psychology, Crime and Law*.

Murphy, C. M. and Baxter, V. A. (1997) 'Motivating batterers to change in the treatment context', *Journal of Interpersonal Violence*, 12: 607–20.

Murphy, T. (2000) 'Coercing offenders into treatment: A comprehensive statewide diversion strategy', paper presented to the Society for the Study of Addiction Annual Symposium, Leeds.

Nelson-Gray, R. O. (2003) 'Treatment utility of psychological assessment', *Psychological Assessment*, 15: 521–31.

Nestor, P. G., Haycock, J., Doiron, S., Kelly, J. and Kelly, D. (1995) 'Lethal violence and psychosis', *Bulletin of the American Academy of Psychiatry and Law*, 23: 331–41.

Nochajsk, T. H. and Stasiewic, P. R. (2005) 'Assessing stages of change in DUI offenders: A comparison of two measures', *Journal of Addictions Nursing*, 16: 57–67.

Novaco, R. W., Ramm, M. and Black, L. (2001) 'Anger treatment with offenders', in C. R. Hollin (ed.) *Handbook of Offender Assessment and Treatment*. Chichester: John Wiley.

Nunes, K. L., Hanson, R. K., Firestone, P., Moulden, H. M., Greenberg, D. M. and Bradford, J. M. (2007) 'Denial predicts recidivism for some sexual offenders', *Sexual Abuse: A Journal of Research and Treatment*, 19: 91–105.

Nurco, D. N., Hanlon, T. E. and Kinlock, T. W. (1991) 'Recent research on the relationship between illicit drug use and crime', *Behavioral Sciences and the Law*, 9: 221–42.

Nussbaum, M. (2006) *Frontiers of Justice: Disability, Nationality, Species-membership*. Cambridge: Belknap Press.

O'Leary, P., Day, A., Foster, G. and Chung, D. (2009) 'Resistant or ready? The challenges of male readiness for offender programs', in A. Day, P. O'Leary, D. Chung and D. Justo (eds) *Integrated Responses to Domestic Violence: Research and Practice Experiences in Working with Men*. Annandale, NSW: Federation Press.

Olver, M. E., Wong, S. C. P., Nicholaichuk, T. and Gordon, A. (2007) 'The validity and reliability of the Violence Risk Scale – Sexual Offender Version: Assessing sex offender risk and evaluating therapeutic change', *Psychological Assessment*, 19: 318–29.

Oxford, M., Gilchrist, L., Morrison, P., Gillmore, M. R., Lohr, M. J. and Lewis, S. (2003) 'Alcohol use among adolescent mothers: Heterogeneity in growth curves, predictors and alcohol use over time', *Prevention Science*, 4: 15–26.

Parhar, K. K., Wormith, J. S., Derkzen, D. M. and Beauregard, A. M. (2008) 'Offender coercion in treatment: A meta-analysis of effectiveness', *Criminal Justice and Behavior*, 35(9): 1109–35.

Patrick, C. J. (2006) *The Handbook of Psychopathy*. New York: Guilford Press.

Payne, J. (2006) *A Discrete-time Survival Study of Drug Use and Property Offending: Implications for Early Intervention and Treatment*, Technical and Background Paper No. 24. Canberra: Australian Institute of Criminology.

Petrocelli, J. V. (2002) 'Processes and stages of change: Counseling with the transtheoretical model of change', *Journal of Counseling and Development*, 80: 22–30.

Piper, W. E. and Joyce, A. S. (2001) 'Psychosocial treatment outcome', in W. J. Livesley (ed.) *Handbook of Personality Disorders*. New York: Guilford Press.

Pithers, W. D., Beal, L. S., Armstrong, J. and Petty, J. (1989) 'Identification of risk factors through clinical interventions and analysis of records', in D. R. Laws (ed.) *Relapse Prevention with Sex Offenders*. New York: Guilford Press.

Polaschek, D. (2009) 'Rehabilitating High-risk Offenders: Pre-treatment Motivation, Therapeutic Responsivity and Change', manuscript under review.

Polaschek, D. and Collie, R. (2004) 'Rehabilitating serious violent adult offenders: An empirical and theoretical stocktake', *Psychology, Crime and Law*, 10(3): 321–34.

Polaschek, D., Hudson, S. M. and Ward, T. (2001) 'Rapists' offense processes: A preliminary descriptive model', *Journal of Interpersonal Violence*, 16: 523–44.

Power, M. and Dalgleish, T. (1999) *Cognition and Emotion: From Order to Disorder*. Hove, UK: Psychology.

Prendergast, M. L. and Maugh, T. H. (1994) 'Drug courts: Diversion that works', *Judges' Journal*, 34(3): 10–14.

Prendergast, M., Greenwell, L., Farabee, D. and Hser, Y.-I. (2009) 'Influence of perceived coercion and motivation on treatment completion and re-arrest among substance-abusing offenders', *Journal of Behavioral Health Services and Research*, 36: 159–76.

Preston, D. L. (2000) 'Treatment resistance in corrections', *Forum on Corrections Research*, 12: 24–8.

Preston, D. L. and Murphy, S. (1997) 'Motivating treatment-resistant clients in therapy', *Forum on Corrections Research*, 9: 51–4.

Prochaska, J. O. and DiClemente, C. C. (1983) 'Stages and processes of self-change of smoking: Toward an integrated model of change', *Journal of Consulting and Clinical Psychology*, 51: 390–5.

Prochaska, J. O. and DiClemente, C. C. (1984) *The Transtheoretical Approach: Crossing Traditional Boundaries of Therapy*. Homewood, IL: Dow Jones-Irwin.

Prochaska, J. O. and DiClemente, C. C. (1986) 'Toward a comprehensive model of change', in W. R. Miller and N. Heather (eds) *Treating Addictive Behaviours: Process of Change*. New York: Plenum Press.

Prochaska, J. O. and DiClemente, C. C. (1992) 'Stages of change in the modification of problem behaviours', in M. Hersen, R. M. Eisler and P. M. Miller (eds) *Progress on Behaviour Modification*. Sycamore, IL: Sycamore Press.

Prochaska, J. O., DiClemente, C. C. and Norcross, J. C. (1992) 'In search of how people change: Applications to addictive behaviours', *American Psychologist*, 47: 1102–14.

Prochaska, J. O., Velicer, W. F., DiClemente, C. C. and Fava, J. (1988) 'Measuring processes of change: Applications to the cessation of smoking', *Journal of Consulting and Clinical Psychology*, 56: 520–8.

Proeve, M. J. (2002) 'Responsivity factors in sex offender treatment', in T. Ward, D. R. Laws and S. M. Hudson (eds) *Sexual Deviance: Issues and Controversies*. Thousand Oaks, CA: Sage.

Proeve, M. J. and Howells, K. (2002) 'Shame and guilt in child sexual offenders', *International Journal of Offender Therapy and Comparative Criminology*, 46: 657–67.

Proeve, M. and Howells, K. (2006) 'Shame and guilt in child molesters', in W. L. Marshall, Y. M. Fernandez, L. E. Marshall and G. A. Serran (eds) *Sexual Offender Treatment: Controversial Issues*. Chichester: John Wiley.

Project MATCH Research Group (1997) 'Matching alcoholism treatments to client heterogeneity: Project MATCH posttreatment drinking outcomes', *Journal of Studies on Alcohol*, 58: 7–29.

Project MATCH Research Group (1998) 'Matching alcoholism treatments to client heterogeneity: Project MATCH three-year drinking outcomes', *Alcoholism: Clinical and Experimental Research*, 22: 1300–11.

Proulx, J., McKibben, A. and Lusignan, R. (1996) 'Relationships between affective components and sexual behaviours in sexual aggressors', *Sexual Abuse: A Journal of Research and Treatment*, 8: 279–89.

Proulx, J., Pellerin, B., Paradis, Y., McKibben, A., Auibut, J. and Ouimet, M. (1997) 'Static and dynamic predictors of recidivism in sexual aggressors', *Sexual Abuse: A Journal of Research and Treatment*, 9: 7–27.

Quinsey, V. L. (1988) 'Assessments of the treatability of forensic patients', *Behavioral Sciences and the Law*, 6: 443–52.

Quinsey, V. L. and Maguire, A. (1983) 'Offenders remanded for a psychiatric examination: Perceived treatability and disposition', *International Journal of Law and Psychiatry*, 6: 193–205.

Quirk, A. and Lelliot, P. (2002) 'Acute wards: Problems and solutions. A participant observation study of life on an acute psychiatric ward', *Psychiatric Bulletin*, 26: 344–5.

Regier, D. A., Farmer, M. E., Rae, D. S., Locke, B. Z., Keith, S. J., Judd, L. J. and Goodwin, F. K. (1990) 'Comorbidity of mental disorders with alcohol and other drug abuse: Results from the epidemiologic catchment area (ECA) study', *Journal of the American Medical Association*, 264: 2511–18.

Renwick, S. J., Black, L., Ramm, M. and Novaco, R. W. (1997) 'Anger treatment with forensic hospital patients', *Legal and Criminological Psychology*, 2: 103–16.

Rice, M. E. and Harris, G. T. (1997a) 'Cross validation and extension of the Violence Risk Appraisal Guide for child molesters and rapists', *Law and Human Behavior*, 21: 231–41.

Rice, M. E. and Harris, G. T. (1997b) 'The treatment of adult offenders', in D. M. Stoff, J. Breiling and J. D. Maser (eds) *Handbook of Antisocial Behavior*. New York: John Wiley.

Rice, M. E. and Harris, G. T. (2005) 'Comparing effect sizes in follow-up studies: ROC area, Cohen's *d* and *r*', *Law and Human Behavior*, 29: 615–20.

Rigg, J. (2002) 'Measures of perceived coercion in prison treatment settings', *International Journal of Law and Psychiatry*, 25: 473–90.

Rogers, R. and Robbins, T. W. (2001) 'Investigating the neurocognitive deficits associated with chronic drug misuse', *Current Opinion in Neurobiology*, 11: 250–7.

Rogers, R. and Webster, C. D. (1989) 'Assessing treatability in mentally disordered offenders', *Law and Human Behavior*, 13: 19–29.

Rollnick, S., Heather, N., Gold, R. and Hall, W. (1992) 'Development of a short readiness to change questionnaire for use in brief opportunistic interventions among excessive drinkers', *British Journal of Addiction*, 87: 743–54.

Room, R., Greenfield, T. K. and Weisner, C. (1991) 'People who might have liked you to drink less: Changing responses to drinking by US family members and friends, 1979–90', *Contemporary Drug Problems*, 18: 573–95.

Ross, E. (2008) 'Investigating the Relationship Between the Therapeutic Alliance and Treatment Outcome in Violent Offender Treatment', unpublished PhD thesis, Wellington, NZ: Victoria University.

Ross, E. C., Polaschek, D. L. L. and Ward, T. (2008) 'The therapeutic alliance: A theoretical revision for offender rehabilitation', *Aggression and Violent Behaviour*, 13: 462–80.

Rossberg, J. I. and Friis, S. (2003) 'A suggested revision of the Ward Atmosphere Scale', *Acta Psychiatrica Scandinavica*, 108: 374–80.

Rutter, M. (2008) 'Introduction', in S. Hodgins, E. Viding and A. Plodowski (eds) *The Neurobiology of Violence: Implications for Prevention and Treatment*, Philosophical Transactions of the Royal Society, 363: 2485–90.

Ryan, R. M. and Deci, E. L. (2000) 'Self-determination theory and the facilitation of intrinsic motivation, social development and well-being', *American Psychologist*, 55: 69–78.

Safran, J. D. and Muran, J. C. (2006) 'Has the concept of the therapeutic alliance outlived its usefulness?', *Psychotherapy: Theory, Research, Practice, Training*, 43(3): 286–91.

Safran, J. D., Muran, J. C., Samstag, L. W. and Stevens, C. (2002) *Repairing Alliance Ruptures. Psychotherapy Relationships that Work: Therapist Contributions and Responsiveness to Patients*. New York: Oxford University Press.

Sainsbury, L. (2010) 'Violent offending treatment for male patients with personality disorder', in A. Tennant and K. Howells (eds) *Using Time, Not Doing Time: Practitioner Perspectives on Personality Disorder and Risk*. Chichester: Wiley-Blackwell.

Sainsbury, L. G., Krishnan, L. G. and Evans, C. (2004) 'Motivating factors for male forensic patients with personality disorder', *Criminal Behaviour and Mental Health*, 14: 29–38.

Salter, A. C. (1988) *Treating Child Sex Offenders and Victims: A Practical Guide*. Newbury Park, CA: Sage.

Schalast, N., Redies, M., Collins, M., Stacey, J. and Howells, K. (2008) 'EssenCES, a short questionnaire for assessing the social climate of forensic psychiatric wards', *Criminal Behaviour and Mental Health*, 18: 49–58.

Schneider, S. L. and Wright, R. C. (2001) 'The FoSOD: A measurement tool for re-conceptualizing the role of denial in child molesters', *Journal of Interpersonal Violence*, 16: 545–64.

Sechrest, L. (2005) 'Validity of measurement is no simple matter', *Health Services Research*, 40: 1584–604.

Sefarbi, R. (1990) 'Admitters and deniers among adolescent sex offenders and their families: A preliminary study', *American Journal of Orthopsychiatry*, 60: 460–5.

Sellen, J. L., McMurran, M. M., Cox, W. M., Theodosi, E. and Klinger, E. (2006) 'The Personal Concerns Inventory (Offender Adaptation): Measuring and enhancing motivation to change', *International Journal of Offender Therapy and Comparative Criminology*, 50: 294–305.

Sellen, J. L., McMurran, M. M., Theodosi, E., Cox, W. M. and Klinger, E. (2009) 'Validity of the offender version of the Personal Concerns Inventory with adult male prisoners', *Psychology, Crime and Law*, 15: 451–68.

Serin, R. C. (1998) 'Treatment responsivity, intervention and reintegration: A conceptual model', *Forum on Corrections Research*, 10: 29–32.

Serin, R. C. (2004) 'Understanding violent offenders', in D. H. Fishbein (ed.) *The Science, Treatment and Prevention of Antisocial Behaviors, Vol. 2: Evidence-based Practice*. Kingston, NJ: Civic Research Institute.

Serin, R. C. and Kennedy, S. (1997) *Treatment Readiness and Responsivity: Contributing to Effective Correctional Programming*, Research Report R–54. Ottawa: Correctional Services of Canada.

Serin, R. C. and Lloyd, C. D. (2009) 'Examining the process of offender change: The transition to crime desistance', *Psychology, Crime and Law*, 15: 347–64.

Serin, R. C. and Preston, D. L. (2001) 'Designing, implementing and managing treatment programs for violent offenders', in G. A. Bernfeld, D. P. Farrington and A. W. Leischied (eds) *Offender Rehabilitation in Practice: Implementing and Evaluating Effective Programs*. Chichester: John Wiley.

Serin, R. C., Mailloux, D. L. and Kennedy, S. M. (2007) 'Development of a clinical rating scale for offender readiness: Implications for assessment and offender change', *Issues in Forensic Psychology*, 7: 70–80.

Serran, G., Fernandez, Y., Marshall, W. L. and Mann, R. E. (2003) 'Process issues in treatment: Application to sexual offender programs', *Professional Psychology: Research and Practice*, 34(4): 368–74.

Shearer, R. A. and Ogan, G. D. (2002) 'Voluntary participation and treatment resistance in substance abuse treatment programs', *Journal of Offender Rehabilitation*, 34: 31–45.

Sheldon, K. and Krishnan, G. (2009) 'The clinical and risk characteristics of patients admitted to a secure hospital-based Dangerous and Severe Personality Disordered unit', *British Journal of Forensic Practice*, 11(3): 19–27.

Sheldon, K., Howells, K. and Patel, G. (submitted) 'An empirical evaluation of reasons for non-completion of treatment in a DSPD unit, using the MORM framework'.

Shumway, M. and Cuffel, B. J. (1996) 'Symptom heterogeneity in comorbid alcohol disorder', *Journal of Mental Health Administration*, 23: 338–47.

Siegert, R., Ward, T., Levack, W. and McPherson, K. (2007) 'A Good Lives Model of clinical and community rehabilitation', *Disability and Rehabilitation*, 29: 1604–15.

Simourd, D. J. and Malcolm, P. B. (1998) 'Reliability and validity of the Level of Service Inventory with incarcerated sexual offenders', *Journal of Interpersonal Violence*, 13: 23–8.

Simpson, D., Joe, G. W., Broome, K., Hiller, M., Knight, K. and Rowan-Szal, G. (1997) 'Program diversity and treatment retention rates in Drug Abuse Treatment Outcome Study (DATOS)', *Psychology of Addictive Behaviors*, 1194: 279–93.

Skeem, J. L., Eno Louden, J., Polaschek, D. and Camp, J. (2007) 'Assessing relationship quality in mandated community treatment: Blending care with control', *Psychological Assessment*, 19(4): 397–410.

Smith, R. J. (1999) 'Psychopathic behavior and issues of treatment', *New Ideas in Psychology*, 17: 165–76.

Stewart, L. (2005) Personal communication, 15 September 2005.

Stiles, W. B. (2000) 'Assimilation of problematic experiences', in J. C. Norcross (ed.) *Psychotherapy Relationships that Work: Therapist Contributions and Responsiveness to Patients*. New York: Oxford University Press.

Stiles, W. B., Honos-Webb, L. and Lani, J. A. (1999) 'Some functions of narrative in the assimilation of problematic experiences', *Journal of Clinical Psychology*, 55: 1213–26.

Stiles, W. B., Morrison, L. A., Haw, S. K., Harper, H., Shapiro, D. A. and Firth-Cozens, J. (1991) 'Longitudinal study of assimilation in exploratory psychotherapy', *Psychotherapy*, 28: 195–206.

Strauss, J. L., Hayes, A. M., Johnson, S. L., Newman, C. F., Brown, G. K., Barber, J. P., Laurenceau, J. and Beck, A. T. (2006) 'Early alliance, alliance ruptures and symptom change in a nonrandomized trial of cognitive therapy for avoidant and obsessive-compulsive personality disorders', *Journal of Consulting and Clinical Psychology*, 74(2): 337–45.

Sturmey, P. (2007) *Functional Analysis in Clinical Treatment*. Burlington. MA: Elsevier.

Sturmey, P. (ed.) (2009) *Clinical Case Formulation: Varieties of Approaches*. Chichester: John Wiley.

Swann, W. B., Stein-Seroussi, A. and Giesler, R. B. (1992) 'Why people self-verify', *Journal of Personality and Social Psychology*, 62: 392–401.

Swanson, J. W., Borum, R. and Swartz, M. S. (1996) 'Psychotic symptoms and disorders and the risk of violent behaviour in the community', *Criminal Behaviour and Mental Health*, 6: 309–29.

Swartz, J. A. and Lurigio, A. J. (1999) 'Psychiatric illness and comorbidity among adult male jail detainees in drug treatment', *Psychiatric Services*, 50: 1628–30.

Taft, C. T. and Murphy, C. M. (2007) 'The working alliance in intervention for partner violence perpetrators: Recent research and theory', *Journal of Family Violence*, 22: 11–18.

Taft, C. T., Murphy, C. M., King, D. W., Musser, P. H. and DeDeyn, J. M. (2003) 'Process and treatment adherence factors in group cognitive-behavioral therapy for partner violent men', *Journal of Consulting and Clinical Psychology*, 71(4): 812–20.

Taft, C. T., Murphy, C. M., Musser, P. H. and Resmington, N. A. (2004) 'Personality, interpersonal and motivational predictors of the working alliance in group cognitive-behavioral therapy for partner violent men', *Journal of Consulting and Clinical Psychology*, 72(2): 349–54.

Tait, L., Birchwood, M. and Trower, P. (2002) 'A new scale (SES) to measure engagement with community mental health services', *Journal of Mental Health*, 11: 191–8.

Tangney, J. P. (1991) 'Moral affect: The good, the bad and the ugly', *Journal of Personality and Social Psychology*, 61: 598–609.

Tangney, J. P. (1999) 'The self-conscious emotions: Shame, guilt, embarrassment and pride', in T. Dalgleish and M. Power (eds) *Handbook of Cognition and Emotion*. London: John Wiley.

Taylor, G. (1985) *Pride, Shame and Guilt: Emotions of Self-assessment*. Oxford: Clarendon.

Tennant, A. and Howells, K. (eds) (2010) *Using Time Not Doing Time: Practitioner Perspectives on Personality Disorder and Risk*. Chichester: Wiley-Blackwell.

Thakker, J., Ward, T. and Navathe, S. (2007) 'The cognitive distortions and implicit theories of child sexual abusers', in T. A. Gannon, T. Ward, A. R. Beech and D. Fisher (eds) *Aggressive Offenders' Cognition: Theory, Research and Practice*. Chichester: John Wiley.

Theodosi, E. and McMurran, M. (2006) 'Motivating convicted sex offenders into treatment: A pilot study', *British Journal of Forensic Practice*, 8: 28–35.

Thigpen, M. L., Beauclair, T. J., Keiser, G. M., Guevara, M. and Mestad, R. (2007) *Cognitive-behavioral Treatment: A Review and Discussion for Professionals for Corrections Professionals*. US Department of Justice National Institute of Corrections.

Thomas-Peter, B. (2006) 'The modern context of psychology in corrections: Influences, limitation and values of "What Works"', in G. J. Towl (ed.) *Psychological Research in Prisons*. Oxford: Blackwell.

Tierney, D. W. and McCabe, M. P. (2001) 'The validity of the transtheoretical model of behaviour change to investigate motivation to change among child molesters', *Clinical Psychology and Psychotherapy*, 8: 176–90.

Timko, C. and Moos, R. H. (2004) 'Measuring the therapeutic environment', in P. Campling, S. Davies and G. Farquharson (eds) *From Toxic Institutions to Therapeutic Environments: Residential Settings in Mental Health Services.* London: Gaskell Press.

Toch, H. and Adams, K. (2002) *Acting Out: Maladaptive Behavior in Confinement.* Washington, DC: American Psychological Association.

Tsuang, M. T., Lyons, M. J., Eisen, S. A., Goldberg, J., True, W., Lin, N., Meyer, J. M., Toomey, R., Faraone, S. V. and Eaves, L. (1996) 'Genetic influences on DSM-III-R drug abuse and dependence: A study of 3,372 twin pairs', *American Journal of Medical Genetics*, 67: 473–7.

Tucker, K. A., Potenza, M. N., Beauvais, J. E., Browndyke, J. N., Gottschalk, P. C. and Kosten, T. R. (2004) 'Perfusion abnormalities and decision making in cocaine dependence', *Biological Psychiatry*, 56: 527–30.

Van der Walde, H., Urgenson, F., Weltz, S. H. and Hanna, F. J. (2002) 'Women and alcoholism: A biopsychosocial perspective and treatment approaches', *Journal of Counseling and Development*, 80: 145–53.

Van der Zwaluw, C. S. and Engels, R. C. M. E. (2009) 'Gene-environmental interactions and alcohol use and dependence', *Addiction*, 104: 907–14.

Velicer, W. F., Prochaska, J. O., Fava, J. L., Norman, G. J. and Redding, C. A. (1998) 'Smoking cessation and stress management: Applications of the transtheoretical model of behavior change', *Homeostasis*, 38: 216–33.

Vess, J. (2005) 'Preventive detention vs. civil commitment: Alternative policies for public protection in New Zealand and California', *Psychiatry, Psychology and Law*, 12: 357–66.

Vess, J. (2008) 'Sex offender risk assessment: Consideration of human rights in community protection legislation', *Legal and Criminological Psychology*, 13: 245–56.

Vess, J. (2009) 'Fear and loathing in public policy: Ethical issues in laws for sex offenders', *Aggression and Violent Behavior*, 14: 264–72.

Vess, J., Murphy, C. and Arkowitz, S. (2004) 'Clinical and demographic differences between sexually violent predators and other commitment types in a state forensic hospital', *Journal of Forensic Psychiatry and Psychology*, 15: 669–81.

Vroom, V. H. (1964) *Work and Motivation.* New York: John Wiley.

Ward, T. (2000) 'Sexual offenders' cognitive distortions as implicit theories', *Aggression and Violent Behavior*, 5: 491–507.

Ward, T. (in press) 'Extending the mind into the world: A new theory of cognitive distortions', *Journal of Sexual Aggression*.

Ward, T. and Birgden, A. (2007) 'Human rights and correctional clinical practice', *Aggression and Violent Behavior*, 12: 628–43.

Ward, T. and Brown, M. (2004) 'The Good Lives Model and conceptual issues in offender rehabilitation', *Psychology, Crime and Law*, 10: 243–57.

Ward, T. and Gannon, T. (2006) 'Rehabilitation, etiology and self-regulation: The Good Lives Model of sexual offender treatment', *Aggression and Violent Behavior*, 11: 77–94.

Ward, T. and Hudson, S. M. (1998) 'A model of the relapse process in sex offenders', *Journal of Interpersonal Violence*, 13: 700–25.

Ward, T. and Keenan, T. (1999) 'Child molesters' implicit theories', *Journal of Interpersonal Violence*, 14: 821–38.

Ward, T. and Maruna, S. (2007) *Rehabilitation: Beyond the Risk Paradigm*. London: Routledge.

Ward, T. and Nee, C. (2009) 'Surfaces and depths: Evaluating the theoretical assumptions of the cognitive skills programmes', *Psychology, Crime and Law*, 15: 165–82.

Ward, T. and Stewart, C. (2003) 'Criminogenic needs and human needs: A theoretical model', *Psychology, Crime and Law*, 9: 125–43.

Ward, T., Bickley, J., Webster, S. D., Fisher, D., Beech, A. and Eldridge, H. (2004a) *The Self-regulation Model of the Offence and Relapse Process: A Manual, Vol 1: Assessment*. Victoria, BC: Pacific Psychological Assessment Corporation.

Ward, T., Day, A., Howells, K. and Birgden, A. (2004b) 'The multifactor offender readiness model', *Aggression and Violent Behavior*, 9: 645–73.

Ward, T., Mann, R. and Gannon, T. (2007) 'The good lives model of offender rehabilitation: Clinical implications', *Aggression and Violent Behavior*, 12: 87–107.

Wasilow-Mueller, S. and Erickson, C. K. (2001) 'Drug abuse and dependency: Understanding gender differences in etiology and management', *Journal of the American Pharmaceutical Association*, 41: 78–90.

Watson, H. and Beech, A. (2002) 'Predicting Treatment Drop-out in Violent Offenders using Pre-treatment Assessments', unpublished manuscript.

Webster, C. D., Douglas, K., Eaves, D. and Hart, S. (1997) *HCR-20: Assessing Risk for Violence – Version 2*. Vancouver, BC: Simon Fraser University.

Weisz, J. R., Chu, B. C. and Polo, A. J. (2004) 'Treatment dissemination and evidence-based practice: Strengthening intervention through clinician–researcher collaboration', *Clinical Psychology: Science and Practice*, 11: 300–7.

Wells-Parker, E. (1995) 'Mandated treatment: Lessons from research with drinking and driving offenders', *Alcohol Health and Research World*, 18: 302–6.

West, D. J. (1965) *Murder Followed by Suicide*. London: Heinemann.

Wexler, H. K., Blackmore, J. and Lipton, D. S. (1991) 'Project REFORM: Developing a drug abuse treatment strategy for Corrections', *Journal of Drug Issues*, 21: 469–90.

White, H. (1990) 'The drug use–delinquency connection in adolescence', in R. Weisheit (ed.) *Drugs, Crime and Criminal Justice*. Cincinnati: Anderson Publishing.

White, H. and Gorman, D. M. (2000) 'Dynamics of the drug crime relationship', in G. Lafree (ed.) *Criminal Justice 2000, Vol. 1: The Nature of Crime: Continuity and Change*. National Institute of Justice, USA.

White, H., Brick, J. and Hansell, S. (1993) 'A longitudinal investigation of alcohol use and aggression in adolescence', *Journal of Studies on Alcohol*, Suppl. 11: 62–77.

Whitehead, P., Ward, T. and Collie, R. (2007) 'Time for a change: Applying the Good Lives Model of rehabilitation to a high-risk violent offender', *International Journal of Offender Therapy and Comparative Criminology*, 51: 578–98.

Wiesner, M., Silbereisen, R. K. and Weichold, K. (2008) 'Deviant peer association on adolescent alcohol consumption: A growth mixture modeling analysis', *Journal of Youth and Adolescence*, 37: 537–51.

Wild, T. C. (1999) 'Compulsory substance user treatment and harm reduction: A critical analysis', *Substance Use and Misuse*, 34: 83–102.

Wild, T. C. (2006) 'Social control and coercion in addiction treatment: Towards evidence-based policy and practice', *Addiction*, 101: 40–9.

Wild, T. C., Newton-Taylor, B. and Alletto, R. (1998) 'Perceived coercion among clients entering substance abuse treatment: Structural and psychological determinants', *Addictive Behaviors*, 23: 81–95.

Wild T. C., Roberts, A. B. and Cooper E. L. (2002) 'Compulsory substance abuse treatment: An overview of recent findings and issues', *European Addiction Research*, 8: 84–93.

Williamson, P., Day, A., Howells, K., Bubner, S. and Jauncey, S. (2003) 'Assessing offender readiness to change problems with anger', *Psychology, Crime and Law*, 9: 295–307.

Winn, M. E. (1996) 'The strategic and systematic management of denial in the cognitive/behavioral treatment of sexual offenders', *Sexual Abuse: A Journal of Research and Treatment*, 8(1): 25–36.

Wittchen, H.-U., Behrendt, S., Höfler, M., Perkonigg, A., Rehm, J., Lieb, R. and Breesdo, K. (2009) 'A typology of cannabis-related problems among individuals with repeated illegal drug use in the first three decades of life: Evidence for heterogeneity and different treatment needs', *Drug and Alcohol Dependence*, 102: 151–7.

Wormwith, J. S., Althouse, R., Simpson, M., Reitzel, L. R., Fagan, T. J. and Morgan, R. D. (2007) 'The rehabilitation and reintegration of offenders: The current landscape and some future directions for correctional psychology', *Criminal Justice and Behavior*, 34: 879–92.

Wright, R. C. and Schneider, S. L. (2004) 'Mapping child molester treatment progress with the FoSOD: Denial and explanations of accountability', *Sexual Abuse: A Journal of Research and Treatment*, 16(2): 85–105.

Wong, S. C. P. and Gordon, A. (1999–2003) *Violence Risk Scale.* Department of Psychology, University of Saskatchewan. Available at: www.psynergy.ca.

Wong, S. C. P. and Gordon, A. (2006) 'The validity and reliability of the Violence Risk Scale: A treatment friendly violence risk assessment tool', *Psychology, Public Policy and Law*, 12: 279–309.

Wong, S. C. P., Gordon, A. and Gu, D. (2007) 'Assessment and treatment of violence-prone forensic clients: An integrated approach', *British Journal of Psychiatry*, 190, Suppl. 49: s66–s74.

Wong, S. C. P., Olver, M. E., Nicholaichuk, T. P. and Gordon, A. (2003) *The Violence Risk Scale – Sexual Offender version (VRS-SO).* Saskatoon, Saskatchewan, Canada: Regional Psychiatric Centre and University of Saskatchewan.

Wong, S. C. P., Van der Veen, S., Leis, T., Parrish, H., Gu, D., Liber, E. U. and Middleton, H. L. (2005) 'Reintegrating seriously violent and personality-disordered offenders from a supermaximum security institution into the general offender population', *Journal of Offender Therapy and Comparative Criminology*, 49: 362–75.

Wright, R. C. and Schneider, S. L. (2004) 'Mapping child molester treatment progress with the FoSOD: Denial and explanations of accountability', *Sexual Abuse: A Journal of Research and Treatment*, 16(2): 85–105.

Wundersitz, J. (2007) *Criminal Justice Responses to Drug and Drug-related Offending: Are They Working?*, Technical and Background Paper No. 25. Canberra, Australia: Australian Institute of Criminology.

Yalom, I. D. (1995) *The Theory and Practice of Group Psychotherapy*, 4th edn. New York: Basic Books.

Yalom, I. D. and Lieberman, M. A. (1971) 'A study of encounter group casualties', *Archives of General Psychiatry*, 47: 427–39.

Yates, P. M. (2009) 'Is sexual offender denial related to sex offence risk and recidivism? A review and treatment implications', *Psychology, Crime and Law*, 15(2–3): 183–99.

Yates, P. and Kingston, D. A. (2006) 'The self-regulation model of sexual offending: The relationship between offence pathways and static and dynamic sexual offence risk', *Sexual abuse: Journal of Research and Treatment*, 18: 259–70.

Young, D. (2002) 'Impacts of perceived legal pressure on retention in drug treatment', *Criminal Justice and Behaviour*, 29: 27–55.

Young, J. E. (1990) *Cognitive Therapy for Personality Disorders: A Schema-focused Approach*. Sarasota, FL: Professional Resource Exchange.

Young, J. E. (1999) *Cognitive Therapy for Personality Disorders: A Schema-focused Approach*, 3rd edn. Sarasota, FL: Professional Resource Exchange.

Zamble, E. and Porporino, F. (1990) 'Coping, imprisonment and rehabilitation: Some data and their implications', *Criminal Justice and Behavior*, 17: 53–70.

Zamble, E. and Quinsey, V. L. (1997) *The Criminal Recidivism Process*. New York: Cambridge University Press.

Zlotnick, C., Clarke, J. G., Friedmann, P. D., Roberts, M. B., Sacks, S. and Melnick, G. (2008) 'Gender differences in comorbid disorders among offenders in prison substance abuse treatment programs', *Behavioral Sciences and the Law*, 26: 403–12.

Index